Developing Literacy
in the **Secondary Classroom**

Sara Miller McCune founded SAGE Publishing in 1965 to support the dissemination of usable knowledge and educate a global community. SAGE publishes more than 1000 journals and over 800 new books each year, spanning a wide range of subject areas. Our growing selection of library products includes archives, data, case studies and video. SAGE remains majority owned by our founder and after her lifetime will become owned by a charitable trust that secures the company's continued independence.

Los Angeles | London | New Delhi | Singapore | Washington DC | Melbourne

Developing Literacy
in the Secondary Classroom

Georgina Barton
& Gary Woolley

Los Angeles | London | New Delhi
Singapore | Washington DC | Melbourne

Los Angeles | London | New Delhi
Singapore | Washington DC | Melbourne

SAGE Publications Ltd
1 Oliver's Yard
55 City Road
London EC1Y 1SP

SAGE Publications Inc.
2455 Teller Road
Thousand Oaks, California 91320

SAGE Publications India Pvt Ltd
B 1/I 1 Mohan Cooperative Industrial Area
Mathura Road
New Delhi 110 044

SAGE Publications Asia-Pacific Pte Ltd
3 Church Street
#10-04 Samsung Hub
Singapore 049483

Editor: James Clark
Assistant editor: Rob Patterson
Production editor: Nicola Carrier
Copyeditor: Gemma Marren
Proofreader: Thea Watson
Indexer: Silvia Benvenuto
Marketing manager: Lorna Patkai
Cover design: Sheila Tong
Typeset by: C&M Digitals (P) Ltd, Chennai, India
Printed and bound by
CPI Group (UK) Ltd, Croydon, CR0 4YY

Library of Congress Control Number: 2016956222

British Library Cataloguing in Publication data

A catalogue record for this book is available from
the British Library

ISBN 978-1-4739-4755-9
ISBN 978-1-4739-4756-6 (pbk)

CONTENTS

ABOUT THE AUTHORS

Dr Georgina Barton is a senior lecturer in the School of Education and Professional Studies at Griffith University, Brisbane, Australia. She is also the Program Director of the Bachelor of Secondary Education and lectures in English and literacy education. Previous to this role Georgina taught in schools for over 20 years including teaching English in South India. She has experience as an Acting Principal, Lead Teacher in literacy and numeracy and has been responsible for whole school literacy planning. She also has extensive experience in teaching the Arts from Prep-Year 12 and in tertiary contexts. Her research interests include: English and literacy education, multi-modalities, arts and music education and teacher education with a focus on international students. She has published widely in these areas including an edited book titled: *Literacy in the Arts: Retheorising Learning and Teaching,* published with Springer.

Dr Gary Woolley is an adjunct senior research fellow with Griffith Institute of Educational Research at Griffith University. Gary's particular professional interests include reading comprehension difficulties, memory, cognition, learning engagement and English as a second language. He has had a broad teaching experience in public and private school systems for over 30 years. During this time Gary taught in both primary and secondary school contexts and was a learning support teacher working with students with diverse needs. Gary has received a number of awards in recognition for his research and publications in the field of literacy and learning difficulties and for the development of the COR Literacy Framework. Author's blog: http//reading4 meaning.blogspot.com.au

ACKNOWLEDGEMENTS

The authors would like to thank the staff at SAGE for their advice and support. They appreciate the continued encouragement and assistance from their spouses, Helen and Robert, especially during the writing process. Finally, they would like to acknowledge the support from Griffith University and the University of the Sunshine Coast.

SAGE and the authors would like to thank the following reviewers whose comments on the proposal helped shape this book:

Paul Grover, Charles Sturt University

Garth Stahl, University of South Australia

Judith Kneen, Newman University, Birmingham

Marcello Giovanelli, University of Nottingham

CHAPTER 1

WHAT IS LITERACY FOR TODAY'S YOUNG PEOPLE?

Chapter objectives

- To understand what literacy is in the twenty-first century and beyond.
- To understand adolescent learners.
- To evaluate the complex nature of education and change.
- To develop an understanding of appropriate instructional approaches for adolescents in literacy learning.

Key questions

1 How does adolescence affect learning in general?
2 How do adolescent learners construct meaning through literate practices?
3 How can educators support adolescents' literacy learning?

Key words: Literacy, twenty-first century, adolescent, education and change, adolescents and literacy learning.

Introduction

Literacy is a dynamic phenomenon that impacts on people's everyday lives. From waking up in the morning and communicating with families to how we commute to daily activities, we draw on literate practices to engage successfully in these day-to-day routines. In considering today's young people, we are faced with an increasing level of diversity, whether cultural, social or economic, along with the complexities that come with adolescent development. What may be important for young people and adolescents in their daily work and personal lives may be quite different to that in school. Also while literacy is often defined in terms of all people, we believe it has unique attributes when considering adolescent engagement and learning.

Literacy within the secondary school context has been given considerable attention over the past few decades (Alvermann, 2001; Barton and McKay, 2016a; 2016b; Freebody, 2007; Moje, 2002; Moje et al., 2004; Moll et al., 1992). It is therefore important to continue solid dialogues between this research and practice. This book aims to provide a strong evidence-base for effective teaching strategies and approaches for teachers and educators to ensure literacy teaching and learning is appropriate and meaningful for adolescent students.

This chapter begins by asking what literacy means in the twenty-first century and beyond. The following conversation focuses on the complex and ever-changing nature of literacy and literate practice, particularly for young people. Rapid and frequent movement in the development of complex texts, modes and channels used for communication coupled with political, social, cultural, economic and technological changes affecting people worldwide has a significant impact on the ways in which we conceive literacy and therefore teach it. So what does literacy mean in the twenty-first century and beyond?

What is literacy in the twenty-first century?

In order to address this question we aim to define the term literacy in a way that can be applied effectively in the secondary school context including the quest to attend to adolescent literacy learning. A well-known literacy educator in Australia, Peter Freebody (2007), notes that literacy is essentially an 'open-textured' concept, meaning that the definition of literacy is constantly shifting depending on its purpose, the people who use it and in which context it is consumed. In some ways the inability to define literacy specifically can be challenging for educators. However, if we understand the features that impact on diverse literate practices more, then we are able to further strengthen students' literacy learning in the secondary classroom context.

The United Nations Educational, Scientific and Cultural Organization (UNESCO) regards literacy as: an attempt to recognise the diversity of definitions attributed to the term, as being beyond simply the set of technical skills of reading, writing and calculating ... to a plural notion encompassing the manifold of meanings and dimensions of these undeniably vital competencies. Such a view, responding to recent economic, political and social transformations, including globalization, and the advancement of information and communication technologies, recognizes that there are many practices of literacy embedded in different cultural processes, personal circumstances and collective structures. (UNESCO, 2012)

Acknowledging concepts such as globalisation, including the advancement of information and communication technologies as well as transnational movement of people, is important as they impact on what literacy means today and into the future. For instance, much research in the area of literacy education considers the ways in which young people communicate with each other through increasingly diverse methods (Jewitt, 2008) such as social media platforms including Instagram, Pinterest and Facebook (Barton, 2014). This clearly has implications for school teaching yet there appears to be a mismatch between the ways in which youth interact with each other and what is expected in formal institutional learning (Cremin et al., 2015). Further, the above definition of literacy recognises 'different cultural processes, personal circumstances and collective structures'.

Understanding and recognising varied cultural practices and learning processes in education is vital to meet the needs of all students. Research in literacy education has for some time explored the concept of multiliteracies (see also Chapter 6) – including two aspects of language acquisition – the first concerns the ranges of meaning making in different social and cultural contexts and the second explores the diverse kinds of digital and technological mediums used to create meaning through communication (Kalantzis and Cope, 2012).

Aside from the complex environments and technologies available today, young people may also experience hardships that were uncommon even 20 years ago. It is therefore important to consider personal, social and cultural implications of learning literacy in this ever-changing complex world. Attempting to address all of these issues and considerations for teachers, as highlighted in the UNESCO definition above, is an ongoing challenge yet we aim, in this book, to provide some appropriate strategies that have been proven to make an impact on young people's lives.

The implications of the above information mean that literacy cannot be measured as a set of narrow skills such as in high-stakes testing. Therefore, if we are to truly improve literacy standards and learning for young people, we need to take into account the multitude of elements 'encompassing the manifold of meanings and dimensions' (UNESCO, 2012) of reading, writing, listening, speaking, viewing, acting; ultimately communicating via multiple modes of meaning making. This is particularly important in relation to considering learning and teaching for adolescents.

Adolescence – a time of great change

Young people aged 11 to 17 years are often referred to as young adolescents or adolescents. This stage of development is complex with many *physiological* changes, including puberty and hormone fluctuations; *intellectual* changes, such as brain development and growth; and *behavioural* changes occurring, particularly as they move from dependence to independence. These changes are often seen as challenges for educators and parents; however, with a thorough understanding of the *how* and *why* of adolescent development mutual benefit can be gained. The aim of this book is to assist leaders, teachers, pre-service teachers, teacher aides, parents and community members to have a better understanding of adolescent learners and what literacy means to them today.

As stated above there are many changes that young people experience throughout adolescence. Physical changes are perhaps the most noticeable and are a result of the onset of puberty. According to Pendergast and Bahr (2005) in this period of our lives we experience the most rapid stage of development, second to our early years of growth. During this time not only does the body change but the brain is constantly changing – and at different rates between boys and girls and of course this also varies between individuals (Nagel, 2005). It is therefore very important for teachers of early or young adolescents through to late adolescents to be aware of these changes and how they may impact on learning, communication and the ways in which young people react to certain situations.

Behaviourally, adolescents are commonly known to be building up their sense of self through a process of independence (Brinthaupt and Lipka, 2002). During this time it is also important to be mindful of supporting and guiding young people in the decisions that they make as well as embracing their strengths.

What's important to young people?

This book takes the premise that all young people we are likely to teach have individual attributes towards learning that need to be met; however, the research also shows that adolescents have some common developmental features worth noting.

From the age of 11 there can be a distinct shift for young people to place more importance on their peers than adults in their lives (Barton and Bahr, 2013). Research across a number of cultural contexts confirms this observation, such as McCrae et al.'s (2002) work. Given that adolescence is a time of great change, feeling valued and understood is incredibly important. Of course this would be the case for any child but often adolescent student voice and choice are missing in teaching practice even though adults' actions are well intended. Many key researchers who are interested in adolescents and literacy emphasise the necessity to consider issues pertaining to youth culture and the individual's own 'funds of knowledge' (Moje, et al., 2004; Moll et al., 1992). This means when we plan and programme learning for young people we need to take into account the knowledge base they already have as well as making learning student-centred rather than teacher-directed.

When young people feel they have ownership over their own learning then more positive outcomes will result. Personal agency is also another aspect to consider. When students are self-directed and are able to make decisions about what they need to know and how, then a more positive learning experience occurs. On the other hand, when adolescents view themselves through a deficit lens, that is by what they cannot do, then motivation and engagement becomes limited (Barton and McKay, 2016a). It is therefore important for educators and other significant people in the students' lives to support a positive outlook on students' capacities to engage with and make meaning through literate practices.

Issues related to adolescents and literacy

In 2000, the Organisation for Economic Co-operation and Development (OECD) administered for the first time the Programme for International Student Assessment (PISA) which resulted in showing 'wide differences between countries in the knowledge and skills of 15-year-olds in reading literacy' (OECD, 2003: 5). While the skills tested in such assessment programmes are important they often discount other rich literate practices present in communities and families. The results from tests such as PISA confirm that measures such as those used in high-stakes testing favour more advantaged communities than those from disadvantaged areas. Students from low socio-economic circumstances do less well than those more advantaged and this gap is widening (Freebody, 2015).

'Closing the gap' is essential if we are to address the concerns related to adolescent literacy learning. This will not be achievable if the focus is always on results from standardised testing. There are many other ways to measure reading and writing success as well as other multimodal ways to make meaning. Therefore much needs to be done in the area of assessment and reporting, and in particular formative modes of assessment, which we will focus more on in Chapter 12. PISA's reading literacy is defined as:

> an individual's capacity to understand, use and reflect on and engage with written texts, in order to achieve one's goals, to develop one's knowledge and potential and to participate in society. (OECD, 2009: 14)

What this kind of definition fails to take into account is the notion that 'texts' can be communicated via a range of modes, not just through the written word. So if we are to address the diversity in the ways young people make meaning, as well as support them in creating effective written texts, then we may be closer to supporting young people to have positive pathways after school.

Understanding literacy and literate practices in the school context

As discussed in this chapter, literacy is both a social and cultural practice and relates to how we make meaning in particular contexts. Literacy is not only about effective communication but also how engaging in literate practices can empower people socially and culturally.

Understanding students and teachers as learners

When developing literacy programmes, it is important for you to understand who your students are and what their interest areas are. This includes what is important to them including the community of which they are a part, as well as their peers. An easy way to do this is to do a SWOT (Strengths, Weaknesses, Opportunities and Threats) analysis of each student. In addition, teachers are always learners so carrying out a SWOT analysis for yourself and other staff members is recommended. Part of this activity could also include a mapping exercise where teachers reflect on their own literacy journeys. Remembering how we as teachers learnt to read and also certain milestones can assist in understanding the process of learning literacy for our students.

Establishing the purpose

It is important for all learning to be meaningful and have a clear purpose. Literacy activities that are purposeful are incredibly important for adolescent students because if they do not see the point of a learning task they will disengage and lose motivation to complete the task. Therefore, at the commencement of any task the teacher should always be clear about the purpose and what the expectations are for the student. Alternatively, teachers can explore key concepts first and then make explicit what the purpose was after the task – it does not necessarily have to be made up front.

Planning and setting up tasks

When planning and setting up literacy tasks for adolescent students it is equally important to create rich learning tasks that not only have a clear purpose but where the students have agency to make decisions about these tasks. Tasks can range from a writing activity to planting a vegetable garden. It is equally important that a range of assessment types are offered to adolescent students for the same task. For example, one group may organise the project, another may do the actual planting and caring of the garden, and another may write a recipe book or play involving a narrative around the garden. Offering a range of assessment types enables students to focus on their strengths ensuring success in the task.

The notion of text

The idea of a text constituting only written or oral scripts is now considered inappropriate for today's classrooms. Social and cultural theorists often define a text as a meaningful artefact of society and culture. The Context-to-Text model of language by Michael Halliday (1973) shows that the context in which a text is created impacts greatly on the sociological and cultural meanings or ideologies represented in the text. Halliday, as a linguist, then deconstructs the text into a number of layers including paragraphs, sentences, word groups and words (combinations of letters or symbols as in alphabets). However, there has been more work done in research that explores modes other than language such as visual image, gesture and sound. Therefore, texts can be an artwork, performance or dance.

Strategies to support literacy learning for adolescents

Often when we are asked to work in schools people are seeking explicit strategies that will ensure improvement in their students' literacy learning outcomes. It is difficult, however, to provide a list of pedagogies that work across every context as each one is different. Therefore, as a teacher you need to understand the environment in which you work from the individual level through to the wider school community level. Drawing on a range of pedagogical practices and strategies appropriately can then be tailored to the learner's needs. Sometimes this is difficult given the amount of change that occurs in schools.

Understanding change in your context

At the heart of educational change is the overall aim to improve student learning outcomes; but sometimes change can be daunting for teachers, particularly if changes are radically different from current practices. It is also difficult if these changes are multifaceted, complex, time pressed, externally driven and poorly resourced and it can lead teachers to feeling overwhelmed. Not only are adolescent learners undergoing great change but teachers' views and philosophies change over time too.

Teachers do not work in isolation and in fact working collaboratively makes the teachers' job much easier and more enjoyable. Increasingly, both teachers and students enter the classroom space with unique learning experiences and skills that may have resulted from socially and culturally diverse contexts. For example, one school may represent up to 30 different cultural backgrounds in their student-base and another 12 within its staff members. Consideration of staff and student strengths and diversity is incredibly important in curriculum planning and assessment in schools otherwise there may be a risk of preferring one ideology or mode of communication over others. Therefore, change in educational contexts requires teachers to continue to consider and reflect on new ways to include and address students' unique attributes and dispositions constantly.

Being a reflective practitioner

Critical and professional teachers need to not only understand the process of change but to also critically reflect on actions and activities within particular conditions. Reflection and reflective practice have been noted as an integral component of the teaching profession (Moffatt et al., 2015). Across the world many teacher education organisations include reflection as a key skill in their professional standards.

Critical and deep reflection has moral purpose at its core and involves reflection on and in action (Schön, 1983). A good model to utilise for reflective practice is the 4Rs model (Ryan and Ryan, 2013) which was adapted from Bain et al.'s (2002) 5Rs model. The 4Rs model highlights the need for students and educators to reflect deeply on the process of learning, including critical incidents, through a process of four levels of reflection. These include:

1 *Report and respond* – where students report on the phenomenon
2 *Relate* – where students relate this experience to something they may have experienced before
3 *Reason* – where students need to reason as to why the incident occurred by referring to relevant theory, and
4 *Reconstruct* – resulting in a reframing or reconstruction for future practice.

In considering the idea that change is constant in education and also the necessity for teachers to be reflective practitioners, then working with adolescents adds further complexities but also excitement in the work we do. Given the nature of multiple levels or phases of change in and across education, teachers' experiences and adolescent learners, it is crucial for teachers to be flexible, responsive and select appropriate instructional methods for learning and teaching. To ensure improved literacy learning outcomes, students, rather than systemic directives, need to remain at the centre of everything we do as teachers.

Knowing your students

The importance of knowing your students may sound obvious but surprisingly many programmes are developed with groups of students in mind rather than individuals. In recent research concerning adolescent learners and literacy carried out by Barton and McKay (2016a) it was found that often the voice of the student is missing in programmes developed to support literacy learners in particular. Barton and McKay (2016a) offer a model that places the student at the centre of learning in contrast to 'top-down' models where more often than not decisions about the students' learning are made by leadership and teaching staff. Simple techniques such as carrying out SWOT analyses on students as well as asking students about their interests make a substantial impact on adolescent learners. Barton and McKay (2016a) also found that when students, even those that struggle, are given more opportunities to teach others and show leadership then powerful and transformative results occur.

For adolescent learners it is important to view their current literacy practices as vital in developing their sense of identity including self-worth. Many students in this age group may communicate via social media platforms; however, it is equally important to consider that many may not. Morrison (2014) for example, found that only 15 per cent of young adolescents had regular access to the Internet at home – this finding is in contrast to Prensky's (2001) idea that young people are 'digital natives' or at least have constant access to digital forms of media and communication. A positive lens, and one that draws on young people's agencies (Moje, 2002), particularly for students who have difficulty reading for example, is crucial for learning success.

A suggested model of effective practice: Learning by Design

The Learning by Design model developed by Kalantzis et al. (2005) acknowledges that teaching and learning is about the ways in which pedagogy and curriculum overlap (see Chapter 6). Curriculum is about content, media and learning processes and pedagogy involves a range of knowledge processes. These are: experiential, conceptual, analytical and applied.

If we consider each of these as verbs they would be experiencing, conceptualising, analysing and applying. When we plan learning episodes we need to consider all four knowledge processes for the learning to be deep not surface learning.

According to Kalantzis et al. (2005) experiencing involves acknowledging students' prior knowledge by drawing on what they already know. Then teachers may introduce new knowledge which is about immersion into new information and also experiences.

The second level is conceptualising which involves defining and applying concepts and theorising by considering these concepts in relation to discipline knowledge. When students understand the differences between the literacies present in curriculum or content areas they have a better chance of comprehending and composing both reading and writing tasks more effectively.

Analysing is a higher order thinking task and requires clear scaffolding. Kalantzis et al. (2005) explain that analysis can occur on two plains. The first is to analyse functionally. This means to identify cause and effect and also inquire into what things are for. The second involves critical analysis. Critical analysis requires investigation into people's purposes, motives, intentions and looking at different points of view.

Finally, while learning, it is important that students are given the opportunity to apply their new learnt knowledge. Often referred to as active or collaborative learning, applying is contrary to a 'traditional' model of teaching where the teacher controls all the learning (Prince, 2004). The Learning by Design model outlines two levels of application: applying appropriately is where knowledge is applied in a typical situation whereas applying creatively is about innovative application of knowledge, or transfer to a different situation.

Teachers as researchers: evidence-based practice

Quality teaching is a theme in much educational discourse and often focuses on evidence-based practice. In fact Pendergast (2015) reports that:

> Teaching has grown as a profession which has a high degree of accountability, is informed by evidence-based practice and is subject to professional self-regulation.

The process of professional regulation is also often addressed through government policy and the media, resulting in increasing pressure for teachers to prove they are doing a good job. For teachers to maintain their professional agency it is important to guide practice by strong evidence. Evidence-based practice means that teachers engage with student data not just to 'determine student learning, but to inform, reflect upon, and modify their teaching practice' (Pendergast, 2015).

Usually this process requires teachers to act as researchers. Many education departments internationally have implemented 'teachers as researchers'

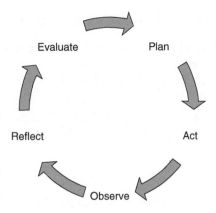

Evaluate   Plan

Reflect   Act

Observe

Figure 1.1 An action learning cycle

programmes allowing teachers to see the value of identifying a problem, thinking of ways to address this problem, gather data, analyse this data, reflect on the findings, implement change and evaluate this practice. Often an Action Research or Action Learning approach is used whereby a cycle of professional learning and investigation takes place.

Vignette 1.1

Leafy High School identified writing as one of their main areas of focus. The school therefore decided to implement a range of strategies to improve the teaching of writing across the entire school programme. These included:

1   Regular allocation of time for students to engage in 'quick' writing activities in each of their content areas.
2   An informal assessment of these tasks by teachers and students.
3   Data cycles that gathered teachers together in pairs with a third member acting as a listener when the teachers discussed the students' work as well as identified areas needing improvement.
4   A more focused programme in the English department on encouraging the students' creative writing – including the establishment of English Excellence classes and an ongoing relationship with a university academic who researches in the area of literacy.

The reason why evidence-based practice, as shown in the above vignette, has become important is not only due to increasing pressure on schools and teachers to be accountable but also that it impacts on, and improves students' learning outcomes, most notably in the area of literacy.

High expectations and leadership opportunities

Michael Fullan's (1993) work on educational change discusses the importance of having moral purpose at the core of teaching and learning practice as it keeps teachers close to the needs of the students. He also highlights the fact that 'change agency' (1993: 12) helps teachers develop more effective strategies to assist in meeting their moral goals. Further, Fullan's work with Hill and Crévola (2006) outlines a Breakthrough model that acknowledges Hill and Crévola's ideas that:

All students can achieve high standards given sufficient time and support

All teachers can teach to high standards given the right conditions and assistance

High expectations and early intervention are essential

Teachers need to be able to articulate what they do and why they do it (theory-based rather than trade-based). (Hill and Crévola, 1997)

Having a belief that all students can achieve is critical in teaching adolescents. So too, is setting high expectations for students. In this sense, for effective and transformational change to happen it is important that teachers acknowledge that their beliefs can be challenged or even 'unlearned'. This is only possible through critical reflection. Fullan (1993), however, notes that this can be difficult due to the systemic constraints and expectations placed on leadership teams as well as teaching teams; often resulting from a 'top-down' approach from policy makers and government departments.

On the one hand, schools are expected to engage in continuous renewal, change expectations are constantly swirling around them. On the other hand, the way teachers are trained, the ways schools are organised, the way the educational hierarchy operates, and the way political decision makers treat educators results in a system that is more likely to retain the status quo. (Fullan, 1993: 12)

Despite the pressures placed upon teachers from external jurisdictions it is possible for transformational change to occur. Chris Sarra, a pioneering Aboriginal principal in Australia, has shown that high expectations produce positive results through his Stronger Smarter campaign. His programme embraces 'a strong and positive sense of what it means to be Aboriginal in contemporary Australian society'. The Stronger Smarter Institute believes that:

Every student deserves to feel safe, respected, valued and happy. Every student deserves to dream, believe and succeed. Unfortunately, this is not the case in Australia. Many children face a culture of low expectations and negative perceptions of who they are. As a result, their self-esteem, achievements and ambitions can be, and so often are, deeply corroded. The solution and the Stronger Smarter approach unlocks the belief and confidence of teachers and parents to give all children the opportunity to be the best they can be. We help people uncover and own habitual patterns that impact on their ways of thinking, seeing, talking and doing and ability to meet challenges. (Stronger Smarter Institute, n.d.)

Therefore creating 'third-space' possibilities (Moje, 2002) is crucial for success when we consider adolescent learners and literacy. The first step is to engage learners through a collaborative and productive model that assumes that all stakeholders have something to offer (Parris et al., 2009). We explore such approaches throughout this volume.

Conclusion

This chapter has explored what literacy is in today's world as we move through a rapid time of growth and movement across the globe. As such, it is important for teachers and educators to be reflective and be able to step back to deeply understand their own literacy learning journeys, their own students and the context in which they work. This will be more and more important given the extensive change that occurs in the education sector as well as the pressures placed upon schools to improve standards and compete with each other. What will be required, however, is an acknowledgement that in order for adolescent literacy standards to be improved we not only value results on high-stakes tests but also well-considered approaches to meeting the individual needs and desires of our students.

    Discussion questions and activities

   Questions

1   What are some everyday literacies that you experience?
2   What are some key attributes of adolescents you would need to consider when planning literacy learning activities in the classroom?
3   How does your social and cultural context impact on the types of literacies you engage in?
4   Create a timeline of your own individual literacy learning journey. Identify significant moments that impacted on your literacy learning. Were they enjoyable or did you experience hardship? How do these influence your own practices in literacy education?
5   Carry out a SWOT analysis on your own competencies or literacies. What are you good at? What areas could you improve? Where and what are the

(Continued)

(Continued)

opportunities and what are the threats? How do you know? Why is it important to know about these?

6   Survey your current literacy and assessment tasks. Is there a clear purpose and is the task meaningful for adolescent learners? Where can you identify the student voice? Are you addressing individual differences in the task as well as in the assessment? Can you identify all four knowledge processes being carried out in the Learning by Design model?

✝✝✝✝ Group activities

1   Carry out an analysis of the context in which you are working. What type of community are you working in? Who are your students? Do a SWOT analysis on each student. What are their personal, social and cultural needs? What are their learning needs? How do you know?

2   Find and document evidence of effective practice from the research on literacy and how this can be implemented with your students and staff. How does this evidence impact on your school's practice?

3   Constantly reflect – allow professional development time to reflect on and in action. Utilise the 4Rs model or an Action Learning model to assist in reflection.

CHAPTER 2

THE ADOLESCENT LEARNER AND LANGUAGE

Chapter objectives

- To develop a solid foundation upon which literacy learning can more effectively take place in the classroom.
- To develop an understanding of the importance of visual, audio, gestural, spatial and tactile forms of language.
- To develop appropriate instructional approaches for the teaching of visual, audio, gestural, spatial and tactile language skills.

Key questions

1   Why is it important for adolescents to discuss social issues in the classroom?
2   How can teachers encourage their students to develop their visual, audio, gestural, spatial and tactile language skills in the classroom?
3   How do adolescents develop their imagination and effectively convey their ideas to others using the appropriate forms of language?

Key words: Speaking, listening, memory, viewing, acting, dialogic interaction, questioning, discussing, elaborating, explaining, showing.

Introduction

Learning a language is an extremely complex process. Many believe that learning language only occurs during the early stages of development. This is not the case. As we move through life we are constantly adding to our vocabulary, learning new forms of expression and consolidating learned skills. At school, young people are exposed to a variety of subject-specific literacies, which require knowledge of specialised and technical language. The importance of oral language for young adolescents who need support should not be overlooked. In order to make language constructive you will need to use the students' knowledge of grammar as a metalanguage to describe how language can be manipulated. Oral and written languages are important modes of communication but each affords different ways of knowing. Grammatical skills can be effectively taught within the context of student writings rather than being taught in isolation (Black and Bannan, 2010).

It is important for students to understand how language works in order to become effective users of language. In particular, teaching students how to use the metalanguage of speaking, listening, viewing and writing will help demystify the process, develop self-confidence, increase self-awareness, self-esteem and empathy for others (Rose, 2009). This chapter will emphasise the importance of rich language and engaging literacy learning environments. It will also explore how language is acquired as well as the central purpose of literacy for adolescent learners. Being literate in an ever-evolving literate world requires learners to set their own goals, monitor their learning and to reflect on what and how they have learned new knowledge and skills.

> Our language can be regarded as an ancient city: a maze of little streets and squares, of old and new houses, of houses with extensions from various periods, and all this surrounded by a multitude of new suburbs with straight and regular streets and uniform houses. (Wittgenstein, 2009: 11)

In the above quote Wittgenstein suggests that language is both ancient and modern. For example many cities, like Rome, are built upon the foundations of ancient structures; the present city is a modern metropolis, and vastly different from 2,000 years ago. The buildings have changed and the technologies that are incorporated within them are worlds apart but Rome retains a certain character and life of its own. Language, like the Roman city, is built upon ancient foundations but is in a constant state of flux depending to some degree upon the literacies, technologies, cross-cultural influences and values that a particular society affords.

Language and society

Literacies of all kinds enable us to make meaning within our society and we use language to shape the concepts that we convey to others. Language is not only used for communication but it is the very substance of thought. We talk to ourselves and this helps us to develop thoughts, solve problems and to control our behaviour. However, language is not just about words as it also incorporates mental imagery and perceived actions. In terms of thinking processes we can self-talk, imagine scenarios and generate moving pictures in our heads. To make meaning in communicative settings we also use oral/aural language, gestures, pictures, symbols and actions.

Today's language learners

In earlier generations learners were viewed as passive readers and listeners or merely observers of television and video. This is in stark contrast to the adolescents in today's Western societies where interactive video games and social media like Snapchat and Instagram position young people in a much more interactive space. They provide a network where ideas can be shared and tested. Digital platforms enable the literacy user to become a more active participant and constructor of meaning.

For previous generations, who grew up in the industrialised world, learning and thinking were influenced by print media and mechanisation. Their world was perceived as being linear: there was a definite beginning and end and knowledge was essentially hierarchical and sequential. All knowledge was concerned with the discovery of truth and absolutes. This was seen to be part of the 'grand narrative' that offered a singular but correct view of the world. The world was predictable in the sense that the economy functioned like a huge machine and jobs tended to be static and unchanging. At the turn of the last century Henry Ford introduced the production line that mechanised manufacturing and mass-produced identical products quickly and cheaply. In order to make commerce and society more efficient the market economy strove for uniformity of language, culture and religion. Nation states developed and their industrialised societies depended on standardisation to make production more efficient. Society was structured in a patriarchal and hierarchical order with essential services run by governments. Knowledge tended to be static and passed on from technocrats to the novice learners. Thus learning became like an apprenticeship with essential knowledge passing from the master to the apprentice. Schools resembled factories with students organised into large age groupings placed in regimented rows of desks in classrooms.

In contrast the post-modern world has been dominated by instant news and images from all over the globe. This globalised trend has given rise to instantaneous delivery of information through satellite communication and Internet connectivity. At the same time, there has been more migration and demographic changes resulting in the blending of cultures along with the introduction of other languages, customs, religions and ideas. The 'grand narrative' no longer has sway because in this ever-changing world there are no longer absolutes but rather a wide diversity of opinions, characterised by many points of view. People are seen as constructors of their own realities rather than as apprentices. This notion has been given momentum by the introduction of a diverse range of mobile technologies, including video games. Identity is in flux as new ideas are easily accessed and information is instant, fragmented and multimodal. Governments have generally adopted neoliberal policies and seek to reduce the influence of the state by transferring more responsibility for welfare to the individual. Thus, deregulation, privatisation and innovation have become paramount. This shift has placed more responsibility on the learner for their choices within what has become known as the 'knowledge society'.

Globalised world regions are becoming more specialised. For example, a car may be assembled in Seoul but the car design might take place in London; the engine may be produced in Melbourne while other car parts are created in Singapore or Shanghai. New technologies bring new words such as 'mobile', 'iPhone', 'Google' and 'texting', and have provided the platform for the hybridisation of English through better communication between countries. New communicative applications, such as Instagram, video conferencing and Google Drive have provided a platform for innovation and collaboration to take place with participants communicating in real time and often thousands of kilometres apart. These newer applications and technologies have provided a catalyst for change in the way people communicate and think. The forms that expressive language embraces are in a constant state of flux with many hybrid forms of literacy emerging such as post-modern picture books, graphic novels, video games, blogs, wikis, Twitter and other multimedia forms such as texting and YouTube.

Language and philosophy

In the early nineteenth century, the Danish philosopher Søren Kierkegaard proposed that language should play a larger role in Western philosophy. He maintained that philosophy has not sufficiently focused on the role that language plays in cognition (Cloeren, 1988). Earlier last century Saussure espoused the notion that knowledge is founded on the 'structures' that make experience possible, such as concepts, and language or 'signs'. Chomsky believed that there is an innate language learning facility within our brain. However, many cognitive scientists and linguists have now discarded Chomsky's concept of 'universal grammar' because the bulk of new research suggests young children acquire and use language by employing various types of thinking processes that may not be language specific (Ibbotson and Tomasello, 2016). Vygotsky, on the other hand, proposed that language is mediated through social interaction. Derrida was another major figure associated with post-structuralism and post-modern philosophy and was best known for developing a form of semiotic analysis known as 'deconstruction' used to unpack the social and contextual meanings embedded within language structures. Halliday (2009) believed that language needed to be grounded in a 'systematic functional analysis', since language had evolved chiefly by being associated with basic human functioning in society. He emphasised that language development involved three elements: learning language, learning through language and learning about language.

National curricula

In recent times, many Western governments have formulated a national curriculum to provide a framework for what they consider to be the core values, knowledge and the skills that their citizens need to know in the twenty-first century. The Australian Curriculum, Assessment and Reporting Authority (ACARA, 2012a) characterises English as a coherent body of disciplinary knowledge that students are to develop over the years, from the formative years through to senior secondary. Three key, interconnected elements that are analogous to those of Halliday were identified: an explicit knowledge about language, an informed appreciation of literature, and expanding repertoires of language use. The content of the language curriculum, however, will always be a contentious issue and needs to be revised regularly due to the changing perception of language in our multicultural and multimodal environment (Atweh and Singh, 2011).

Grammar

Earlier last century English grammar became unpopular and had virtually disappeared from the curriculum by the 1960s. However, by the 1980s the trend had been reversed and a revival of the teaching of grammar took place and grammar is now central to most Western curriculums. As a result many of today's teachers will have a partial or fragmented knowledge about the structure of language (Harper and Rennie, 2009).

Why is grammar important?

1. Explicit awareness of grammatical structures helps students to become more expert particularly when language structures are made more explicit in multicultural contexts.
2. The knowledge of metalanguage enables teachers and students to discuss their language performance and to explore particular communicative aspects of the different genres that incorporate visual, audio, gestural, spatial and tactile forms of language.

3. Language grammar reflects and shapes how a culture thinks and per-
    ceives the world around it. Grammar is an essential part of teaching
    English as a second language because it helps to make explicit the intrica-
    cies and nuances of the new language.
4. Language is the substance of thinking and knowledge of grammar enables
    students to make more logical and meaningful connections with new
    concepts.
5. Language competency develops a more critical response to the ways in
    which language is encountered in society. (Hudson and Walmsley, 2005)

Language in context

There have been universal concerns that past generations have suffered from
a lack of explicit teaching of grammar in schools. Australia is not alone in the
resurgence of the explicit study of language in English curricula. Grammar
teaching has also become a central part of the English curriculum and literacy
policy in the UK (Myhill, 2005). Such a renewed interest in grammar instruction embraces a broader concept of grammar than in previous times. This is
evidenced by a shift from the traditional prescriptive and decontextualised
approach to one that enables the rhetorical power of grammar in enhancing
meaning making and writing development (Jones and Chen, 2012).

In England the Bullock Report (Department of Education and Science,
1975) proposed, 'the traditional view of language teaching was, and indeed
in many schools still is, prescriptive. It is a set of correct forms and prescribed
that these should be taught' (1975: 170). A traditional approach to language
instruction operates in a bottom-up fashion that begins with separate frag-
ments of texts and then when the parts are assembled meaning is realised.
For example, orthographic and phonic elements form the basic building
blocks of words. Generally, this approach progresses from parts of words to
words, to phrases and then to sentences and paragraphs. In contrast functional pedagogy is a top-down process approach that focuses on the
communicative intent and social purposes of language (Kalantzis et al., 2016).
The Bullock Report deplored the teaching of grammar that was 'prescriptive'
and which identified a 'set of correct forms' (Department of Education and
Science, 1975: 170). For many contemporary practitioners the teaching of
grammar in context is essential and avoids the worst excesses of prescriptive
grammar. Such an approach gives impetus by way of a systemic-functional
approach to grammar, which emphasises language in use (Myhill, 2005).
Today most Western countries have a highly contextualised approach to
teaching language. Hence, grammar is related more to patterns of meaning
in texts and to particular contexts of usage (Love et al., 2015).

In Australia over the past 20 years, researchers and practitioners have
also been implementing methods based on Halliday's functional approach

to language in social settings in order to make the kinds of meanings that are important in our daily lives, in school learning and in the wider community. The functional approach was introduced through a genre-based pedagogy in the 1980s so that students would have access to the linguistic resources needed for success in school. The emphasis was on making content more explicit by 'deconstructing' genre by noting its social forms and conventions. The genre approach was, in part, a reaction to the process writing and whole language movements of the 1960s and 1970s based on the work of Chomsky. These latter approaches were naturalistic and child centred and viewed language learning as self-directed. It was assumed that language would flourish with teachers acting as facilitators providing the appropriate conditions. However, the naturalistic approaches were eventually considered as being devoid of structure and content (Derewianka, 2015). In contrast, genres reflect various purposes for which language is used within the socio-cultural context. As the complexity of purpose increases so does the genre (Derewianka, 2012). Hybrid genres and genres within genres have begun to appear. For example, the *Twilight* series has enormous appeal to adolescents with its mix of vampire genres and the romantic teenage genre.

While traditional grammar was typically taught in decontextualised ways, a functional approach to teaching grammar establishes an intimate relationship between contexts and language functions. At the holistic level, the language system has evolved within the context of particular cultures to meet the needs of that society (Derewianka, 2012). A functional model of language describes how language varies from context to context. It shows, for example:

- how the language of history differs from the language of science
- how the language we use in everyday conversations with friends differs from giving a formal oral presentation to an unfamiliar audience
- how spoken language is different from written language
- how the language choices we make when writing a narrative differ from those we make when writing a report or a scientific explanation.

Multimodal forms of language

Mobile phones have become increasingly popular throughout the world as a primary means of accessing Internet resources. Resistance to the use of mobiles in the classroom continues to hinder their adoption in many schools. However, a growing number of schools are finding ways to benefit from this technology. Among adolescents there is also a strong interest in electronic books and electronic note pad applications, which have the capacity to augment basic literacy functions. These new applications support not only immersive experiences but also support social interaction. These experiences are changing our perception of what it means to read and engage with literacy. Mobile technologies enable abundant access to information, social networks, tools for learning and productivity. Mobile devices continue to change and evolve and have been given impetus with the development of more affordable and reliable broadband networks (Johnson et al., 2015).

In recent times oral and written forms of language are blended with other modes that convey meaning in the electronic cyber space. Thus, new forms of multimodal representations also include icons, pictures, illustrations, video, music, sound effects, facial expressions, gesture and tactile modes of expression (Cloonan, 2011). Coupled with these multiple modes of expression are increasingly complex demands, which are placed on students as readers/ viewers (see Chapter 7). Students need an ever increasing set of skills to decode, read fluently, critically comprehend more complex and difficult multimodal texts and remain motivated to independently continue to improve their reading and responding activity (Rennie, 2016).

However, it is obvious that teachers and students need a metalanguage (or system of 'signs') to talk about oral and written forms of language to integrate multimodal forms such as visual, audio, gestural, spatial and tactile meanings (Macken-Horarik, 2011). Without a metalanguage for describing multimodal texts, understandings remain tacit rather than explicitly articulated and brought to consciousness (Cloonan, 2011). This is an issue of grammar. The development of a multimodal metalanguage is a pressing need for educators and students alike (New London Group 1996; 2000). Cope and Kalantzis (2000) developed this notion by designing a framework that incorporated linguistic, visual, spatial, gestural and audio categories, which were each explored in terms of five dimensions of meaning: representational, social, organisational, contextual and ideological (see Chapter 6).

Dimensions of language

Language, as a thinking activity, has three dimensions that shift the focus of language according to the type of thinking process that is required (see Chapter 10 for more detail). The *representational* dimension requires the learner to focus on the surface features of text in a type of bottom-up or data driven process. The *cognitive* dimension works in a top-down fashion whereby the learner combines the new information with prior knowledge. The *reflective* dimension acts in a metacognitive mode whereby the learner monitors thinking processes and looks at future possibilities. In terms of language the New London Group (1996) viewed meaning making in the multi-literate environment as design (see Table 2.1 below). This concept connected with the notion that learning and productivity are the results of the designs or structures of complex social systems influenced by environments, technology, beliefs and texts. Thus, the concept of the designer places the learner as an actor on the literacy stage.

Table 2.1   The dimensions of language

Cognitive dimension (Woolley, 2011)	Designer (New London Group, 1996)
Representational	Design
Cognitive	Designer
Reflective	Redesign

Designing is the process of re-representation and re-contextualisation. What this means is that meaning is constantly being fashioned and reshaped through various semiotic systems. Knowledge is transformed to produce new constructions and representations of reality. The *designer* uses available designs in ways that transform them to create new uses with old materials. Therefore, listening, viewing, reading, writing, speaking and acting are all activities that enable new understandings to develop from the various kinds of texts that are encountered in the process of design. *Redesigning* is the process of forming new meanings in different contexts; it is grounded on cultural patterns and shared forms of meaning. Redesign is also the production of new products or resources that are being reproduced or transformed (New London Group, 1996).

The term designer implies that the learner is placed at the centre of creative language production. From another perspective the learner must interpret and use the designs or products of their society. This requires the learner to deconstruct language and its meanings from multiple perspectives: representational, social, organisational, contextual and ideological (see Table 2.2 below).

The design paradigm positions the learner from the perspective of the producer while the semiotic conventions position the learner as consumer of the language product. Each of the representational, social, organisational, contextual and ideological dimensional elements can be applied to the various modes of language such as: linguistic, visual, audio, gestural and spatial (see Table 2.3 below).

Table 2.2   Some different perspectives of the dimensions of language

Cognitive dimension (Woolley, 2011)	Designer/producer (New London Group, 1996)	Semiotic conventions (available designs)/products (Cope and Kalantzis, 2000)
Representational	Design	Representational
Cognitive	Designer	Social Organisational Contextual
Reflective	Redesign	Ideological

Table 2.3 Dimensions of multimodal meaning framework (see Chapter 6)

Dimensions of meaning	Modes of meaning				
	Linguistic	Visual	Audio	Gestural	Spatial
Representational					
Social					
Organisational					
Contextual					
Ideological					

Critical literacy

English education has, in many cases, been disconnected from the diverse lives of student populations ignoring the increasing trend of racial, cultural, linguistic and social class diversity (Skerrett et al., 2015). Any critical literacy engagement in the classroom should be guided by flexible definitions that encompass a variety of existing text forms and should take into consideration the diversity of user approaches when interacting with language. Critical engagement in literacy is not a static process, but is reflective and ever changing depending upon the current social expectations. For this reason it is important that you are aware of the ways in which students engage with texts, when they interact with one another face-to-face or online, and to incorporate the kinds of activities that will engage the students meaningfully. This knowledge should form the basis for opportunities to involve discussion, debates, questioning and sharing ideas related to text (Leu et al., 2004). The types of questions (see Table 2.4 below) should model the reflective thinking that individuals should use when engaging with aural language, gestures, pictures, symbols, and actions. This self-questioning approach will make possible the utilisation of the funds of knowledge that students bring into the classroom. Furthermore, paying attention to the ways in which adolescents engage with texts outside of school, can lead to more motivated and engaged learners (Kurki, 2015).

Popular culture

Hip-Hop is a cultural identity that incorporates rapping, breakdancing, graffiti and deejaying while encompassing notions of community, subculture and self. In particular rap takes poetry and music into a distinct contemporary context where social concerns are often considered and expressed (Love, 2014) (see Chapter 10). With direct and critical inquiry in secondary classrooms, Hip-Hop has the capacity to expose white adolescents to diverse racial representations and discourses that undermine dominant paradigms of race and invite youth to reflect on how race

Table 2.4   Guiding questions to accompany the critical engagement continuum (sourced from Kurki, 2015)

Type of questioning/ response	Guiding questions
Analyse	*Representational*: Where does the text come from (source)? How is the text being produced?
	Social: What is the purpose of the text? Why is it produced? Is the message real/fake or true/false?
	Organisational: Is only one source used to find out more about a text?
	Contextual: What is the message/meaning of the text? Are generalisations made about the text's meaning?
	Ideological: Who is/is not involved in producing the text? Why?
Evaluate	Do I like/dislike, agree/disagree with the message?
	Are there personal responses with little or no reasoning provided (i.e. I like, I think …)?
	Is the text shared with others (with little or no reasoning given for sharing)?
	Am I comfortable even if the text's message does not align with my personal beliefs?
	If the quality of text is judged – how will this affect the overall meaning?
	Am I, as reader, skeptical of the message in the text?
Challenge	How does the text affect me and/or others (personal–global responses to the text)?
	Are connections to other texts or experiences made?
	Do I question the message(s) of the text (does it disrupt the status quo)?
	Should the text be shared with others (consider collaboratively)?
	Which social justice issues are addressed by the text? How?
Transform	How am I moved to act/respond because of the text's message?
	What existing views of mine are transformed because of the text (text as catalyst to transform ideas)?
	Is there reflection and action occurring (praxis)?

operates in their own lives and society at large (Netcoh, 2013). Hip-Hop not only connects with contemporary social issues but it can be a fascinating launch pad for the study of more traditional forms of music, art and poetry.

Vignette 2.1

Mr Thomas introduced Hip-Hop culture into his history lessons as a way of initiating a unit of work on the development of black American history and culture. He also wanted to show how this musical trend has influenced local youth culture and democracy by giving the poor and underprivileged a voice. They explored

(Continued)

(Continued)

aspects of Hip-Hop culture, including a viewing of exerts of the film *8 Mile*. *8 Mile* is a 2002 American semi-biographical drama film set in 1995. It is an account of a young white rapper named Jimmy 'B-Rabbit', who attempts to begin a music career in rap, a genre dominated by African Americans. After viewing and discussing the film the students were asked to form small research groups and use their mobile technology to find newspaper articles related to racial tensions in the United States. The groups were then asked to discuss the issues raised and to use a brainstorm chart to list their thoughts with the view of responding using a linguistic, visual, audio, gestural or spatial mode of literacy. One group, for example, decided to make a rap music composition and to perform it at a future school assembly.

Questions

1 Is popular culture a suitable topic to discuss in class? Why/why not?
2 By giving students a project to work on it will decrease the time that could be devoted to delivering other course content. How can you overcome this problem? What are the benefits/problems?

Film-making

Film-making and media production can support student engagement with their world in a sensory and embodied way by interacting with tangible environments and people inhabiting those spaces. In other words their world can be perceived through the mind and kinaesthetically as the body moves through space and time. It can provide a sense of place where culture can be localised (Mills et al., 2013).

Vignette 2.2

Johnston Central High School organised a special half-day each week for a whole school term where students could choose from a number of activities associated with their interest areas. The range of activities involved drama, writing, art and many other aspects of literacy. The overall theme was to discover personal identities and meanings related to the place in which they interact and live. The students were to be engaged across disciplines and would integrate aspects of science, history and art.

Mrs Parker decided to conduct sessions on documentary filming. She had a group of 20 students and three interested parents who had some experience with filming. She organised the students into four groups of five with a film camera for each group. One group decided to explore the local nature park and interview people that visited the area. Another group chose the war memorial as a focal point and interviewed people that had relatives who had served in the armed forces by posing the question, 'What does the memorial mean to you?' The third group interviewed a migrant community and collected personal stories of their experiences in their new location. The fourth group interviewed people from the local art society and explored cityscape and land-scape paintings over time.

The groups were introduced to basic filming and media production skills such as making a storyboard, using filming techniques such as long shots, panning and using zoom. They were also introduced to various software and apps to help with the production such as a storyboard app, 'iMovie', a soundtrack app and timing apps. Interviewing techniques, lighting and how to use a microphone on-site were also important techniques that the students would need to make a professional production. Editing and voice-overs using 'iMovie' were also impor-tant elements of the production. The volunteer parents rotated between groups to advise on some aspects relative to their experience.

Questions

1   How could the teachers of history, art and science use the documentaries as a discussion point in their own disciplines?
2   What other activities could you add to the repertoire of topics?
3   How would aspects of community, place and culture be enhanced using this activity?

Literacy in the teaching context

When transitioning to early secondary schooling, a large number of students have difficulties with the increased complexity, abstraction and technicality of the language required for learning in high school (Christie and Derewianka, 2008). For example, students studying history often rely solely on their exist-ing literacy knowledge and skills. However, this particular domain of knowledge will require learners to strategically focus on the relationship between genre, writing, personal belief and new knowledge (Allender and Freebody, 2016) (see Chapter 7).

Harnessing technology

Keeping pace with the rapid proliferation of information, software tools and devices is challenging not only for students but for teachers as well. The chal-lenge is exacerbated by the fact that digital technologies morph and change quickly at a rate that generally outpaces curriculum development. As a teacher you will need to engage with new technologies, ideas and ways of teaching in the ever-changing technological and digital landscape. The technologies you use are increasingly Cloud-based and tutorials can be accessed via YouTube or by way of specialised and topical blogs. Online professional collaboration between teachers can also help you to make effective changes in your practice with a deeper awareness of your own professional and technological needs.

English language learners

In the United States in the academic year 2012–13 almost one out of every 10 K-12 students was classified as an English language learner (ELL) (Kena et al., 2015). Some regions are experiencing more rapid demographic shifts and some schools are underprepared to meet the needs of their ELL students. Often students are placed in mainstream classrooms regardless of their English language proficiency after only one year in specialised instructional settings with other ELL students. Braden et al. (2016) found that even teachers who were untrained in teaching ELL learners had the potential to engage students in effective learning but they emphasised the importance of personalised student–teacher interaction. For example, in addressing a student's vocabulary needs you, as the teacher, to select the appropriate known small words to explain the 'big words'. In other words it is important to ask students what they think. This will give you valuable insights as opposed to relying just on your own understanding. You should consider the question, 'How did my students show me how I made the input comprehensible for them?' This not only empowers the student but it also empowers you as the teacher.

Social justice issues and language

In modern Western multicultural and democratic societies social justice issues have become paramount. Language that is presented and used in the classroom can empower or disempower individuals or groups of individuals. This is because words (or signs) and the relationships between words and groups of words can convey deeper meaning that is emotionally laden.

Conclusion

Visual, audio, gestural, spatial and tactile language skills often combine in different ways according to the medium and the purposes intended. Traditionally they have been taught as separate and often isolated elements.

However, in the multimodal and multimedia worlds in which adolescents are situated they are exposed to combinations of these elements in a myriad of different ways. However, what is important is that there needs to be a distinction between the process and the product of literacy. Too often the content or product is emphasised while the process is neglected. The process involves three dimensions that include representational, cognitive and reflective aspects. This emphasis gives a central role to the 'designer' who utilises different modes of communication in what has become a much more instant and interactive communicative environment. The student of the twenty-first century must take more responsibility for their creative literacy endeavours and must be critically aware of the persuasive power of language.

Discussion questions and activities

Questions

1   How might it help students to talk about a task together before attempting it?
2   What are the advantages for adolescents of working collaboratively?
3   When is it most appropriate for the teacher to be involved in group discussions?
4   Under what conditions is it more appropriate for teachers not to take part in dialogic interactions during group activities?

✝✝✝✝ Group activities

1   Divide the class into discussion groups and answer the following question by creating a brainstorm chart and writing the group's thoughts on the chart. What are the advantages of having the students contribute their own ideas during group discussions?
2   Choose a topical discussion. Set up a fish bowl activity by nominating a small group discussion and having the rest of the class observe and make notes on the interactions within the focus group. Ask them to discuss the dynamics within the group. What were the positive and negative aspects of the group discussion?
3   Divide the class into groups of about five students and provide used photocopy paper, Sellotape and paper clips. Ask the groups to make the largest tower possible using the materials given for a competition between groups. Each group will be given 10 minutes to try and build the tallest freestanding paper tower in the time given. The students will be primed to think about the dynamics of the group for a reflective discussion at the end.
4   The same groups (as in group activity 3) will be asked to discuss the notion of assigning roles to individual members as a way of structuring groups. What roles can be given to group members? What are possible barriers to assigning roles to individual group members? How can these be overcome?

CHAPTER 3

DIVERSE LEARNERS AND LITERACY

Chapter objectives

- To understand the scope and nature of learning difficulties within contemporary high school classrooms.
- To develop appropriate instructional approaches to accommodate and adjust to individual needs within the literacy learning classroom.
- To develop a repertoire of strategies to foster literacy engagement and reading independence.

Key questions

1 What is a learning difficulty/disability?
2 How do you re-engage the disengaged students in literacy classrooms?
3 How can you adjust your teaching strategies and use classroom accommodations to engage adolescents with meaningful learning?

Key words: Literacy, diversity, inclusion, language, adaptations, accommodations, learning difference.

Introduction

This chapter considers learner diversity with the focus on adolescents who learn differently including gifted and talented learners. Biological, cognitive and behavioural factors combined with external causes impact on a student's ability to learn and often lead to a cycle of underachievement in literacy. From recent research studies there is now considerable evidence that learning difficulties may not be attributed solely to intrinsic deficits within the adolescent, but may, to some degree, be related to the learning experiences provided for students learning to engage with literacy. There is an acknowledgement that some learning difficulties are resistant to good evidence-based pedagogical practice and that a team approach may offer a wider pool of expertise. Response-To-Intervention (RTI) is an example of a whole school three-tiered team approach that is gaining increasing acceptance as a process to assist students that may need support with their literacy learning.

RTI emphasises the importance of the identification of student strengths rather than weaknesses. In inclusive classrooms the teacher is required to make reasonable adjustments to differentiate the curriculum so that all adolescents will be able to perform literacy tasks to their full potential.

> The cause of learning difficulty usually cannot be attributed to a single factor. Most learning problems arise from a complex interaction among variables such as the learners' knowledge and experience, learners' cognitive ability, learners' confidence and expectation of success, teachers' instructional method, complexity of teachers' language, the perceived relevance and value of the curriculum content or task, and suitability of resource materials. Until recently, teaching methods and instructional materials were rarely investigated as possible causes of a learning difficulty. (Westwood, 2015: 7)

In the above quote Westwood suggests that students experiencing learning difficulties are not a homogeneous group and the basis or origin of their learning problems can vary quite considerably (Alexander, 2010). He also acknowledges that in recent years there has been a major shift to a much broader view of learning difficulties. It is assumed that educators will seldom be able to change many of the factors within the learner but are more able to adjust the curriculum and teaching methods to provide a more supportive learning environment that will enhance the students' ability to self-regulate learning with improved learning outcomes.

Social justice

Notions of equality and human rights have come to prominence in Western education systems, particularly since the civil rights movement of the 1960s in America. This is not just a recent phenomenon but it is part of a general trend that has stemmed from the social justice ideas generated from Ancient Greek philosophical traditions to French and English philosophers since the time of the Renaissance. The notions of equality and the building of an inclusive society have been further reinforced through the Universal Declaration of Human Rights (United Nations, 1948). The notion of human rights and anti-discrimination in terms of gender, race, religion and disability has gained traction from anti-discrimination and freedom of information legislation in many countries. Many contemporary inclusive schools apply social justice principles by exercising transparent and non-discriminative practices while endeavouring to cater for human diversity in all its forms leading to a fairer and more just society.

Inclusive schools populated by adolescents in most Western countries are generally not homogenous; they are diverse academically, economically, socially, culturally and linguistically (OECD, 2010). The term inclusion also implies that all students have different needs and will be catered for in mainstream classrooms (Reid, 2013). Inclusive education should be viewed as a flexible concept that includes all adolescents in suitable environments where they learn best (Warnock and Norwich, 2010). As a teacher you will also need to foster a classroom culture of inclusion that is influenced by positive attitudes, appropriate school policies and distinct departmental guidelines.

Learning differences

Thus, in recent times there has been a fundamental change in direction from what was often labelled as the medical model towards a social model, which shifts the emphasis from individual deficits to a school systems paradigm (Skidmore, 2004). A common method to identify students with a learning disability was to determine the discrepancy between their actual academic achievement and their perceived ability. This discrepancy was normally determined by measuring potential learning ability using an Intellectual Quota (IQ) test (usually in the form of the Wechsler Intelligence Test) by comparing it with reading tests to measure actual academic performance at school. It was assumed that if the gap was sufficiently large enough the child would be classified as having a learning disability. However, the so called 'discrepancy method' assumed that all learning problems were located within the learner and ignored other fundamental factors outside of the learner such as the suitability of the literacy teaching and learning environment. As a consequence, there was a tendency to 'blame the victim' rather than to adapt or adjust the teaching style and curriculum to accommodate for the diversity of learning needs.

The Australian Curriculum, Assessment and Reporting Authority (ACARA, 2014) has taken a broad view whereby the term, 'students with special needs' includes those with disabilities, health conditions or learning difficulties.

Westwood (2015) maintained that such terms could be confusing and denote different groups depending on which country or region in which they are situated. In reality, in most Western classrooms today there is a much broader spectrum of additional learning needs and learning styles that do not fit neatly into clearly definable categories. What is certain is that many learning problems are often long lasting and resistant to normal classroom interventions, particularly with adolescents who may have struggled with underachievement over many years of their school education. In the UK as many as one fifth of all school aged adolescents are identified as having additional education needs (Alexander, 2010; Rose, 2009). The situation in Australia and New Zealand is similar where it is estimated that 10 to 20 per cent of students are failing to reach literacy benchmarks (Louden et al., 2000; Rohl and Rivalland, 2002; Skues and Cunningham, 2011).

This chapter will use the term 'learning difficulties' as a broad term that not only includes students with learning disabilities but also encompasses students who are likely to have non-permanent cognitive or behavioural difficulties or whose poor school performance results from external environmental, social or cultural conditions (Louden et al., 2000). What is certain is that students with learning difficulties will most likely experience considerable problems with literacy in all its many forms. For example, adolescents who struggle academically with reading will present with immense academic challenges, particularly in middle and high school classrooms because texts of all kinds, at this stage of their development, are cognitively demanding (Droop and Verhoeven 2003; Perfetti, 2007). This is due to the fact that adolescents can expect to encounter more complex grammatical structures, newer and more unfamiliar domain-specific content and they are increasingly required to use higher-order text processing and research skills such as inference generation and comprehension monitoring as they progress through middle and high school (Cain and Oakhill, 2006; 2007).

To teach such a diverse group of adolescents you need to consider a range of learning related factors such as: learner characteristics and teacher

Figure 3.1 Factors influencing learning

responses, literate teaching practices, and socio-cultural influences (see Figure 3.1). These issues will be further discussed below.

Socio-cultural influences

Ideas about human gender, sexuality, race, class and even what is regarded as being normal also have a large impact on learning. In society these views have been changing over time and from place to place and various groups of people negotiate these meanings differently. However, one of the main theoretical frameworks driving the move towards inclusion is social constructivism, which proposes that knowledge and meaning are constructed by the interactions between people and society. The notion that humans are part of widening spheres of influence (Bronfenbrenner, 1992) and learn best in social contexts (Vygotsky, 1978) will be discussed further in Chapter 5. Moreover, the types of literate practices available in the home, such as having access to, and being able to use computers or smartphones and having familiarity with books, have been found to affect the diversity of literacy outcomes at school. Other factors such as socio-cultural and language differences between home and school, social class, educational experience of the parents, and family income will also profoundly influence school literacy outcomes (McNaughton et al., 2004; Rohl and Rivalland, 2002).

Collaborative context

Invariably there will be tensions between the needs of the class as a whole and how the needs of the individual student can be met (Warnock, 2012). However, many problems can be overcome when schools develop a team approach by taking advantage of expertise and resources within their wider community to provide a systematic and whole school line of attack. For example, you as the classroom teacher may seek the assistance of the multi-disciplinary team when you become aware that classroom-based interventions or accommodations may not be working effectively for a particular student.

It should be acknowledged that some students do not respond adequately to the normal evidence-based pedagogy. What is often required in these circumstances is to meet each adolescent's unique academic needs with a responsive team teaching approach to each individual's academic, social and emotional needs. RTI, for example, is such a framework in which a three-tiered evidence-based intervention is provided to support all learners in general education settings (Allington, 2012). It provides a structure for the provision of increasingly intensive interventions that are informed by frequent monitoring and assessment of each student's progress. Tier 1 is considered to be accessible to regular classroom education and received by all students. Tier 2 interventions increase in duration and intensity with progress more frequently monitored than for Tier 1 interventions and will often involve differentiated group work. Tier 3 would involve referral to a specialist learning support teacher and access to specialised short-term withdrawal intervention programmes.

Factors that impact learning

In most developed countries however classroom teachers are expected to have the necessary skills to adjust their teaching environment and teaching methods to support adolescents with individual differences. Before entering into a discussion about what should be done and how teachers can accommodate for diversity in the classroom we must first examine the types of factors (see Figure 3.2 below) that may impact on a student's ability to learn effectively. There are broadly three types of factors: biological, cognitive and behavioural, which will be discussed below.

Biological/sensory

For many adolescents, particularly for those with dyslexia, there may be genetic predisposition as a possible cause for their continuing literacy difficulties (Bender, 2002). However, not all reading difficulties can be attributed solely to a genetic origin. There is evidence that neurological abnormalities may be caused by biochemical and other environmental factors, such as poor diet, poor food quality, environmental toxins, bacterial or viral infections, which may have an ongoing negative influence on their literacy development. In our modern technological environment there are many chemicals present that may contribute to certain types of learning disorders (Cortiella and Horowitz, 2014; Needleman et al., 1979). For example, adolescents with high levels of lead in their bodies have been found to score lower than other adolescents on several important variables including verbal performance, language processing and attention.

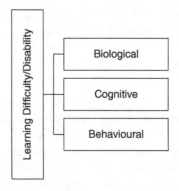

Figure 3.2   Factors that impact learning

Furthermore, many common substances such as food additives, refined sugars, eggs, corn and milk can also cause allergic reactions that may be associated with other learning disabilities. If a student has sensory deficits related to vision or hearing they are more than likely to have major problems in literacy.

Cognitive factors

Cognitive deficits are often related to the functioning of working memory and often, but not always, will have a biological origin. For example, a child with attention deficit hyperactivity disorder (ADHD) may have an immature neurological condition, which affects his/her cognitive functioning. It often translates into an executive cognitive deficit that exhibits as an inability to consistently focus attention, maintain concentration and manipulate, store and retrieve information in working memory. However, cognitive deficits are often influenced and reinforced by factors outside the learner such as poor parenting or poor teaching practices. For example, language proficiency is normally influenced by the home environment and also by the quality of the teaching and social interactions at school. As language is an integral part of the thinking process and the foundation for reading, any language-processing difficulties will translate into broader literacy deficits.

Behavioural factors

Adolescents who have literacy difficulties often develop behavioural issues that compound their learning problems. They tend to read less in and out of school when compared to their more successful peers and are often reluctant to engage with literacy tasks. As a consequence, they are frequently described as disengaged learners who have a limited range of effective literacy skills (Guthrie and Davis, 2003; Saenez et al., 2005; Westwood, 2015). This behavioural disengagement frequently leads to a widening academic gap between themselves and their more successful peers who have more exposure to texts of all kinds and subsequently develop more breadth and depth in reading vocabulary and generally more advanced literacy skills (Stanovich, 1986).

Cycle of failure

Having a learning difficulty can often lead to a complex cycle of failure, particularly in regard to literacy (see Figure 3.3 below). Most struggling students typically lack confidence, especially after comparing their own academic performance to that of their more successful adolescent peers often resulting in anxiety and reluctance to participate in future reading activities. As a consequence they appear to be less motivated. They are often reluctant to try because they expect to fail and seek to avoid embarrassment, particularly if they are required to read in front of others thereby developing what is often referred to as 'learned-helplessness'. Learned helpless students tend to believe that it is better to avoid performing a learning task than to attempt the task only to experience more failure.

In some cases their avoidance strategies will take the form of overt or distracting classroom behaviours. Often the response for such disruptive behaviour is exclusion from the unwanted activity. However, this inappropriate teacher response reinforces the unsatisfactory behaviour and ensures that it will be repeated in the future. A typical example is James, who had often been sent to sit outside the principal's office for disruptive behaviour. This happened on several occasions and meant that he succeeded in avoiding the embarrassment that he would have to face in front of his peers. Alternatively, many learned helpless students will exhibit much more passive avoidance behaviours causing their teachers to view them as being lazy or unmotivated. Most students with learning difficulties are not lazy or unmotivated. On the contrary, they will often be highly motivated to avoid tasks that they perceive as contributing to their poor self-perception.

Such behaviours often contribute to their teacher's low expectations and are frequently associated with the setting of lower academic performance goals. As a result, it then becomes a self-fulfilling prophecy because when you expect less from students they tend to meet those low expectations. Thus, the lower the expectations and the lack of literacy challenges and less exposure to new words result in a restricted vocabulary and scarce reading skill practice (Stanovich, 1986). Consequently, the gap begins to widen between those who have more literacy skills and those who don't. As literacy impacts on other domains of the curriculum struggling adolescents will begin to experience failure across the domains of learning. What is certain is that their continuing poor school performance will lead to fewer rewards, which further contributes to a lack of confidence and greater performance anxiety. And so the cycle continues but each time round the negative cycle of academic disengagement becomes even stronger (see Figure 3.3 below).

Thus, disengaged students are less intrinsically motivated and generally attribute their lack of success to factors outside of themselves, which they perceive as beyond their control (Ryan and Deci, 2000; Wigfield et al., 2004). For example, they may attribute their failure to the perception that they are just 'dumb' or that the work is 'stupid'. As a result they are reluctant to try because they believe that by not trying they can protect their self-esteem by thinking, 'I did not succeed because I just did not try' (Paris et al., 2001).

Motivation and the cycle of achievement

Often when students are assessed the emphasis is on looking for their weaknesses, which can contribute to a negative view of the student (Alexander,

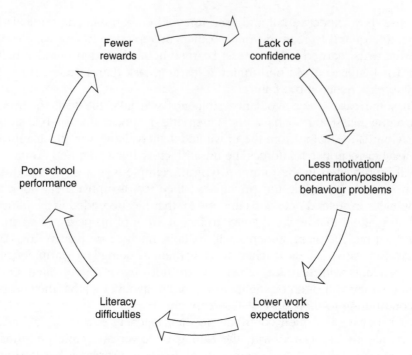

Figure 3.3 Cycle of failure

2010). This often leads to a deficit view of the individual in that the adolescent's problems are viewed solely as being within the learner. For example, on many report cards there are typical comments such as Jack 'lacks interest', 'is unmotivated' and 'often will not try'. These comments usually reflect the tendency to 'blame the victim' and will most likely ignore the fact that behaviour can be influenced by altering the teaching style, learning environment and the task demands.

Intrinsic motivation

Many teachers and parents still hold the mistaken belief that student motivation is part of a global personality trait and view students are either being motivated or unmotivated across all domains of learning (Bong, 2004). What is certain is that motivation is strongly influenced by the kinds of experiences adolescents have at school. Moreover, it has been shown that most students' motivation and academic beliefs are differentiated across subject areas (Bong, 2004; Wigfield et al., 2004). It should be emphasised that many adolescents with learning difficulties have foundational funds of knowledge, can be very creative, and can make valuable contributions in the classroom particularly when their strengths are acknowledged and catered for (Reid, 2013). Moreover, all adolescents will have a number of strengths; you will need to acknowledge their particular abilities and achievements as part of the move towards developing them as more motivated and engaged learners (Reid, 2013). Thus, motivation will be enhanced when adolescents are provided with meaningful choices among different activities based on their individual learning interests within a lesson. When they perceive that they have more control over their learning and are provided with the skills to enable them to exercise choice they will be more intrinsically motivated and engaged (Guthrie and Davis, 2003; Wigfield et al., 2004).

To make this happen you will need to develop realistic expectations for the struggling adolescent learner. This means intentionally transferring the locus of control to the learner within each activity. To do this you will need to design tasks that are interesting, relevant and challenging but are not beyond their academic capability. This requires that you explicitly teach the necessary skills needed for each assigned task and that the student knows why, how and when to use them. Thus, intrinsic motivation requires fostering three domains of student strength: competence (skills and understandings needed for the task), a degree of autonomy (locus of control), and related-ness (interest and relevance) to the topic and to the audience or community of learners. Improved literacy outcomes will be the result of the joint func-tioning of motivational processes together with the fostering of cognitive comprehension strategies, social interaction and the development of concep-tual knowledge (Guthrie and Davis, 2003). To reinforce these factors you will need to give more timely and appropriate feedback as part of a positive and upward cycle of achievement (the final chapter on assessment will focus on the role of teacher feedback in more detail). This involves attribution training: part of the shift to locus of control is the notion of attributing success or failure to the effort and skill applied to the task.

Researchers have found that high quality teaching is the most important element in adolescents' literacy learning (Westwood, 2015). Thus, successful teaching depends on your knowledge and your ability to find teaching meth-ods and strategies that provide suitable learning environments for those students identified as having difficulties in literacy (Alexander, 2010; Rohl and Rivalland, 2002). Good teaching will be contingent upon the ability of you, as the teacher, to adequately assess individual students and to provide the appropriate literacy interventions by differentiating the curriculum.

Literate practices, products and purposes

The differentiation of the curriculum usually entails making accommodations for student differences and making reasonable adjustments to the curriculum and to the teaching delivery. For example, a student with ADHD may need to be placed in a classroom without too many distractions and with explicit rou-tines that are listed on a poster board in the classroom. The quieter environment and the explicit listing of the classroom routines will help all students to concentrate and provide them with a predictable working environment. Some teachers may have the view that struggling learners take up too much of their time and effort. However, research demonstrates that students with learning difficulties rarely receive as much attention from their teachers compared to their more successful peers (Woolley, 2011). These concerns can easily be addressed with appropriate planning, accommodation and forethought. Most accommodations are simple adjustments to teaching methods and are easily implemented in the modern classroom situation. It must be emphasised that in an inclusive classroom all adolescents should be treated fairly and so the accommodations or adjustments should not disadvantage other students. On the contrary most accommodations do not impede the learning of others and many accommodations should benefit all students.

Vignette 3.1

Sarah has a minor hearing impairment and a history of underachievement in many subject areas, particularly those that require her to process language. She performs well in mathematics, art and physical education and appears to be a very bright person. The learning support teacher, together with some of her teachers, has designed a number of accommodations that will help her in her classes.

For example, in English, Ms Johnson always makes sure that Sarah sits at the front of the room so that she can clearly hear the instructions and observe the teacher's body language and mouth movements. Ms Johnson also makes other simple accommodations such as making sure that instructions are clear and delivered in shorter sentences. The important instructions and concepts are also written on the white board. Wherever possible Sarah's teacher supplements verbal concepts with diagrams, graphic organisers and illustrations using the interactive white board or other teaching aids. When asking questions in the classroom Ms Johnson allows extra time for Sarah to process the question before answering.

Questions

1 What were some of the accommodations made by Sarah's teacher?
2 How would these accommodations benefit Sarah?
3 Did these accommodations have a negative impact on the rest of the class?
4 In terms of fairness, did the accommodations place Sarah in an unfair situation?

Accommodations

In making accommodations you will need to address a number of facets of learning to develop a self-regulating environment. Your initial approach to instruction should involve a well-balanced curriculum that builds upon an adolescent's existing background knowledge and skills (Vellutino et al., 2004; Woolley, 2014a). This balance should integrate three thinking levels: task, cognitive and metacognitive levels, that consider a whole range of reader and text factors. The task level is concerned with the instructional product, with the navigation of text, with facts and with basic learning outcomes. The cognitive level is more concerned with the learning strategies and thinking processes that are used to comprehend and construct new understandings. The metacognitive level focuses on the learning process itself. It is concerned with the formation of learning goals, the monitoring of the learning goals, reflecting on what was learnt and the efficacy of the learning goals.

Products

According to Gunning (2003) inappropriate or unsuitable readability levels of reading material is one of the significant causes of students experiencing reading difficulties. In writing it may mean that students need to have the necessary writing or keyboard skills to put their thoughts into words. For a literacy task to be motivating and involving, it is essential a text should be age appropriate, challenging but not too difficult, and related to the interests and goals of the readers.

At this surface level of engagement the struggling literacy learner may often be overwhelmed with the sheer complexity or enormity of the task. To make the learning task more considerate for an adolescent with a difficulty certain adjustments and adaptations may need to be made so that the task provides enough of a challenge without becoming frustrating for the student. For example, when introducing a new literacy learning activity new vocabulary could be introduced and discussed before the reading of the text. A concept map could be introduced to develop the concept's connections to known words and ideas. When discussion is involved all students, including the student with a learning difficulty, may benefit from tapping into other students' funds of knowledge.

Processes

Students with learning difficulties are not always aware of the funds of knowledge they bring to the reading situation (Pearson and Johnson, 1978). Research tells us, for example, that less proficient readers have more difficulty preventing unimportant information from overloading their working memories. They may use up more capacity in working memory than their more skilled peers who are better able to inhibit or resist potential interference from irrelevant information (Bayliss et al., 2005; Kendeou et al., 2009). To reduce this overload you will need to model and guide the appropriate reading processes for selecting the relevant information and asking suitable questions so that an integrated understanding of the text can be suitably constructed (Alfassi, 2004).

Purposes

The available evidence suggests that very few teachers provide adequate instruction to their pupils on how to develop self-regulating skills (Fielding-Barnsley et al., 2005; Zimmerman, 2002). Self-regulation is strengthened when teacher feedback focuses on the students' progress, not only in terms of learning product or content, but also on the process of learning itself (Guthrie et al., 2000). Adolescent learners will be more motivated and focused if there is a prior goal or reason for learning tasks. When you expect

Table 3.1 Making adjustments and accommodations in the classroom (adapted from Woolley, 2014a)

Classroom adjustments

Levels	Accommodations	Examples of adaptations
Product	What	Allow alternative formats for products of work, use a voice-to-text-conversion computer program, use the cloze procedure by placing only the important information in the gaps
	Where	Provide specific places to hand in work or to find materials, keep the layout and format of work consistent
	When	Before students encounter new material, discuss the new vocabulary, use a feature analysis chart, use concept maps, show how to use an online dictionary, show how to use the context to construct meaning
	Why	Discuss the content with students before reading, provide top-level structuring (model genre types), use diagrams and coloured markers to highlight important information, use supplementary material dealing with the same topic, use repeated readings, provide audio tapes or CDs of the text
Process	Attention focus	Break the instructions into short sentences, follow a routine, write instructions on the white board, ask the child to articulate the instructions, prioritise steps in completing assignments, provide a checklist, assign a teacher aide as a guide
	Comprehension	Discuss pictures, use graphic organisers, use reading guides, teach skimming and scanning skills, use reciprocal teaching techniques, use self-monitoring (see below).
	Differentiation and quality	Use real-world tasks, allow for spelling errors, use a peer helper or teacher aide as a scribe, use a word processor with a spell checker
Purpose	Metacognition	Set goals, ensure that students are familiar with the procedures, provide advanced notes, teach self-monitoring techniques, self-monitor progress, use checklists, give specific and targeted feedback, reflect on outcomes and apply insights

Source: Shaddock et al., 2007; Woolley, 2011; 2014a

them to set their own goals for instruction it helps them take ownership and gives them clear direction for learning (Schunk, 2005). In setting goals a number of affective considerations need to be taken into account such as motivation, self-concept, attitude and interests (Schunk, 2000). Active student engagement also requires practice combined with frequent applications of self-monitoring and reflective strategies together with adequate and timely feedback (Saenez et al., 2005; Tam et al., 2006). The development of self-regulation skills by an adolescent with a learning difficulty is one of the most important factors contributing to the successful social integration of that child into a regular classroom (Westwood, 2015).

Students with learning disabilities

Approximately 1.4 per cent of students in the UK have additional educational needs severe enough to warrant an official statement of those needs and how they should be met (Alexander, 2010; Rose, 2009). These figures and the process of identification are similar in present day Australian and New Zealand contexts. If the learning needs for adolescents with learning disabilities are severe enough they warrant an Independent Education Plan (IEP) or Individual Support Plan (ISP) to draw together a team of stakeholders such as: education practitioners, paraprofessionals, other professionals, parents and administrators under the guidance of an assigned team manager. In the US these students are referred to as 'exceptional' whereas in the UK they prefer the term 'special education need' (SEN); in Australia they are usually referred to as 'students with learning disabilities'. This individualised intervention process aims to: identify, individualise, simplify and prioritise the teaching of the agreed essential elements of the curriculum for the student so that all stakeholders can work in harmony.

Gifted and talented students

It has been estimated that approximately 1–5 per cent of the student population are regarded as potentially being intellectually gifted (Mastropieri and Scruggs, 2010). However, identification has been difficult due to the fact that there has been no clear definition of what giftedness entails. It is generally recognised that giftedness is usually innate and that it may occur in one or more knowledge domain areas. Renzulli (2002) posited that there were three characteristics of giftedness: superior ability, creativity and task commitment. Talents are related more to acquired skills and interests that are cultivated. In both cases your role will be to recognise these abilities and to provide a safe and supportive learning environment.

In catering for the additional needs of gifted and talented adolescents you will improve your teaching skills and provide a better learning environment for all students. What is needed is appropriate assessment and planning as a response to these academic challenges so that you may adapt and accommodate their unique learning needs. Most teachers are very resourceful and the solutions are rarely beyond their teaching ability.

On the surface it would seem that these students are easily accommodated for. However, this is often an oversimplified response and a gifted adolescent may try and dumb down their giftedness so that they do not appear different from their peers. After many years of underachievement their gifting may be hard to detect.

There are three main approaches to cater for this group:

- Individual: use adaptations to differentiate your teaching by making accommodations and adaptations for product, process and purpose (see Table 3.1).
- Class: use small group work, open-ended questions, open-ended assignments, a compacted curriculum, acceleration (skip a grade level), attend a class for a particular subject in a higher grade, attend a business college course for a particular subject, identify interests, use Gardner's eight intelligences to organise pedagogy, use Bloom's taxonomy to develop questions and learning projects, and problem-based learning assignments and learning stations.
- Whole school: small group withdrawal settings, clubs, special interest groups, extra-curricular activities or events, debates, chess and tournaments of the minds as additional sporting options, inter-school competitions, whole day or half day activities (e.g. maths day), mentor programmes and community projects.

It is important that there is a whole school enrichment model for the development of the gifted and talented. This will require teachers to collaborate with the administration, parents, students, volunteers, local businesses and allied professionals.

Vignette 3.2

Jason is a gifted Year 8 student but his academic performance indicated that he seemed to lack motivation. He had been regarded by most of his teachers as being bright and most thought that he could do better in class. However, his giftedness was not fully recognised until Mr Johnson noticed that his behaviour began to change when he was given particular challenges.

As Jason's home teacher Mr Johnson decided to organise a meeting with the learning support teacher, his parents, some of his other teachers and Jason as well. This meeting was designed to ascertain Jason's aspirations and interests, and to identify his personal goals and explore options to cater for his educational needs. At the end of the meeting a number of priorities were set using an individual learning plan and responsibilities and learning tasks were shared with the members of the team. His classroom teachers also agreed to make a number of accommodations and adjustments to their teaching such as: providing open-ended questions, more options for assignments and challenging extension activities to supplement other work.

As Jason's interests centred on robotics Mr Johnson decided to develop a mentor programme for him and some other gifted students in the school. The idea was that Jason would design an original project that would be supported by the school and his parents with a signed contract. He would also be given a mentor during his study period to guide and support the project. At the end of the set period he gave an oral presentation, along with the other mentees, at a special event.

Questions

1   What are some other options for the classroom teacher to accommodate their teaching for gifted students?
2   What are some other options that the school could provide?
3   How can a 'team approach' help other students?

Some students may be referred to as twice exceptional; they may be gifted but also have a disability. For example, a student with autism may have a special gifting in computer programming from a very early age. Other students may have comorbid or multiple disabilities/learning difficulties. Therefore it is imperative to provide a thorough and timely assessment.

Conclusion

Within most middle school and high school classrooms in Western countries there are diverse populations of learners with unique learning styles and interests. Some factors that lead to an adolescent's underachievement at school are found within the students themselves but other factors are influenced by social or cultural circumstances, teaching practice and social opportunities that are located outside of the learner. What is required is a systematic and collaborative approach to teaching that maximises the wider community resources. Good evidence-based pedagogy is important to differentiate the curriculum but often what is required is that you accommodate and adjust your teaching to diverse learner needs in your classroom. This situation often necessitates some curriculum adaptations and modifications by focusing on learner products, processes and purposes. These are often very simple modifications that are easy to implement in most classrooms and not only benefit struggling adolescent literacy learners but should enable all students to attain academic outcomes consistent with their potential ability.

What is important is that you view the diversity of learner needs as exciting challenges that demand creative solutions rather than as added burdens. By understanding inclusion, acknowledging the differences, recognising strengths and planning for practice you should be able to make an important difference for many of your students. Above all, every student (whether they are struggling or gifted) will be more responsive when the curriculum is anchored in authentic or real-world applications and supported in classrooms with an emphasis on cooperation and a sense of a community.

Discussion questions and activities

Questions

1   Why should students with learning difficulties be included in the regular classroom?
2   What is meant by a team approach and how should it be applied in the regular classroom? Give examples from your experience.
3   Give an example of an adolescent learning differently and how the curriculum was/was not adjusted/differentiated to accommodate his/her needs.

†††† Group activities

1   Ask students to think of a student in a class they have visited and to give an outline of their strengths and educational needs. Brainstorm ideas by noting key words in three columns: strengths, weaknesses and classroom adaptations.
2   Alternatively, present the group with a scenario and do the same as above.
3   Each group will be given a topic to research using their mobile technologies: ADHD, dyslexia, gifted and talented or ESL (English as a second language). Make up a chart showing their particular educational, social and emotional needs. After 30 minutes ask the groups to share their findings with the whole class.
4   After completing activity 3 show how you would adapt the activities for a child with ADHD, dyslexia, who is gifted and talented or ESL. Each group could choose one of these conditions and report back to the whole group with their adaptations.

Whole class activity

Discuss the following:

1   What does fairness mean?
2   What is the difference between equality and equity?
3   Research: Thomas Edison, Albert Einstein and Tom Cruise.

   i   What were their learning difficulties?
   ii   Why do you think that they did not achieve at school but achieved to a very high degree in their post-school lives?

CHAPTER 4

COLLABORATION AND PEER SUPPORT

Chapter objectives

- To understand the nature of learning collaboratively.
- To develop the notion that learning takes place simultaneously at three cognitive levels.
- To understand how motivation can drive individual and cooperative group achievement.

Key questions

1 Why is collaborative learning so important in contemporary education?
2 How does providing choice motivate students to learn and build self-regulation?
3 How does inquiry learning develop the skills needed for the citizen of the twenty-first century?

Key words: Collaboration, collaborative learning, peer support, motivation, project-based learning, problem-based learning, inquiry learning, dialogic interaction.

Introduction

When considering the teaching of reading, writing and literate practices in general it is important to embed collaborative learning strategies, including peer assistance, to teaching and learning. Collaboration is a concept that particularly lends itself to twenty-first-century learning because it enables adolescents to consider a wider range of possibilities. Evidence suggests that young people and adolescents value and benefit from the contribution that peers can make to an individual's learning. The involvement of students in collaborative group discussions before, during and after a literacy activity has been shown to lead to improved learning, particularly when the teacher asks questions, or prompts students to describe what they have been researching. This chapter focuses on the concept of the teacher as a facilitator of learning. Inquiry and project-based learning are particularly suited to a student-centred and collaborative style of learning. With this transfer of responsibility for learning to students, social and motivational aspects of group and individual learning become crucial. The important thing is that students learn to support one another and become reflective learners.

> If you can run the company a bit more collaboratively, you get a better result, because you have more bandwidth and checking and balancing going on. (Larry Page, CEO, Google)

In 2016 Google surpassed Apple as the world's most valuable company and possibly the best-known corporation. It began as a student project in 1996 by two Stanford University graduates – Larry Page and Sergey Brin. It soon grew from a mere 10 employees working in a garage in Palo Alto to over 10,000 employees operating in many parts of the world by 2009. Google became the most frequently used Web search engine on the Internet with over 1 billion searches per day in 2009. 'Googling' is now a common term used to describe searching for information on the Internet. Google has also developed other innovative applications such as Gmail, Google Earth, Google Maps, Picasa and the use of driverless cars.

Google was ranked as the number 1 'Best Company to Work For' by *Fortune* magazine in 2007 and number 4 in 2010. What has made Google such a success? One would have to look at the way in which decisions are made to answer this important question. The management is in the hands of a triad: Larry Page and Sergey Brin hired Eric Schmidt to help manage the company by consensus. It is also common practice for small teams to tackle problem solving collaboratively; the employees are encouraged to work cooperatively by influencing each other using informed data and persuasion.

Collaborative learning

Google has risen out of a globalised environment where there is more competition and a wider range of ideas and products. To function well in such an environment, the twenty-first-century citizen must consider a wide range of possibilities and this often requires not only diverse skills for literacy but also depth and quality of the information content. Not only are there more diverse ways to communicate ideas, in most instances, there is a much broader and diverse audience. The Internet and Web 2.0 digital technologies also provide a broad platform to enable collaboration and communication that expands creative possibilities far beyond what could have been envisioned a decade ago.

In school, collaborative learning models have been shown to improve student engagement, achievement and motivation, particularly for disadvantaged students. The challenge is to make literacy learning more personalised and at the same time more cooperative. This can be achieved easily through inquiry-based learning strategies such as problem-based learning and project-based learning. However, it is not just a matter of throwing together groups of students and expecting them to come up with some solutions to a problem. As with all teaching there must be careful planning and some clear guidelines for personalised and collaborative learning to work successfully in the classroom. The benefit for students is that each individual is given the opportunity to contribute in a collaborative setting while also being able to take ownership of his or her own learning.

Recent research demonstrated that teamwork and cooperative learning environments strengthen student engagement and performance. A report by the European Commission, 'Survey of Schools: ICT in Education' (Wastiau, 2013), showed that approximately 40 per cent of European grade 11 students engage in collaborative work at least once a week. Methods such as project- and challenge-based learning strengthen group work by developing common goals for collaborative problem solving. What has given impetus to this trend is the situation whereby an increasing number of teachers are sharing best practices and participating more often in collaborative online professional development opportunities where they can learn from each other (Johnson et al., 2015).

Theoretical underpinnings

Behaviourism is a theoretical notion that depicts learning as a process of responding to external stimuli. Early education theorists who subscribed to behavioural principles viewed learning as a passive cognitive activity largely governed by data-driven and memory-based processes (McKoon and Ratcliff, 1992). Essentially the construction of meaning was data-driven or developed when the learner was responsive to external stimuli. It was thought that a student's recall of information was the best indication of learning. The role of the teacher was one of an 'expert' instructing and imparting knowledge to the 'learner'.

Cognitivism was another learning theory that rose to prominence in the 1960s. It viewed learning as an active process of acquiring and storing information. It is essentially concerned with the way in which knowledge is constructed, stored and retrieved in the mind of the learner. This approach emphasised conceptually-driven processes whereby existing knowledge structures in memory are used to enable the learner to assimilate new information by identifying new and relevant information. Transfer of knowledge occurs when the new information is applied to novel situations. The process of learning was likened to an information processing system with learning and behaviour regulated by thinking processes such as: mental planning, goal setting and organisational strategies. Teachers who subscribe to this theoretical notion take on the role of a facilitator augmenting the optimisation and organisation of information.

Constructivism is another theoretical position that puts forward the notion that meaning is continuously 'constructed' through student involvement and reflection. The learner's existing 'schema' is a flexible knowledge structure that organises and economises on the amount of information they need to process. This teaching orientation was supported by an earlier notion of learners utilising flexible knowledge structures known as a schema to describe the active and fluid organisation of past experiences that can then be used to structure newer information (Bartlett, 1932). Some theorists have viewed this construction of meaning as both a data-driven and conceptually-driven process that operates in a simultaneous and interactive fashion. It proposes that learning is an active process of constructing and reconstructing understandings by developing appropriate connections between new and existing knowledge and experience. A constructivist teaching approach is based on the belief that learners essentially develop an understanding by the interaction of their own ideas with experiences as they seek solutions to real-world problems.

A social constructivist approach treats learning as a social process through interaction with the socio-cultural environment rather than relying only upon directed teacher input or independent learning. This follows on from Vygotsky's notion that learning is a process mediated in various social contexts. In a cooperative learning context this theoretical construct implies that collaboration between students is fruitful when the beliefs of the members differ but the learning tasks are structured in such a way that learning will take place and joint understandings will be drawn. Effective groupings of students within the classroom will operate effectively if there is a common purpose or authentic reason for the group's existence. Effective constructivist teaching requires the teacher to be a facilitator of learning rather than an imparter of all knowledge. Thus, the facilitation of learning should provide opportunities to explore, cooperatively develop, reflect upon and share understandings and knowledge with others.

While these models diverge in some respects, the majority of contemporary learning models highlight the active, constructive and social nature of the learning process. Thus, learners are viewed as active operators who develop their own individual knowledge structures based on their ability to combine new information with what they already know.

The classroom as a community of learners

Higher student achievement and more positive social, motivational and attitudinal outcomes have also been found to occur in collaborative and dialogic learning contexts (Gambrell et al., 2007; Woolley, 2007). It has been demonstrated that, when reading and thinking processes are taught to students through dialogic interaction with peers, it will increase students' control and engagement of the learning processes (Cole, 2002; Guthrie and Davis, 2003; Hareli and Weiner, 2002).

Meaningful collaborative interactions necessitate involvement in authentic tasks, routines, skills and social behaviours that learners use when engaging with others. Thus, group participants will require systematic instruction, practice and scaffolding along with adequate opportunities for your students to experience frequent success. However, the necessary discussion skills will need to be taught explicitly such as: restating what another person has said; inviting someone else to participate in the conversation; agreeing; disagreeing; focusing or refocusing the conversation; elaborating on a point that someone else has contributed or offering an example of a point that someone made. If, for example, you want to promote elaboration as a discussion skill you should model a question such as: 'Does anyone want to add a little bit to what Juan had to say about that point?' or 'Do you agree with Cindy's statement? Why or why not?' Prompts, such as these, model the types of questions that promote student-centred dialogue.

During student discussion time you should step back to allow more talk to take place between the students while providing frequent monitoring and timely feedback. Cue cards are an example of one way to provide scaffolded prompts for students to guide their discussion questions around key issues. When students are working in groups there should be a progression from teacher direction to student self-regulation (Pressley, 2002; Snow, 2002). This is an important component for the development of meaningful learning; however, it will not just happen without your input (Gambrell et al., 1987; Woolley, 2006).

Levels of cognitive engagement

Whatever the activity, students will need to process information at three levels of cognition if effective learning is to take place. At the surface level the students will need to attend to the task and this often requires them to focus on the factual content. At a deeper or conceptual level the students should comprehend, problem-solve or form opinions about the content. This often requires students to create new understandings and meanings. At an even deeper level, students will be required to mentally step back and consider their own learning by reviewing their goals, monitoring their own performance, making decisions about learning contributions, and reflecting upon their own understandings.

Prompts

You will be able to support learning at these particular levels by using suitable questions and prompts. Prompts enable students to identify learning difficulties more quickly and invite students to invest more effort by planning and implementing fix-up strategies in order to enhance their learning.

Prompts should target learning at three levels:

1. *Perceptual*

   - What is this passage saying?
   - Does it sound right?
   - Does it make sense?

2. *Conceptual*

   - What comprehension strategies will I use?
   - What questions can I ask about the task?
   - What are the relationships that connect with other parts of the task?

3. *Metacognitive*

   - What is the goal of the activity?
   - Are the strategies that I am using helping me achieve my goals?
   - What have I learned about:

     o the topic?
     o myself as a learner?

The key to using prompts is to use them strategically for each phase of the learning task.

Motivational engagement and personalised learning

As groups are composed of individuals we must first seek an understanding of what motivates students. A motive is a condition within a student that affects his/her readiness to initiate any activity or set of activities. Learners will differ in the quality of their motivation and their motivational orientation. Individuals may be motivated by a number of competing psychological needs. For example, a student may be motivated to read a chapter of a book in class but may also be motivated to switch attention to a diversion beyond the classroom window. What is certain is that all human behaviour is goal directed. The success or failure to attain those goals will draw corresponding positive or negative motivational responses (Linnenbrink and Pintrich, 2002; Sideridis and Padeliadu, 2001). Thus an individual's underlying goals and attitudes will provide the basis for deeper engagement with literacy and other learning activities. Ryan and Deci (2000) identified three important drivers that determine a learner's goal which will lead to purposeful learning engagement: autonomy, competence and relationship (see Figure 4.1. below).

Autonomy

Autonomy involves one's need to know and understand it also relies on the learner's desire for significance and self-actualisation. This is usually determined by a sense of purpose and perceived control over learning. Autonomy is a condition that you should be aiming to develop in all learners. It is of utmost importance that learners become autonomous, self-regulating and resourceful. After all, you would expect that when you finish teaching your students they will be able to select appropriate content, use appropriate learning strategies and skills, and transfer their learning to new situations.

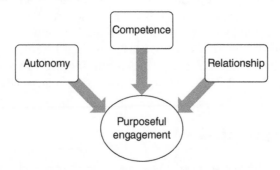

Figure 4.1 Motivational drivers

Thus, the aim of your teaching should be to produce autonomous learners that are able to solve problems and learn independently in their everyday world. This does not imply that you are not needed but it assumes that you are an important relational catalyst for the development of autonomous learning.

Competence

Purposeful engagement requires that the learning task should not be beyond the student's current level of ability. For example, most tasks require a certain amount of prior knowledge on which to build. In general a good learning task should be composed of 20 per cent new knowledge and 80 per cent existing knowledge. Therefore, as the teacher, you will need to know your students fully and be aware of what they already know about the particular topic they are investigating. However, students are often unaware of what they already know and how this knowledge may be applied to new information. You can easily overcome this problem by filling in the knowledge gaps by providing films, excursions, independent study and other discovery activities that will provide opportunities for the students to share their knowledge and ideas. Thus, through open discussion, knowledge gaps within the group can be filled using the wealth of knowledge and relevant life experiences that each student contributes to developing new knowledge and understandings.

Relationship

The third essential element of motivation is relationship. It is influenced by the learning orientation and the value that the individual places on a learning task. It is strongly influenced by the adolescent's expectation of success or failure at completing a set task. Your interest and engagement with the students is important and students' interests can be nurtured when there is a clear purpose in performing a task and when they can see the value in successfully completing it. Therefore, your role as a teacher should be to support and facilitate knowledge accessibility, relevance and utility and students should be encouraged to take ownership of the learning process in meaningful ways. Learners who view the task as highly relevant and believe themselves to be competent and self-determining are more likely to persist when confronted by difficulties or competing distractions (Paris et al., 2001).

Teaching approaches

As mentioned in the last section, a teacher-centred approach, such as a lecture or an explicit lesson devoted to teaching a particular skill or strategy, may be preferred from time-to-time. This method gives the teacher more direct control over what is taught and how learners are presented with information. At other times, learner-centred approaches, sometimes referred to as discovery learning, inductive learning or enquiry learning, are more desirable. Learner-centred approaches are based on the notion that adolescents construct meaning using their background knowledge, experiences and previous understandings to make connections with new knowledge.

Peer tutoring

Peer tutoring is a type of collaborative learning that enables cooperation on a one-to-one basis. Peer tutoring has the advantage of providing greater congruence between individuals: peers are often better able to understand the difficulties that are encountered and are better able to share a common language that makes it easier to engage in effective dialogue. One of the benefits of peer tutoring is that both participants learn to help each other. Normally students are matched within their class or age range. Cross-aged tutoring arrangements that feature older students assisting younger ones also have good outcomes. At-risk students, in particular, have been shown to have better outcomes from being assisted by older students who were at-risk learners themselves (Woolley and Hay, 2007).

In the classroom, a constructionist approach requires students to use active methods such as experiments, real-world problem solving and their own research-based inquiry projects. A collaborative context provides the best space where students can share ideas and opinions and learn from one another. In this way the teacher becomes a facilitator and a guide, helping students to find information by providing guidance, suggestions, prompts and resources, and can assist students to clarify ideas, ambiguities and misconceptions. This is a much more open style of learning and requires more careful monitoring and assessment at each stage (Killen, 2013).

In the literacy classroom the inquiry approach works well, particularly for students with diverse needs, by providing them with choices and learning at appropriate levels. For example, students with English as a second language or students who are gifted or talented can be easily included and accommodated using classroom groupings. Choice within a range of activities, topics and mode of delivery of literacy products, be they compositions, reports, films or blogs, empowers students particularly when they feel that their interests are also valued and appreciated.

Rethinking how teachers work

Recent trends in education are driven by innovative learning approaches, emerging technologies and research-based methodology. Teachers are seeking to use more authentic real-world applications for the engagement and deeper learning of their students. There is also an increasing trend for the use of blended learning and STEM (science, technology, engineering and mathematics – see Chapter 11) learning in particular (Johnson et al., 2015). These trends promote a much more fluid approach to teaching and learning with more emphasis on cooperative learning, problem-based learning or project-based learning. Such approaches may challenge the strict timetabling of lessons and the division of learning domains and are characterised by a multidisciplinary nature and creative application using new digital technologies. Consequently there is a shift from students being mere consumers of information to a more active one whereby they are seen as being creators of knowledge.

Vignette 4.1

Mr Johnson developed a science-based unit on the reintroduction of wolves in Yellowstone National Park with his Year 6 class. At the beginning of the unit he introduced a KWoL chart on the interactive white board to list all the things that the students already knew about wolves and these were recorded on the chart. After this initial brainstorming activity the students were asked to think about what they wanted to learn about wolves. The 'o' (organisation) and the 'L' ('What have I learned?') would be filled in during the middle and end of the unit. Often the KWL strategy is used in individual lessons but Mr Johnson decided to use a variation called 'KWoL' (Woolley, 2011) to organise the unit.

Questions

1   Why do you think that Mr Johnson chose to use the KWoL strategy to launch this unit of work?
2   Why would it be better to start the unit with the KWoL strategy rather than say watch a video on wolves?
3   How could this strategy be used to facilitate other project-based units of work?

Collaborative scaffolding and task engagement

Adolescence is a time when young people are forming their own opinions of the world and often have a desire to share their ideas. Vygotsky (1962) viewed learning and cognitive development as essentially a social process that occurs when individuals interact with one another. It is a communicative process whereby knowledge is shared and negotiated in culturally structured settings. Vygotsky's notion of the zone of proximal development (ZPD) is a key element in this social orientation. The ZPD is the learning space in which the learner is given a learning task pitched at just about the level of learning that can be independently performed. In collaborative learning situations students work as a team to attain shared goals. The roles of the group members are often differentiated and individuals may be responsible for specialised sub-goals. Individual contributions are pooled and the group-learning task is the product of the group's collaborative efforts.

This cooperative learning space often requires some scaffolding by the teacher in order to move the students beyond their level of comfort into the zone of proximal development where optimal learning may take place. Keep in mind that when instructions are unrealistic or pitched beyond the student's level of ability they are more likely to become frustrated and less inclined to persist with the learning task. On the other hand, if the goals and task requirements are pitched too low the students may not be sufficiently challenged. Therefore, your role is crucial in facilitating optimal learning, particularly when individuals have different understandings, ability levels and background knowledge. Group discussions will require your skill as a facilitator to develop a climate of sharing and responding appropriately. Forethought and preparation are necessary before fruitful group discussions can take place. Dialogue within the group will develop some consensus for the construction of suitable guidelines for group interactions to take place. For example, respect for the opinions of others is essential and an important principle for all literacy discussion groups.

Group discussion is usually more effective when the students are expected to contribute their own knowledge and experiences to the topic. Thus, when each student contributes from their own experiences with their unique funds of knowledge they are more empowered and the resulting dialogue is often much richer. Quite often students are more able to pitch their conversation and ideas to an appropriate level to their peers. This will provide a fruitful platform for the development of shared ideas and language development. Vygotsky's notion of inner and outer speech is also an important concept in this situation because it implies that external language can model inner language and thought processes. Thus, guided discussion should provide a foundation for the development of more appropriate thinking tools, which students need for problem solving and independent thinking (Hammond, 2001).

Hence, effective collaborative learning aims to promote task engagement as well as positive interaction in diverse groupings that may include individuals with disabilities, or of different races, ethnicities or genders (Johnson and Johnson, 2014; Woolley, 2014b). Research suggests that diverse students who are regularly engaged in collaborative learning generally achieve higher grades, retain information longer, have improved communication and collaboration skills, and are less likely to drop out of school (Johnson et al., 2000; Terenzini et al., 2001). It is important to track group progress with clear guidelines and deadlines. You should also meet with each group regularly and highlight group progress by using planning sheets or checklists in group-folders that show a time line for sub-tasks or goals (Oakley et al., 2004).

Assigning interdependent roles to students within a group has been shown to increase students' learning and engagement (Johnson and Johnson, 2014; Slavin, 1996). The emphasis should be placed on each individual's contribution as being essential to the team goal particularly when students are encouraged to actively help one another. To encourage this, personal learning goals that supplement shared group task goals should also be established. This requires you as a teacher to progressively release the responsibility of the learning process to the learners: in essence it is the transferral of the locus of control from the teacher to the student (for more on the Gradual Release of Responsibility model see Chapter 7).

Learning through inquiry

Inquiry-based learning is proving to be an effective pedagogical approach to cooperative learning. It involves students sharing in the construction of new knowledge based on personal and team explorations and experiences (Johnson et al., 2015). Inquiry-based teaching/learning methods have the power to engage students in creating, questioning and revising knowledge. As part of the process they develop skills in research, critical thinking, collaboration, communication, reasoning and the synthesis of ideas (Barron and Darling-Hammond, 2008).

Inquiry is essentially about literacy engagement and the establishment of a specific purpose to enable adolescents to set their own reading goals and obtain answers to self-generated questions. However, it is important to realise that while engaging in inquiry students need to know how to navigate and use appropriate study or investigation skills. Many of these skills are needed no matter whether the sources of their research are books, letters, diaries, plays, presentations, websites, films or social media such as Facebook. For example, in some paper-based texts the following types of skills are needed: knowing how to use an index, table of contents, chapter headings, captions and illustrations. In contrast, some of the types of navigation skills that are required when using digital electronic technologies will include: knowing how to use the URL, homepage, menus, tool bars, drop-down menus, breadcrumbs, footers, etc.

Project-based learning (PBL) is built on a pedagogical platform, which emphasises that students learn best by experiencing and solving real-world problems. Often students who participate in a project-based science curriculum outperformed students using just a traditional textbook (Barron and Darling-Hammond, 2008). No matter what pedagogical processes are put in place, effective teaching and learning occurs when there is a deliberate practice aimed at attaining mastery of a learning goal, when there is feedback given and sought, and when there are active, passionate and engaged people (teacher, students, peers) facilitating the learning processes.

PBL is complex and many teachers may find this quite challenging and difficult for an entire faculty or professional learning community to take on board at once. Designing, managing and assessing projects usually involves a wide range of teacher decision-making. However, rollouts of digital technologies in the school may provide a catalyst for change due to the interactive and social aspects of learning in the electronic space. After participating in a whole school or between school professional development programme a couple of teachers may choose to do a pilot study by introducing PBL into their curriculum design. Following this, a school may then decide to implement PBL in certain disciplines such as science, technology, engineering, and mathematics (STEM) or they may engage in it a few times per year. No matter what type of arrangement is chosen, PBL will provide added benefits and rewards for students and teachers (Boss, 2015).

During PBL projects, you should facilitate effective learning by deliberately emphasising evidence-based strategies such as formative assessment, feedback, learning from errors, setting goals and self-monitoring. You should avoid inquiry that is too unstructured, which may not deliver robust results, and encourage students to design projects with specific learning goals in mind. This works for a broad range of students: girls and boys, and students from diverse racial, ethnic and socio-economic backgrounds.

Project-based learning projects have a number of benefits that can enhance teaching and learning; they include providing real-world relevance and preparation for the twenty-first-century work environment, longer retention and ability to apply knowledge of lessons learned, and exposure to using technology to solve problems (Johnson et al., 2015).

Public or classroom presentations can add impetus to learning projects as they encourage full participation and promote accountability (Barron and Darling-Hammond, 2008). Group contracts can also help to keep students accountable. Typically, groups collectively agree upon norms and expectations at the beginning of projects, while reflecting on the group process and product.

Problem-based learning is another practice, which tackles a problem but doesn't necessarily include a student project as with project-based learning. Like project-based learning it also involves a complex task but does not necessarily involve student presentations, or creating an actual product or artefact. Students first need to experience the problems that render demonstrated knowledge useful (Schwartz et al., 2011). In contrast, being told about a concept and procedure before problem solving can inadvertently undermine the learning and development of new knowledge structures. Effective problem-based learning, on the other hand, requires some form of guided discovery: some teachers may be somewhat reluctant to engage their students in what seems to be a more unstructured classroom environment. However, the following seven-step procedure that sets up the problem for students should help teachers to avoid common mistakes (adapted from Hung, 2008).

1. *Define the content.* What exactly do you want the students to achieve? What skills do your students need to perform the task?
2. *Identify the context.* Brainstorm to identify the relevant contexts for the content of the project.
3. *List possible problems.* Following on from Step 2, list possible problems that could come out of different contexts.
4. *Describe potential solutions.* Describe the most plausible solution to one or more of these problems and formulate possible pathways to demonstrate the solution. Identify the skills needed and how they can be organised to deliver or present the learning outcomes.
5. *Calibrate your project.* This requires you to match the intended outcomes in Step 1 with the outcomes identified in Step 4. What, if any, adjustments need to be made to bring the students into alignment? What time constraints, resources and skills are essential?
6. *Describe the task.* What type of scaffolding will be required and are there any gaps (skills or abilities)? How will you overcome them – teaching or mentoring? Clearly identify a small set of goals.
7. *Reflect on the learning.* Embed reflective methods such as a journal or other reporting/recording types to monitor their own progress towards their initial goals. The final assessment should clearly outline the project (for example, a final report, presentation or follow-up question or problem). More importantly it should allow students to reflect upon their overall learning and problem solving process. Accountability is important at the group/project level and at the individual level. Thus, group success should be based on the premise that each person in the group has achieved or exceeded their individual goal expectations. In other words, the group should have agreed upon goals and individuals should also have their own personal goals.

Learner choice

Each learner has unique needs and abilities, so providing choice and giving responsibility to the student is a vital aspect of the overall learning process. Through negotiation and guidance, learners should be given as much choice and control as is feasible over what and how they learn, how much time they will spend on particular activities, and the criteria by which they will be assessed. To achieve high levels of student self-direction, teachers need to engage students in specific activities that offer them opportunities to make decisions and solve problems on their own, as far as possible and with minimal supervision. Cooperative learning and research projects are teaching strategies that can help to foster your students' self-direction. As a consequence your students are more likely to develop self-confidence, particularly when they are encouraged to become more reflective about their own learning processes. However, student self-direction should not be at the expense of the teacher taking an active role in the classroom. Learning engagement will necessitate you guiding and focusing learning endeavours (Killen, 2013). Above all the learning activities should be purposeful and meaningful by resembling, as far as possible, real-life activities.

Most students have a unique learning style and tend to gravitate towards particular types of learning activities. This is because not all students are the same; they have different talents, abilities and interests. Gardner has identified seven intelligences that can be useful in designing activities to support the curriculum (see Chapter 9). The idea is that students can be given a choice of activities according to their particular interest orientation.

Vignette 4.2

Ms Franks designed a learning activity to enhance the participation of her students, particularly those students who were experiencing difficulty communicating and learning science through traditional print modes. She formed working groups and suggested a number of problems for her students to choose from to solve using an appropriate scientific methodology. The emphasis was placed not only on the product or solution to the problem but also on the strategic process that the students used to solve the problem.

This media arts approach also required students to plan how they would create their video shots using a storyboarding app on the iPad. They recorded the most important shots with their iPads in line with their storyboarding plan, and then captured, edited and sound-dubbed their production. In doing so, they repeated the science process and used the video to revisit the science discoveries accompanied with description, scientific methodology, explanations and their reasoning. This was then presented to the whole class so that others could learn from their efforts.

Questions

1   Do you think that the time taken to produce a video demonstration is worth the effort?
2   What are the benefits of doing a problem-based activity such as this and how could you design a problem-based project in other subject areas?
3   How could you use the video demonstrations to include a much wider audience?
4   How would you ensure that diverse learners could be equitably engaged in such an activity?

Metacognition and collaborative engagement

A collaborative approach incorporating techniques such as questioning and peer prompting in which students adopt cooperative roles in analysing texts has been shown to greatly enhance metacognitive processes (McKeon et al., 2009). When reading and thinking processes are taught to students through dialogic interactions, student engagement and control of the literacy learning process is increased (Cole, 2002; Guthrie and Davis, 2003; Hareli and Weiner, 2002; Whitehurst and Lonigan, 1988) with higher student achievement and more positive social, motivational and attitudinal outcomes (Gambrell et al., 2007; Overett and Donald, 1998; Woolley, 2007). For example, the involvement of students in group discussions before, during and after reading, listening or viewing information has been shown to lead to improved comprehension, particularly when the teacher models questions or prompts students to describe what they have encountered (Gambrell et al., 2000). Teacher-directed questions are effective when focusing attention on the relevant text segments containing information being sought (Taboada and Guthrie, 2006). Moreover, when adolescents are encouraged to give explanatory answers to focused questions it generally leads to better comprehension of the text and enables a more deliberate use of language (Snow, 2002). Requiring students to self-explain promotes active learning and leads to significant improvement incorporating the use of more effective metacognitive strategies.

Dialogic interaction used in association with visualisation, film or drama can be augmented by metacognitive strategies such as: comprehension monitoring, self-explanations, identification of the main idea, previewing, predicting and summarising text, etc. (Kirby and Savage, 2008; Woolley, 2011). Wherever possible metacognitive thinking strategies should be included in all instructional frameworks to support the integration of new and existing strategies. You will, however, need to ensure that a metacognitive focus will lead to student self-regulation and self-determination (Zimmerman, 2002).

Collaboration in digital environments

In a digital learning environment collaboration occurs when students have access to task materials, share a text-editor with their group members and communicate through a chat facility. Providing these tools, however, does not guarantee that students will adequately finish their task or have high quality discussions. In this situation you should act as a facilitator. You should, for example, offer thoughts that deepen or broaden the discussion and keep track of the progress that groups of students are making on the task (Van Leeuwen et al., 2015). To provide effective and adaptive support, you will need to be aware of the students' activities in order to identify relevant events, including those that require intervention.

A large body of research has focused on supporting students with a variety of digital tools and learning analytics that enhance students' awareness of the activities of their group members. These so called group awareness tools can provide students with information about social or cognitive characteristics of the group such as knowledge, attention and attitudes of each group member. Awareness tools may guide students in their collaboration by stimulating discussion of the displayed information by giving the student groups feedback (see Chapter 12) about the state of the collaboration concerning a range of indicators (Van Leeuwen et al., 2015). Students can develop co-regulation strategies in online learning environments designed to give feedback to support the setting of collaborative goals, adapting them, making plans, developing strategies, and assessing current skills and solutions to problems. Thus, successful co-regulation would be expected to consist of goal-directed and co-constructed knowledge for the group members (Zheng and Huang, 2015). The development of social skills with careful teacher guidance is essential in this learning environment. The development of a set of group rules and discussion guidelines that are developed by the group members will greatly enhance the group sense of ownership and engagement.

Conclusion

The learning intentions and the success criterion are two aspects in planning and organising classroom lessons. For you to be a proactive teacher and to provide a classroom environment that is conducive to learning and good behaviour requires some thought and organisation. An effective teacher should provide: a supportive classroom environment, a connected community of learners, the promotion of excellence, and recognition of the diverse abilities and interests of your students.

 Discussion questions and activities

 Questions

1 What are the advantages and disadvantages of using whole class, group work or peer tutoring? Make up a pros and cons chart to use for this brainstorming activity.
2 When would you use open-ended activities in the classroom and/or direct teaching methods?
3 What would you need to consider when making groupings of diverse students?
4 What type of feedback should you give group participants?
5 How could you use a contract system to organise project-based learning?

†††† Group activities

1 Group knot. In groups of eight, each person is in a standing circle facing one another. Each person reaches out to two different people on the opposite side of the circle. When all participants are holding two different people's

hands ask them to unravel the 'knot' without letting go. At the end of the activity discuss the notion of collaboration.

2   Tower building. In groups of seven or eight have the students build a tower using photocopy paper, Sellotape and paper clips. Tell them that they have five minutes to compete against the other groups to build the highest free-standing tower. At the end of the activity they will be expected to show how they interacted with the other members of the group. Ask, 'What does this tell you about metacognition?' How can students reflect upon their learning in a collaborative activity?

3   Fish bowl activity. Design a group task centred around a reading passage for one group of eight students. Have the rest of the class sit in a circle around the targeted group. Ask the observers to note the types of interactions that occurred in the group while performing the task. Discuss the following:

- Were there any problems?
- What were the strengths of the group?
- Would there be an advantage in giving specific roles within the group?
- What sort of accommodations could be made for a student who is blind?
- Would there be an advantage in making a set of rules for group discussion? If so what would some of these be? How would you go about deciding what the rules would be?

Whole class activity

1   With your mobile device look up 'Bloom Gardner matrix' and discuss how this could be used as an alternative way to organise a learning activity.

2   Read the article 'Wolf wars' from *National Geographic* or a similar article about the reintroduction of wolves into national parks in Scotland or Portugal and design a mini unit of work for a particular grade level of your choosing (http://ngm.nationalgeographic.com/2010/03/wolf-wars/chad-wick-text). How could you design group projects based on this article for your subject area(s)?

3   De Bono (1976) emphasised the importance of teaching students appropriate thinking skills or ways of moving from one level of knowledge to a higher one. He argued that students needed to be taught how to think constructively. Using a mobile device (e.g. smartphone, tablet or laptop) conduct an Internet search to find out about De Bono's six thinking hats and answer the questions below:

- How can the six thinking hats be used in group work activities?
- Why do you think that students need to use this type of thinking structure?
- Often this technique is used for gifted students. Why do you think this is appropriate?
- Do you think that this could help students with learning difficulties? Why? Why not?

CHAPTER 5

SCHOOL, FAMILY AND COMMUNITY PARTNERSHIPS

Chapter objectives

- To understand a socio-constructivist view of literacy education.
- To explore the importance of school, family and community partnerships for adolescents.
- To provide some ways to improve these partnerships in a variety of contexts.

Key questions

1   What does a socio-constructivist view of literacy education for adolescent learners look like?
2   Why are school, family and community partnerships important for adolescent learners?
3   How can schools improve these important partnerships?

Key words: Socio-constructivist, socio-cultural literacy, community and collaboration, home and school literacies.

Introduction

This chapter explores the important role that school, family and community partnerships play in improving literacy learning outcomes for adolescent students in secondary school settings. It firstly presents a prevailing view of literacy and literacy education as socio-cultural practices. The chapter also aims to provide ways in which schools can consider their own partnerships with families and communities by focusing on their own particular context.

Developing strong partnerships for all stakeholders is important for improved literacy learning outcomes, even for a secondary school context. In fact, schools play an extremely important role in communities yet often the links between schools and communities are for the most part limited if not superficial. So why is it important to strengthen these relationships? And how can these partnerships impact on literacy learning outcomes for adolescent students?

A socio-constructivist view of literacy

For some time, authors have investigated how literacy and learning are influenced by both social and cultural practices (Barton and Hamilton, 1998; Freebody, 2007; Gee, 1999; Street, 1995). These views stemmed from early research on sociological perspectives of human activity and in particular Vygotsky's work. According to Au (1998), 'social constructivist research on literacy learning focuses on the role of teachers, peers, and family members in mediating learning, on the dynamics of classroom instruction, and on the organization of systems within which children learn or fail to learn (Moll, 1990)' (1998: 300). Therefore, if we left literacy learning only to what happens in schools there is potential for this one environment to overlook rich literate practices occurring outside of school.

There are other perspectives that researchers have used to consider best practices for literacy learning. Psychological investigations for example may study linguistic and/or dialogic (Ball and Freedman, 2004) or cognitive (Woolley, 2014a) processes engaged with during reading and writing (Uhry and Ehri, 1999). A developmental approach to early stages of literacy (emergent literacy), middle stages (decoding) and working towards the fluency stage has proliferated within the psychological literacy research area.

While many studies from the psychological perspective investigate these areas of literacy acquisition, Paris (2005) notes that research results can be dubious given a distinction he has made between 'constrained' and 'unconstrained' skills related to reading development:

> constrained skills such as alphabet knowledge are most related to decoding in early childhood, whereas unconstrained skills such as vocabulary are related to a wide range of academic skills throughout life. (Paris, 2005: 188)

He argues that despite the differences between these literacy competencies, research methods and measures on reading fluency tend to be administered as if all reading skills are constrained – that is distinctly measurable given the 'small number of rules that are assessed' (Paris, 2005: 188). Paris, however, continues to claim that 'unconstrained' skills are those that may take some learners more time to accomplish for a number of reasons – *unequal learning, mastery, universality* and *co-dependency* – and therefore the use of 'psychometric data are necessarily skewed' (2005: 189).

Paris continues to discuss possible reasons why children's acquisition of literacy skills varies and suggests that there are strong correlations with socio-economic status and the impact this may have with 'preschool experiences, parental education, amount of parent–child interactions or quality of children's literacy materials at home' (2005: 197).

This aligns with research by Keith Stanovich. His work focuses on the 'cumulative advantage', also known as the *Matthew Effect*, whereby how much text is read in the fluency stage directly influences the ability of children to read. When this happens in the negative:

> reading for meaning is hindered; unrewarding reading experiences multiply; and practice is avoided or merely tolerated without real cognitive involvement. (Cunningham and Stanovich, 2001: 137)

This can mean that the more children read and are encouraged to read at home the more likely they will become literate citizens through a schooling system.

According to Snow, Burns and Griffin (1998: 315) reading can be typically acquired relatively predictably if children:

- have normal or above average language skills
- have had experiences in early childhood that fostered motivation and provided exposure to literacy in use
- are given information about the nature of print via opportunities to learn letters and to recognise the sublexical structure of spoken words, as well as about the contrasting nature of spoken and written language; and
- attend schools that provide coherent reading instruction and opportunities to practice reading.

While these conditions are achievable they are not always possible and many children still struggle with foundational literacy skills impacting on learning through the adolescent years. Snow (2004), however, asks what type of literacy skills are we expecting children to achieve in today's context? She argues that:

> Conceptions of literacy, and definitions of what counts as literacy, vary enormously, and that those varying conceptions are reflected a) in divergent claims about how well children are doing, b) in differing conclusions about whether some early childhood accomplishments really matter to later literacy development,

c) in differing foci for the design of early childhood education and intervention programs, and d) in varying emphases on skills selected for inclusion in the assessment of literacy in the early childhood period. (Snow, 2004: 274)

She continues by outlining two divergent views of literacy prevalent in the literature:

1. The first view emphasises a 'commitment to a notion of literacy that is social, community-based, culturally-defined, varied, and potentially transformational' (Snow, 2004: 4) – here Snow refers to the work of Gee (1996), Street (1995; 2003) and Barton et al. (2000).
2. The second view sees literacy 'as an instructed skill, accomplished by the child operating individually, as a technical achievement exercised primarily and most crucially in school settings, analysable into component skills' (Snow, 2004: 5).

However, this usually applies in western contexts so it is also important to consider the diverse literate practices that occur in other cultures.

Literacy in diverse cultural contexts

Another 'social' observation by psychologists was the work of Scribner and Cole (1981). Their research on the Vai in Liberia was one of the first to explore literate practices in informal settings rather than just in schools. The impact of this study on literacy investigation was profound. Heath (1999) notes that:

> No longer regarding literacy as a mark of individual achievement, many psychologists and other social scientists came to understand it as a phenomenon interlaced with numerous symbol systems – verbal, visual, gestural – and located within social contexts marked by differential power distribution. (1999: 103)

Sociologists unsurprisingly take this observation further by looking at what the functions of literacy are in context (Gee, 1999; Moje et al., 2000; Moll, 1990). Are literacy practices meant to serve people so that they can function and participate successfully in society? Or should they allow people to have the capacity to interrogate these practices – so as to 'unmask the ideological operation of texts' (Walton, 1993: 61)?

A concern with the first perspective is that much research and policy work that aims to inform and improve the 'work of literacy' in the classroom context tends to be 'knee-jerk' responses targeting early years' literacy programmes and skills and when they are still unsuccessful those responsible then disguise broader social problems as individual problems (Fairclough, 1989). This results in research philosophically embedded in the second perspective – challenging the status quo in present society.

In this sense literacy education is 'tailored to particular features of the script of a language, and the educational, institutional and cultural contexts in which they need to be put to work' (Freebody, 2007: 6). As such, a sociological investigation has understandingly altered over time according to change in symbolic systems, technological advancements, access to these and so forth and there have been many who believe this is controlled by 'differential power distribution' (Heath, 1999: 102; Freebody, 2007) resulting in the New Literacy Studies phenomenon (Street, 2003).

While a sociological evaluation of literacy education starts to question a Euro-centric view of education and schooling it is the work of anthropologists that considers indigenous, multi-lingual and ultimately culturally responsive approaches to the teaching and learning of literate practices (Barton et al., 2000; Prinsloo and Breier, 1996). This perspective acknowledges social and cultural elements of literate practices in the community and therefore supports inclusive and equitable approaches to literacy learning.

Prinsloo and Janks (2002), for example, critically examine curriculum documents in South Africa with Prinsloo noting:

[the] education system prepared children differently for the positions they were expected to occupy in social, economic and political life under apartheid. The curriculum played a powerful role in reinforcing inequality. What, how and whether children were taught differed according to the roles they were expected to play in the wider society. (Department of Education, 2002: 4, as cited in Prinsloo and Janks, 2002: 21)

Others have confirmed this observation in Australia with statistics showing that Indigenous students are less likely to succeed in the current educational system (Alloway et al., 2002). This work has led to the concept of 'Closing the gap'; however, evidence suggests that this gap is actually widening. Even back in 2009 Geoffrey Yunupingu stated that:

And the 'gap' that politicians now talk of grows larger as we speak, as I talk: ... as the next speech is given by the next politician, the gap gets wider. I don't think anyone except the few of us who have lived our lives in the Aboriginal world understand this task that is called 'closing the gap'. There is no one in power who has the experience to know these things. ... No one speaks an Aboriginal language let alone has the ability to sit with a young man or woman and share that person's experience and find out what is really in their heart. They have not raised these children in their arms, given them everything they have, cared for them, loved them, nurtured them. They have not had their land stolen, or their rights infringed, or their laws broken. They do not bury the dead as we bury our dead. (Yunupingu, 2008: 37, as cited in Simpson et al., 2009)

Much has been achieved by anthropological approaches to literacy teaching and learning; however, little has changed in terms of what happens in schools. This is largely due to overarching political and economic agendas of relative educational jurisdictions. Unless a discrete and concerted effort is made to not only acknowledge multiple methods to literacy learning but to align both development and assessment of these skills with diversity then there will always be children or young people 'left behind'. Continuing practices in literacy education in this way may diminish the capacity for students whose cultural and social experience rests outside the narrow boundaries of Euro-centric views to reading and writing.

Wagner (1999) acknowledges the importance of indigenous approaches to transmission and acquisition of social, cultural and ecological literacy practices:

> In such [indigenous] societies the functions of literacy cannot be uniquely defined by governments or agencies, since many indigenous literacies have histories that go back several centuries and are likely to continue well into the future. Instead of viewing indigenous education and indigenous literacies as impediments to or competitors with development policies, national planners would do well to consider such literacies as resources. The reality is that a real and substantial portion of the world's children acquire literacy skills in indigenous schools. (1999: 286)

In Chapters 1 and 2 we explored the notion of literacy being wide-ranging and diverse and having particular features and functions relevant to adolescent learners. In order for adolescents to succeed at school it is important to create a supportive and positive partnership between home and school environments. Much evidence suggests a need for greater parental involvement in adolescent learning, particularly in relation to the school's academic and behavioural expectations. Such involvement results in positive attitudes towards school, improved homework and study outcomes, reduced truancy and ultimately improved literacy outcomes.

Better education outcomes are directly related to the extent that parents, carers and extended family and/or community are involved in their child's learning. Sharing responsibility for literacy learning across a wide range of relationships is an important part of a child's development and socialisation and is critical to achieving literacy improvement. The challenge of course is to ensure consistency and complementary approaches within these important relationships in terms of learning objectives, expectations and standards for literacy learning. As such, schools, families and communities should work collaboratively to identify strengths and areas for improvement. Partnership approaches provide an influential lever in enabling positive change.

Research shows a direct correlation between low school literacy levels and poverty (Alloway et al., 2002). This is particularly apparent in English language learning communities. It is important to recognise that students may possess other literacies important in their 'out of school' contexts yet struggle with school-based literacies. Similarly, parents, carers and other significant adults in the adolescent's life may have a strong interest in the student's learning but little connection with the school or classroom teacher. In this light, strong literacy partnerships between school, home and community are pivotal to building greater levels of engagement, active participation and achieving success.

Many external factors influence adolescent students' lives including social, cultural, economic, and political factors. To gain a greater understanding of the influence of these factors, the following discussion will explore the Bronfenbrenner ecological model.

Bronfenbrenner's ecological systems theory

The Bronfenbrenner model explores child and adolescent development from the context of a system of relationships (1990; 1994). Not only does the adolescent's own biology impact on their growth but so does the interaction between this and others' environments. Both family and community are important in their influence on adolescents' progress through schooling and beyond. Any changes in the web of relationships surrounding adolescents can impact on this progress.

The ecological model acknowledges a number of layers or systems that form a person's environment. These are:

1. the microsystem
2. the mesosystem
3. the exosystem
4. the macrosystem
5. the chronosystem.

The microsystem is the level closest to the student and therefore refers to close family, friends and community members. The mesosystem allows a connection between elements in the microsystem such as between the parent/carer and teacher. The exosystem is the larger social system that impacts on a student such as a parent's workplace or community organisations. The macrosystem involves cultural and traditional values and beliefs. This level, in many ways, has power over the other layers. Finally, the chronosystem is about the student's journey through life and time and is related to change and events.

It is important to understand and acknowledge each of these layers in relation to adolescent learning. A full picture is not possible without considering how these levels influence students as well as educational practices in schools.

Bronfenbrenner argues that the instability and unpredictability of family life resulting from the economy is the most destructive force to an adolescent's development (Addison, 1992). Economic forces and their impacts on family members, extended family and the broader community mean that young people often do not have consistent and regular mutual interaction with important adults that is necessary for development.

According to the ecological theory, the breakdown of relationships in the immediate microsystem means young people develop without the necessary tools to engage and interact with other aspects of their environment. The typical guidance that comes from key relations between the adolescent and parent, caregiver or other important adult is impeded and so young people seek attention in other ways that may be harmful, less positive, risky or disruptive. The gaps in developmental guidance present and play out especially in adolescence as anti-social behaviour, lack of self-discipline and inability to provide self-direction (Addison, 1992).

Bronfenbrenner's model has significant repercussions for teaching practice. Teachers have potential to be a strong and positive influence in adolescents' lives but such efforts may have marginal impact when the relationships at home and more broadly are disrupted. Moreover, the sporadic contact in a typical school day cannot make up for the hours of contact, deep connection and caring from relationships at home when they are missing.

According to Bronfenbrenner, the primary care relationship needs to be developed and nurtured by a person and people within the student's immediate circle of influence. Consequently, schools and teachers may play an important secondary role, but cannot provide for the complexity of interaction required of adults by developing adolescents. Nor should schools be drawn into addressing economically driven issues with poor work–life balance, conflict and family breakdown and dysfunction arising from economic stress. In Bronfenbrenner's view, schools do, however, have a primary role in supporting caregivers by providing a welcoming and nurturing environment for families and communities.

The importance of school, family and community partnerships in improving literacy learning outcomes

What are school, family and community partnerships?

> Family–school partnerships are collaborative relationships and activities involving school staff, parents and other family members of students at a school. Effective partnerships are based on mutual trust and respect, and shared responsibility for the education of the children and young people at the school. (Australian Government, n.d.)

Many educators and policy makers acknowledge the significant importance of strong school, family and community partnerships yet there are blurred definitions or applications of what this actually means. This is largely due to the fact that every school is different and so too are communities. The quote above highlights that effective partnerships must be based on trust and respect as well as a shared responsibility.

School, family and community partnerships have potential to improve results for students particularly those at high risk of disengaging or with poor performance in literacy, numeracy and other subject areas. At the same time, it's important to acknowledge that such partnerships don't typically occur by default but require a robust approach that's systematically organised, supported by school leadership and teaching staff alike with a specific focus on improving literacy outcomes for students through partnership with a wide range of stakeholders who take responsibility for student learning. Drawing on the evidence of successful models elsewhere it is clear that literacy partnerships require resourcing and an action team comprising representatives from each of the stakeholder groups involved. Schools play a key role in leading and coordinating such collaborations. Shared ownership and responsibility are commonly identified as key ingredients to achieving success through the partnership model.

Why are school, family and community partnerships important?

The literature identifies a range of potential positive benefits and outcomes that can be achieved through school, community and family partnerships. These include:

- raising awareness about literacy
- building stronger relationships with the student, family and community
- developing partnerships that specifically address literacy needs
- influencing positive values and behaviours that support literacy learning in contexts outside of the school
- increasing effectiveness of classroom-based activities focused on literacy
- increasing the efficiency in responding to literacy challenges when identified
- drawing on the capability and capacity within the home and community context to assist engagement, literacy learning and achievement
- better tailoring and targeting of literacy support and interventions to students who need it most.

Raising awareness about literacy

Drawing on the available evidence shows that school, family and community partnerships can be effective in raising awareness about literacy. A critical component in doing so rests with ensuring that the overall focus and objectives of school, family and community partnerships is geared towards addressing a principal concern such as literacy improvement. Partnerships that disperse their efforts across too many fronts become unwieldly and ineffective and their impact is diluted.

The concept of overlapping spheres first flagged in the work of Epstein et al. (2002) notes the cumulative effect of addressing literacy needs across a range of fronts, points of influence and contexts, which can not only bring attention to literacy concerns but also enable the school to have a stronger base on which to address literacy needs. Further, such approaches provide avenues for addressing literacy that are much more nuanced to the needs of particular community stakeholders thereby making them more relevant, engaging and more likely to create a positive impact.

Building strong relationships with the family, student and community

Another positive benefit of school, family and community partnerships identified in the literature rests with building stronger relationships with students, their families and communities. One of the underlying tenants of partnership approaches is the notion that these enable greater equity within the school environment by engaging families and communities who may be estranged from formal education institutions. A more inclusive school environment means families feel welcome and can contribute to the school and their children's learning. Similarly, community stakeholders are more likely to take an active interest in the welfare of the school and the students if they feel valued, their roles are clearly defined and the input required of them sits within their capability and capacity.

Developing partnerships to address literacy needs

Aside from resulting in more positive experiences for students, school, family and community partnerships also support the development of collective action to address literacy needs. In this sense literacy needs can be used as a galvanising force to drive focus and efforts across school, community and family partnerships when there is shared clarity around the overall objective of the partnership, particularly driven by a priority to improve literacy results. Various stakeholders can then focus on developing and supporting specific strategies and interventions which when combined can address literacy needs in a much more profound and powerful way than simply through classroom-based literacy activities.

Influencing positive values and behaviours that support literacy learning

School, community and family partnerships have significant potential to influence positive values and behaviours that support literacy learning.

Reinforcement helps to model expected literacy skills and demonstrate their importance by example through measures such as:

- consistent messaging
- efficient deployment of best practices strategies and tools for supporting literacy learning
- effective identification and follow-up of students struggling with literacy demands
- support, encouragement and training for those involved in the lives of children such as parents, significant carers or other stakeholders.

Similarly, supporting positive literacy behaviours through rewarding, effective and sustained reading as well as providing tools such as reading resources for both the student, their family and significant others works to elevate the importance of literacy learning in and out of school contexts.

Increasing effectiveness of classroom-based literacy activities

Increasing class sizes, higher levels and more complex literacy needs, increasing student diversity particularly ESL/EAL students, curriculum crowding as well as teachers' own proficiency and confidence with teaching literacy means that practitioners have limited time, bandwidth and capacity to address literacy within the school and classroom context. School, family and community partnerships therefore provide an opportunity to leverage classroom-based literacy activities (Epstein et al., 2002). The multiplier effect of bringing family and community stakeholders into the mix of supporting literacy learning increases the capacity of the teacher to improve literacy outcomes particularly in contexts outside of the classroom where students spend the majority of their time. Moreover, these contexts outside of the classroom are often governed by individuals and groups who play a prominent and significant role in the lives of students. The valuing of literacy outside of school and the extension of literacy best practices and interventions means students can access a range of support where it may be more socially and culturally acceptable to do so.

Increasing efficiency in responding to literacy challenges

School community partnerships have potential to increase the efficiency of schools responding to literacy challenges. Firstly, a number of literacy issues can be addressed simultaneously on multiple levels and in multiple contexts. Secondly, cultural and social obstacles which inhibit or reduce student engagement and literacy performance can be addressed directly at the coal face of issues rather than remotely through the classroom. A strong school community and family partnership that is robust, systematically organised, sustained and supported by management has the capacity to respond to new challenges as they arise. Collective planning, priority setting and problem solving have the potential to improve the quality of interventions developed but also the speed of their deployment. Community stakeholders or family members are aware of the need to focus on literacy and pay attention to some of the warning signs for poor literacy performance, which can escalate if not supported appropriately.

Having a robust network or partnership with a wider range of stakeholders important in the student's life gives much more insight into some of the challenges and issues that may impact on their ability to improve their literacy. As a result, partnerships provide an opportunity to improve the tailoring and targeting of literacy support and interventions to students who need these most. Further, partnership enables a more nuanced and responsive approach that addresses issues that may be impeding students' learning, supports the identification of potential gaps either in the student support system, access to resources or in terms of specific issues students may be struggling with.

Drawing on capability and capacity within the home and community

Classroom teachers, support staff and school leadership can draw on a wider base of capability and capacity both within the home and community context to assist with engagement around literacy learning and achievement. Reinforcement of core concepts, ideas and learning strategies within the home and community contexts can add value and significant strength to interventions. Further to this, the home and community context can potentially address issues more intensively where there's simply not enough time within the classroom context for a teacher to work individually with students around particular issues. These interventions outside of the school context are not meant to replace the work of the teacher but to complement, support and extend that work. Complementary literacy learning activities in the home and community context can bolster work done within the classroom and create further variety for students to gain and keep their interest and engagement as well as continue their learning.

Ultimately, effective school, family and community partnerships should aim:

- to connect students with their communities
- to enhance the health and wellbeing of students
- to broaden vocational options and skills
- to improve learning outcomes for students. (Clerke, 2013)

How to strengthen home, school and community partnerships in the high school

In Chapter 1 we explored the idea of teachers as researchers as well as the importance of using a strong evidence base to improve literacy learning for all students. Undertaking a contextual analysis of school settings in order to understand what approaches work best is critical for school improvement. This should include ways in which schools can work alongside families and their local communities.

Cairney's (2000; 2016) work has explored the nature of home, school and community partnerships and found that six elements can support transformative practice for children and their families. These are that families:

1. know what is best for their children
2. vary in relation to the resources available to support their children
3. have unique cultural resources and experiences
4. have varied school experiences that impact on how they view school
5. are capable of supporting their children's education
6. want to know about their children's experiences at school and their progress.

Beginning with these premises is critical for strengthening home, school and community partnerships. If there are misunderstandings present between the school and community, then progress may be limited. The following vignette shows how one school strengthened its partnership with families and its community, with even more room for improvement.

Vignette 5.1

Treetops High School recognised that more of their students who were beginning high school needed robust support around the area of reading. They therefore developed the Treetops High Reading Project. The project involved a number of stakeholders including:

-   the leadership team at the school
-   the school staff
-   the school's support staff including teacher aides
-   community volunteers
-   the local feeder primary schools
-   a partner from a national charity organisation

With a targeted and multi-pronged approach, the school reinvigorated their approaches to teaching reading, which ultimately improved students' pathways

(Continued)

(Continued)

after school. However, it did take some time for the school to realise that their initial method may not have been the best approach.

First, the school enhanced their learning support programme for the students needing more support. They did this by gathering more information about the students' current skills through various diagnostic tests as well as information from primary school teachers. They then implemented both phonics and comprehension commercial programmes which improved the students' decoding skills and basic comprehension levels.

This first phase of improving literacy for Treetops students could be described as a top-down model whereby the school administration, although happy to support the programmes run by the learning support team, were not directly engaged with the process. Figure 5.1 shows how the learning support lessons with the help of teacher aides were disconnected from the everyday work of the school and solely the responsibility of the learning support coordinator. Other classroom teachers were essentially unaware of what was occurring in these lessons and the students' voice was also missing (at the bottom of the framework).

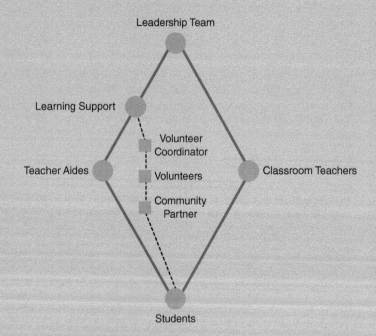

Figure 5.1 Model of the Treetops High Reading Project practices at the beginning (Barton and McKay, 2016a)

Reprinted with permission from the Australian Literacy Educator's Association

For a comprehensive whole school approach, it was essential for the whole community (including all of the stakeholders mentioned above) to be hands-on and involved for positive change to occur.

Therefore, realising that just focusing on the learning support lessons was not enough (as the results were plateauing) the school aimed to find more help so they employed a volunteer coordinator who sourced volunteers from the local community. In addition, a community partner from a charity organisation became one of the key drivers for a collaborative, community approach model to improving literacy for all students.

Through shared leadership they developed innovative support structures that materialised in the form of community partnerships. A collaborative approach enabled a shared responsibility of teaching literacy and the moral purpose of the school moved beyond relying on the skills of the teachers to the beliefs of the school community.

Figure 5.2 presents an alternative model for effective reading instruction for adolescent learners. It places the students at the centre of the literacy intervention and illustrates the complexity of the literacy process and in particular the affective and socio-cultural elements. Managing these influences on adolescents, who are experiencing difficulties mastering literacy skills, is particularly challenging for teachers of

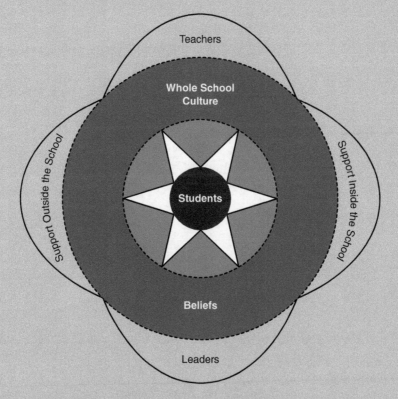

Figure 5.2   An effective model of reading instruction for adolescent learners: a collaborative, community approach (Barton and McKay, 2016a)

Reprinted with permission from the Australian Literacy Educator's Association

(Continued)

(Continued)

adolescents. The four petals surrounding the centre identify key stakeholders in the process of developing adolescent literacy skills and present a timely reminder of the value of a community approach. All stakeholders – the leadership team, the teaching team, the learning support team (including teachers and teacher aides), and community partners (including parents, volunteers, community organisations) – have an integral role in supporting young people to achieve positive results in their schooling and beyond. In relation to the teaching of reading all parties need to have a deep understanding of the reading process (not just the learning support team). This is why it is important for professional development to be ongoing. Most secondary teachers have not had training in this area of learning so it is vital that all teachers are provided this opportunity.

In the middle section of the flower we see the 'big six' of effective reading instruction – phonics, phonological awareness, oral language, fluency, vocabulary and comprehension (Figure 5.3). These aspects are all integral to effective reading. For adolescent learners, however, there are also other impacting factors

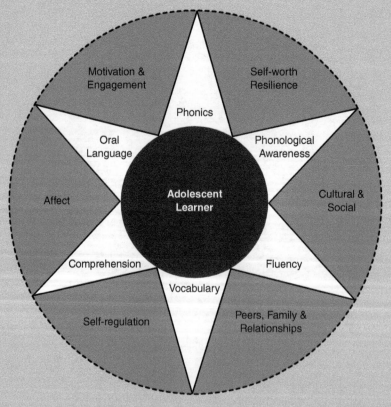

Figure 5.3 The centre of the collaborative, community approach to effective reading instruction (Barton and McKay, 2016a)

Reprinted with permission from the Australian Literacy Educator's Association

on their learning that early years' learners, for example, do not have to face. These include self-worth and resilience, cultural and social aspects, relationships with peers, family and community, self-regulation, affect and motivation and engagement. For an adolescent these influences are different and need to be taken into consideration in order for positive learning outcomes to be gained.

If these influences are taken into account, and all stakeholders take an active role in improving literacy learning outcomes, then students will have more positive pathways after school.

The importance of parent/carer involvement in home literacy learning

The significance of parents/carers and significant others in an adolescent's life cannot be understated. Even though young people begin to move from dependence to independence throughout their secondary schooling the presence and impact of their families, community and friends on their learning outcomes is substantial. In fact, according to the Ofsted Report (House of Commons, 2015) schools that outperformed others had strong parental/carer involvement in the school's activities and environment.

Epstein et al.'s (2002) work, for example, shares six types of involvement parents and schools can create with each other. These are listed below:

1. *Parenting*. Assist families with parenting skills, family support, understanding child and adolescent development, and setting home conditions to support learning at each age and grade level. Assist schools in understanding families' backgrounds, cultures and goals for children.
2. *Communicating*. Communicate with families about school programmes and student progress. Create two-way communication channels between school and home.
3. *Volunteering*. Improve recruitment, training, activities and schedules to involve families as volunteers and as audiences at the school or in other locations. Enable educators to work with volunteers who support students and the school.
4. *Learning at home*. Involve families with their children in academic learning at home, including homework, goal setting and other curriculum-related activities. Encourage teachers to design homework that enables students to share and discuss interesting tasks.
5. *Decision-making*. Include families as participants in school decisions, governance and advocacy activities through school councils or improvement teams, committees and parent organisations.
6. *Collaborating with the community*. Coordinate resources and services for families, students and the school with community groups, including businesses, agencies, cultural and civic organisations, and colleges or universities. Enable all to contribute service to the community. (Epstein et al., 2002)

Another consideration is the rising prevalence of home schooling and other alternative education practices. There is evidence to suggest that enrolment and involvement are increasing in virtual schools, distance education, home schooling and/or faith schools that have distinct relationships with their communities. More and more parents and/or carers are seeing the benefits of strong community and family-based schooling systems. It is important then to consider the ways in which parents and/or educators are optimising learning and in particular literacy learning in these environments.

Peer support in and for literacy learning

In Chapter 10 we explain how adolescents prefer to learn, including collaboratively via student-centred approaches. Secondary school students also appreciate opportunities to show leadership skills (Barton and McKay, 2016a) as well as support each other through group work and tutoring. Topping's (1996) work on peer tutoring provides some solid evidence as to appropriate approaches to tutoring young people in the home as well as contexts other than traditional schooling methods. Further, Luca and Clarkson (2002) explain that peer tutoring is based on a socio-constructivist view of learning or social interaction in context. This in turn improves motivation (Hartman, 1990) and is more intellectually rewarding (Benware and Deci, 1984).

Conclusion

This chapter has aimed to explain what a socio-constructivist view of literacy education entails. This includes how any literate practice, whether in or out of school, is a socially and culturally constructed one, meaning that the ways in which we communicate with each other are influenced by the society and culture in which we live. The chapter has also outlined the critical importance of schools developing effective and productive partnerships with the community and their families.

Discussion questions and activities

Questions

1   What does a socio-constructivist approach to literacy education mean?
2   Why is it important to build strong partnerships between students' homes, schools and communities?
3   How is your school working with students' homes and communities?

4   What are some ways these partnerships can be improved?
5   Think about your own home and community life when you went to school. Did your school consciously bridge these environments for you? Or was there little connection between your home life and school life?
6   Consider the reasons why it is important for adolescent learners to have strong connections between their home life and the community in which they live in their schooling practices.
7   Look at your teaching plans, for example a term's unit of work. Identify some places where you could involve a community member in the learning cycle. Many people who work and live in your school's community are keen and happy to be involved in the day-to-day learning in your school. For example, many schools have had artist-in-residency programmes set up for the students which have proven to be extremely positive experiences for both artist and students.

†††† Group activities

1   Refer back to Chapter 1 – what were the results of your analysis of the school context in which you are working? What did you discover about your community? What did you find out about your students' personal, social and cultural needs?
2   Brainstorm some ways in which your school could communicate information about your students' learning and activities at the school with your community. Are there more diverse ways you could share this information?
3   Thinking about your own school's context, what are some ways you could improve and enhance the partnerships you already have with your students' home lives and the community?

CHAPTER 6

MULTILITERACIES AND MULTIMODALITIES

Chapter objectives

- To define the concepts of multiliteracies and multimodalities.
- To consider comprehension and composition of multimodal texts.
- To understand and apply Cope and Kalantzis' Learning by Design model.

Key questions

1 What do multiliteracies and multimodalities mean?
2 What are the implications of this knowledge on teaching and learning?
3 How are these considered in curriculum, planning and assessment?

Key words: Multiliteracies, multimodalities, multimodal text, design elements, Learning by Design model.

Introduction

In Chapter 1 we explored the notion that literate practice in the twenty-first century is multifaceted, involving the ways in which people communicate across borders and across modes and mediums. Back at the turn of this century Bill Cope and Mary Kalantzis (2000) edited a seminal book entitled: *Multiliteracies: Literacy Learning and the Design of Social Futures.* Interestingly the concept of designing social futures implies that the education of young people has potential to impact on prospective generations. The importance of this cannot be understated. A socially just view of education means that boundaries can be broken, power can be shifted and young people can ultimately aspire to achieve their own personal and educational goals.

What does 'multiliteracies' mean?

Multiliteracies is a term that encompasses a range of literate practices that we might engage in. Cope and Kalantzis' (2000) idea of multiliteracies works on two levels and these are texts and practices. In relation to texts, the use of language across a range of platforms such as new information and communications media constitutes multiple meanings that are increasingly multimodal. No longer are oral and written linguistic modes dominant in communicating this meaning. Cope and Kalantzis (2000) discuss the importance of recognising the ways in which language interfaces with audio, gestural, spatial, tactile and visual patterns of meaning in the contemporary classroom and everyday world (from http://newlearningonline.com/multiliteracies).

In addition to the complexities of the types of texts we experience every day, the ways in which we engage with or create these texts are influenced by our prior experiences, particularly from what we learn both socially and culturally. Cope and Kalantzis refer to this as 'variability of meaning making in different cultural, social or domain-specific contexts' (from their website http://newlearningonline.com/multiliteracies) and note the importance of socio-cultural aspects to communications environments. They believe that:

> it is no longer enough for literacy teaching to focus solely on the rules of standard forms of the national language. Rather, the business of communication and representation of meaning today increasingly requires that learners are able to figure out differences in patterns of meaning from one context to another. These differences are the consequence of any number of factors, including culture, gender, life experience, subject matter, social or subject domain and the like. Every meaning exchange is cross-cultural to a certain degree.

Therefore, it is critical to understand multi-contexts, multi-cultures and multi-literacies within and across communities when planning for learning in the secondary classroom.

What does 'multimodalities' mean?

An important component of a multiliteracies framework is the notion of multimodality. According to Anastopoulou et al. (2001: 1), 'multimodality is based on the use of sensory modalities by which humans receive information'. Modes can be auditory, tactile or visual and can be used in combination in the same transaction. A multimodal interaction therefore is where a user may receive information through visual and auditory modes but may respond by voice and through touch. Similarly, multimodal texts use a range of modes so that meaning can be communicated through synchronisation of modes – this may include spoken and/or written language, still and/or moving images and sound and silence. These may be produced on paper, in three dimensions or on an electronic screen.

Print form multimodal texts include books such as information books, newspapers or magazines. Non-print texts include film or video, emails, digital media and/or artworks or performances. Understanding the modes present in a range of texts helps us to explicitly teach our students to both comprehend and compose similar texts effectively. It is therefore important to know information about each design process and element deeply.

The design elements

The New London Group's framework of multiliteracies consists of three processes of design: available designs, design and redesigned (see Chapter 2). These are used to describe the activities of an individual as they identify, read and create new text using various semiotic codes. The three processes allow us to make patterns of meaning from the multiliteracies around us.

Available designs refers to any *text* (in Chapter 1 we noted that text can refer to 'meaningful artefacts of society and culture') that inspires us in creating new texts. Exploration of the grammars of language, different semiotic systems such as film, photography and embodied communication occurs so that people can gain greater understanding of texts and artefacts. These elements are then utilised to influence creators of new design and objects and the redesigned is the finished product or work.

Within each of these three design processes we can identify six design elements. Table 6.1 depicts this relationship:

Table 6.1 The relationship between design processes and elements (Cope and Kalantzis, 2000)

Available designs		Design		Redesigned	
Adjustable resources	Aurality and sound	Embodiment and movement	Language and linguistic resources	Spatial design	Visual resources
Multimodal resources					

←   →

The above framework allows us to understand how we make meaning when reading, viewing or engaging with a text. Related to this is the process of intertextuality, which 'draws attention to the potentially complex ways in which meanings … are constituted through relationships to other texts' (Cope and Kalantzis, 2000: 30).

The following section will unpack each of the design elements in relation to multiliterate practices and comprehending and composing multimodal texts.

Aurality and sound

The use of music including sound effects and silence contributes greatly to meaning within multimodal texts, including literary and non-literary texts such

Table 6.2 Music features for emotive response

Tonal features	Rhythmic features	Articulation and dynamics	Timbral features
Includes Ellis and Simons' model (2005)	Includes Ellis and Simons (2005)	Attacks/releases	Instrumentation and sound quality (Gundlach, 1935)
Major key – positive valence	Slow tempo – low arousal	Short	Layers and textures – how many instruments and what type
Minor key – negative valence	Regular rhythm or meter – low arousal	Sustained	
Intervallic relationship – 2nd, 3rd – close proximity; 4th, 5th – open sparse effect; 6th – harmonic consonance; 7th – harmonic dissonance	Fast tempo – high arousal	Delayed	Wooden, metallic, shimmering, breathy
	Irregular rhythm – low arousal	Flowing	Techniques on instruments
	Repetition	Disjointed	
	Rhythmic motifs	Irregular/regular	Sustained chords/notes
Melodic suspension and resolution	Increase in tempo	Soft	Muted
Melodic motifs (with the use of the above)	Intensity	Loud	Types of mallets
Repetition	Layering	Increase in volume	Combination of spatial organisation (Rahn, 1998)
	Uneven	Decrease in volume	
	Smooth (Gundlach, 1935)	Layering	Vibrato/tremolo
		Intensity	

as narratives and persuasions. In 1999 Theo van Leeuwen wrote a book titled *Speech, Music and Sound* that detailed how music and sound are used to communicate meaning across a range of contexts. Similarly, Barton and Unsworth (2014) unpacked how a music soundtrack can contribute to meaning by exploring the short film *The Lost Thing* by Shaun Tan. They demonstrated how image, movement and sound work together as an ensemble in making meaning. An analytical framework to assist in the deconstruction of music soundtracks in relation to the narrative was offered. A number of features are explored in this framework: tonal, rhythmic, timbral, articulation and dynamics or volume (see Table 6.2).

Embodiment and movement

Gestural action and interaction has been said to constitute approximately 80 per cent of our communication. A gesture is a form of non-verbal communication and involves some form of movement of the body including facial expression or body language. Elements such as speed, stillness (Anstey and Bull, 2010), direction and articulation all contribute to gestural meaning.

Work carried out by Dael et al. (2013) highlighted the importance of understanding gestural movement in relation to emotion and emotive responses. In particular, they investigated how emotion is expressed through body movement such as arm movements. Emotional arousal, valence and potency are all related to spatio-temporal characteristics in arm gestures – meaning the bigger the arm movement the bigger the emotional arousal (Dael et al., 2013). Table 6.3 shows some of their findings from a literature search.

Dael et al. (2013) note that ME represents the *main effect* of the gestural movement and IE is the *interaction effect*. They believed that the effects of potency and valence were larger when there were high arousal emotions present.

The significance of such research is that movement and gesture plays a crucial role in making meaning from 'texts' that feature movement, in particular embodied movement. Think, for example, about particular characters in movies

Table 6.3 Gesture dynamics with expressed emotion dimensions (from Dael et al., 2013: 645)

Expressed emotion dimension	Perceived gestural arm movement	Evidence from Dael et al.'s study
High/low potency	Forceful/weak	ME, IE × arousal
	Expansive/contracted	ME, IE × arousal
Positive/negative valence	Fluent/abrupt	ME, no IE × arousal
	Higher/lower in space	No ME, IE × arousal, IE × arousal × potency
High/low arousal	Abundant/few movements	ME
	Fast/slow	ME

that you have watched. How has their movement, posture, gesture all impacted on the portrayal of character? It is therefore important for young people to be aware of these elements when comprehending or composing multimodal texts and especially when they are required to present through dramatic or dance forms.

Language and linguistic resources

It is undeniable that language is a central part of much communication. Whether written or oral, language has paved the way for both ancient and modern civilisations. Language is comprised of a number of linguistic resources such as letters, vocabulary, structure, as well as grammar. According to Michael Halliday (1978) language comprises of three areas of meaning: field, tenor and mode.

Field is concerned with the subject matter and involves participants (or characters or objects) and circumstances (or contexts). Field also refers to topic areas such as those found in science and history. It focuses on 'who is involved, what is the topic, what is happening and where?'

Two examples are featured in Figure 6.1.

Tenor refers to the ways in which these characters, objects and contexts relate to the reader or listener of the language. Tenor reflects the concept of audience and explores whether the 'status, level of expertise, age, ethnic background, and gender of the participants can have an impact on the language used' (Derewianka, 2012: 132). It also refers to the ways in which particular texts might persuade or engage the reader and asks 'who is involved but also what kind of relationships are being established?'

In the first example in Figure 6.1 below we could consider the process 'wandered' suggests that the black cat is curious and relaxed while walking through the woods – this creates a visual image in our mind. Let's consider the sentence if we altered it to the following:

The black cat wandered through the woods.

Participant	Process	Circumstance
The black cat	wandered	through the woods.

The destruction of a rainforest can impact greatly on habitat.

Circumstance (nominalisation)	Participant	Process	Circumstance
The destruction	of a rainforest	can impact greatly	on habitat.

Figure 6.1 Sentence examples

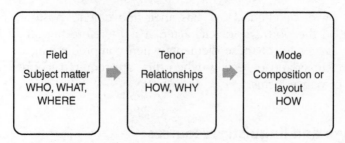

Figure 6.2   Concepts of field, tenor and mode

The scraggly old black cat wandered fearlessly through the mysterious woods.

The tenor or relationship with the reader has now changed. The use of extended noun groups (the addition of a number of adjectives) as well as an adverb (fearlessly) added to the process allows us to visualise a particular type of cat – one who can face confronting situations fearlessly.

In relation to the second sentence in Figure 6.1 – one typically found in an informative text – we can surmise that perhaps someone who disagrees with destroying rainforests has constructed the discourse. This is particularly evident through the use of the extended verb or process group 'can impact greatly'. We can often see a certain bias even coming through texts written in science and history through the use of modality such as the word 'greatly'. If the writer had chosen the word 'somewhat' instead the meaning would be different as the modality is mid-range rather than high.

Mode is about the ways in which authors utilise language in creating cohesion across texts and how words and images are represented including how they are placed on a page. Mode is about the channels of communication being used by the author and therefore it is important to explore how these may be different from what students are commonly used to.

A simpler way to explain field, tenor and mode is illustrated in Figure 6.2.

Spatial design

According to Anstey and Bull (2010: 1) spatial design, as one of the five semiotic systems, includes features such as 'proximity, direction, position of layout and organisation of objects in space'. This means that how objects or text are placed on a page and the relationship between these contributes to the overall meaning of the text, as illustrated in Figure 6.3.

Spatial resources not only include realistic or abstract images alongside text but also graphs, charts and other diagrams. Most importantly it is how these are positioned and the relationship between them on a page, website or even within a moving image screen that constitute spatial design. Diagrammatic

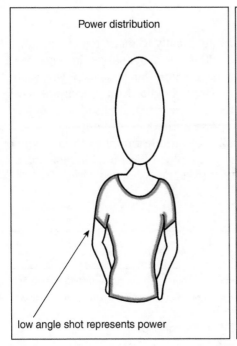
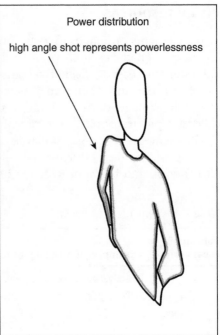

Figure 6.3 Power/spatial distribution in images

representations, particularly in scientific or factual texts, often display information that compares or organises. These can fall under one of three categories:

1. Ecosystem designs
2. Geographic designs
3. Architectonic designs

Ecosystem designs may represent subsystems that are linked to a core idea or topic. An example would be a food web or chain. Mind or concept maps, Venn diagrams and flow charts are also examples of ecosystem designs.

Geographic designs include information that shows the difference between the main information on the page as well as minor or subordinate information. In history, for example, a text book page might explain the medieval feudal system with some images that have smaller font-sized paragraphs below the images explaining them, rather than including this information in the main text. Other geographic design materials include maps and strata organisational resources.

Architectonic designs are about how organisational and comparative information is displayed or what Mills (2010: 21) explains as 'material qualities of design and structure'. Common examples of these are margins, tables, matrices and general formatting features.

Visual resources

Visual elements or images in texts contribute greatly to meaning; even though for much literacy research prior to the 1980s visual resources in texts were not often discussed. Work by literacy researchers such as Len Unsworth, Gunther Kress and Theo van Leeuwen has highlighted the important work that visual image does in a range of text types, from narratives, such as children's picture books, to technical reports and advertisements.

The elements of image shown in Table 6.4 are important to discuss when working with students (please also refer to Chapter 12 in Lorraine McDonald's (2013) book and Humphrey et al. (2012: 119–121).

Table 6.4 Elements of visual image

Element of visual image	Examples of meaning making
Colour • Warm tones • Cool tones	Red, yellow and orange tones amplify emotion and bring energy and excitement. Blues, greens and cooler colours are more muted and detached or emotionally withdrawn. Brown and grey indicate a more depressed/dark mood.
Vector • Line of sight	Vector is about 'reading pathways'. They can be horizontal, vertical or diagonal. The vector often follows where the character is looking. These are important as they can show movement in the picture. Think of shapes and directions:
Camera shot and angle • Focalisation • Affect • Attitude	There are generally 3 types of camera shots: • close-up • mid shot and • long shot Close-ups indicate more of an intimate relationship with the viewer while long shots create a distant relationship.
Layout and positioning Levels of power distribution	The angle of the shot also impacts on meaning. A high shot shows the viewer as having more power while a low shot portrays the viewer with less power. Eye-level is equal. If a participant in the photo or image is looking directly at the viewer this is called a 'demand' whereas if they are looking away it is an 'offer'.
Framing and salience	Framing has the viewer focus on a specific part of an image while salience is the most 'attention-grabbing' part of the image. This includes part of the image that might be in sharp focus, high contrast and involve foreground and background. Is it a two-page spread? Is there a frame around the page?
Texture: smooth rough scratchy etc.	Texture in images is important as it creates certain emotions. Scratchy and rough backgrounds can make the viewer uncomfortable while a smooth background such as using silky cloth can depict cosy environments. The colour also impacts on texture – e.g. pastel and smooth, dark and rough.

Understanding and using the above design elements in learning and teaching is critical in today's multi-literate world. In fact, many curriculum outlines note the importance of acknowledging and implementing a range of texts within the classroom particularly in relation to understanding and composing multimodal texts.

Adolescents and literacy in a multi-literate world

As described in Chapter 1, we are faced more and more with diverse modes of communication, we engage in a range of literate practices, and create new and unique works or texts continuously. Much research has shown that the ways in which we communicate has exponentially increased over the past decade, and that this trend is predicted to continue (Jewitt, 2008). Equally reported in the literature is the mismatch between the ways adolescents use and consume technologies or other socially and culturally appropriate forms of communication within their communities as compared to within school (see Hull and Schultz, 2002). While young people's lives outside of school are certainly different from inside school many have noted the need to make more links between these contexts so that learners can see connections between their everyday literate practices and the new knowledge being learnt in the school context (Cairney, 2002). Connecting students' prior knowledge to school content ensures a greater understanding of the topic at hand. It also allows students to have more agency and autonomy and therefore feel more engaged in relation to learning.

For adolescents, a social approach to learning is critical for engagement and motivation. The work of Louis Moll (1993), for example, provides strong evidence to change approaches to learning and teaching from individualised to a community of practice for young people. This aligns with Vygotsky's (1978) socio-cultural approach to learning which notes that when students are challenged appropriately and with the right support they are working within their zone of proximal development or, as Csikszentmihalyi (1997) believes, they are in flow, which is the optimal learning phase. For researchers such as those mentioned above part of this experience includes tapping into students' prior learning experiences and knowledge base. Moll et al. (1992) term this 'funds of knowledge'. Moje et al. (2004) state that it is important to acknowledge these, including:

> homes, peer groups, and other systems and networks of relationships that shape the oral and written texts young people make meaning of and produce as they move from classroom to classroom and from home to peer group, to school, or to community. (2004: 38)

Without accessing the knowledge base and experiences that adolescents bring with them to the classroom it can be difficult to make links or use effective strategies, such as when comprehending new texts, in order to make meaning. One approach that explores good pedagogy for learning is Kalantzis et al.'s (2005) Learning by Design model. This model applies particularly well to when students are required to engage with and utilise a range of modes when exploring multimodal texts.

Comprehending and creating multimodal texts in a multi-literate world: Learning by Design

In Chapter 1 we introduced the Learning by Design model by Kalantzis et al. (2005). We explained that the model involved a range of knowledge processes: experiential, conceptual, analytical and applied. This means that when students engage with texts, learn about new topics and participate in meaningful discussions, it is vital that all knowledge process levels are met for deep learning. Table 6.5 highlights what each level entails.

You may notice that these processes are similar to the levels of understanding in Bloom's taxonomy in relation to factual knowledge (experience), conceptual knowledge (conceptualise), procedural knowledge (apply), and metacognitive or critical thinking (analyse); see also Anderson and Krathwohl (2001) and Krathwohl's (2002) revision on Bloom's taxonomy.

The knowledge processes form an integral part of a multiliteracies pedagogy, but it is equally important to know what experiences can activate these processes. Kalantzis et al. (2005) believe that there are different ways of knowing and that these operate differently in and through the learning process.

A major consideration for adolescents and learning is what knowledge they bring with them into the school context. Often termed 'funds of knowledge', recognising what students are already familiar with and how they can share these 'life learnings' is incredibly important to understand for teachers in high schools.

Table 6.5 The knowledge processes (Kalantzis et al. 2005)

To experience	To conceptualise	To analyse	To apply
What the learners will gain from the experiential work they do: what they will gain from immersion in texts, real-world problems, community experiences, etc.	What the learners will gain from the conceptual work they do: the main concepts they will learn, and the theory.	What the learners will gain from the analytical work they do: understanding causal relationships, critical thinking skills.	What learners will gain by applying their knowledge: solving a real-world problem, communicating meanings, etc.

The Learning by Design model therefore suggests beginning new learning with *experiencing the known* followed by *experiencing the new*. This is where field knowledge is built around and about the topic at hand. New knowledge can be introduced via different activities such as listening, viewing, visiting, locating or immersing. Next, *conceptualising*, as a knowledge process, involves *identifying or naming* through glossaries, labelling, sorting and/or categorising. When students conceptualise they also *theorise* by working on concept maps, discussing cause and effect, comparing and contrasting, making decisions, summarising or making analogies.

Analysing occurs both *functionally and critically*. Classroom activities such as explanation, story boarding, modelling and flow diagrams assist students when analysing with purpose. Critical analysis is a deeper level that can include debating, predicting, reviewing, identifying stereotypes and exploring human interests and motivations. Finally, checking for understanding through *applying appropriately and creatively* needs to be carried out. Creating texts for an audience and with purpose through the use of appropriate technologies, using suitable and contextual language and other modes as well as innovating by applying to a different setting or reforming problems is the final learning process in the Learning by Design model.

The following section shares ways in which teachers can implement a Learning by Design model in their curriculum planning and assessment.

Vignette 6.1

Topic: Climate Change

Experience – the known

When introducing the topic of climate change to students a good place to start is by asking them what they already know about climate change. Ask students to write any ideas they have on Post-it notes and place them on a large cardboard tree at the front of the classroom. Then ask the students to nominate a classmate to read out each of the notes.

Encourage discussion about the ideas and concepts students are already familiar with in small groups through the following guiding questions:

- What do you already know about climate change?
- How do you know these topics are related to climate change?
- What is your opinion about climate change?

(Continued)

(Continued)

Experience – the new

Invite a guest speaker from a relevant government department on climate change to visit the class and share their views and/or policies. Have the class discuss and debate what the guest speaker has revealed. Then use Al Gore's film *An Inconvenient Truth* (2006) as a stimulus text as well as finding further evidence through research of counterclaims to expand the students' knowledge in the area.

- What is your opinion on the guest speakers' presentation? Do you agree with their views?
- How is Al Gore's evidence presented? e.g. What images/data are used? What do the graphs tell us? Do you think they are accurate? How do you know?
- What are some counter arguments against Al Gore's film? What evidence do these claims provide? Is this accurate?

Conceptualise – identify and name

Instruct the students to research further by identifying and naming aspects related to climate change. Much of this research could focus on scientific information such as the greenhouse effect, carbon levels in the atmosphere, etc. Students could also explore the outcomes of the Paris Climate Change Conference in November 2015 and other key events such as the Kyoto Protocol.

- Define the issue/s being explored
- What are the arguments for and against these issues?
- Where is your evidence?
- What was the purpose of the climate change conference? Were these goals achieved?

Conceptualise – theorise

Support and encourage students to theorise the new information they have gathered. This is where they start to form a stronger and evidence-based opinion about climate change.

Invite students to have a discussion on issues related to climate change, before focusing on theories related to climate change which include images on the carbon and nitrogen cycles, the greenhouse effect and changes in earth temperatures and water levels.

Then show students information from the following website: www.bbc.co.uk/news/resources/idt-5aceb360-8bc3-4741-99f0-2e4f76ca02bb (accessed 22 November 2016) and proceed to allocate groups to look at the different numbered topics:

1   What is the problem?
2   Why is this happening?
3   What are the effects?
4   What does the future hold?
5   What can be done?
6   How can we limit the damage?

Analyse – functionally

The students need to then verify their exploration and information with experts in the field by writing letters, visiting and interviewing people.

Analyse – critically

Students start to develop their own ideals and debate with their classmates and other members of the community.

Apply – appropriately

Students form groups for assessment purposes. Students decide who they would like to work with, e.g. other peers with the same views; other peers with differing views; other peers with similar skills such as technological savvy, artistic flair, reporting/journalistic abilities; or a group of peers with a range of skills.

Apply – creatively

Students work in their groups to present findings of their research on climate change. For example, one group may perform a dance that displays their view about climate change – this performance could also feature data as projected on a screen throughout the performance; another group may decide to do a dramatic performance and write a script about their findings; while another creates a newspaper or scientific report.

Assessment of this topic can be wide and varied and should be decided upon by the students themselves. The assessment should focus on the question: Is climate change real? Assessment could also be multimodal in presentation, i.e. with images, graphs, diagrams, sound and audio, music, movement, etc.

Take the following students for example. What would be the best approach for them to present their ideas related to the assessment task?

(Continued)

(Continued)

Meet Alex

Alex, an Indigenous student, utilises various ways in which to communicate with her friends every day, particularly Snapchat and Instagram but also Facebook. For Alex, learning for understanding involves images as she is a strong visual learner. Alex is therefore very good at visual art and design. She believes this is the case with many young people as information needs to convey meaning quickly. Alex explained that the most used 'word', as indicated by the Oxford Dictionary, was an emoji.

She therefore believes that communication has changed greatly and that this knowledge should be drawn on more in the classroom. Alex therefore has chosen to create an interactive digital poster to display her knowledge and opinions about climate change.

Meet John

John is a keen gamer and often uses Skype to talk to his friends and YouTube to learn about topics of interest. Orally communicating with his friends via Skype, John believes, is easy, reliable and cost-effective. He also thinks YouTube is a valuable resource for new information and in particular learning new skills. Gaming, in particular, is a way for John to socialise. He believes the process requires team building as it involves trust on the part of each participant and requires deep problem solving and thought processes. John thinks his life out of school appears to be irrelevant to his schooling. He believes that school does not value or recognise the skills he learns through gaming with his friends online and understands that learning at school is more static and teacher-centred. John has therefore decided to develop six short news reports utilising animation methods that explore concepts such as sustainability and climate control with his peers that will be presented on their own YouTube channel.

Meet Zong-Xian

Zong-Xian (or Kevin) recently arrived in Australia from China and is fluent in Mandarin, Cantonese and English, although he has yet to learn Australian colloquialisms. Kevin said that many people assume he cannot communicate well in English and therefore he attends an ESL class at school. He likes this class as he helps the other students but he said he is bored with his studies as he attended an international school in Hong Kong for some of his school years. He enjoys writing reports for a small magazine back in Hong Kong about his experiences in Australia. Kevin therefore has organised to write a magazine article that compares pollutants and strategies to alleviate impacts on the environment in Australia and China (including Hong Kong).

Using a Learning by Design model can therefore positively impact on and benefit every student in the class.

Conclusion

Given both the diversity of texts and literate practices across the globe it is important that teachers acknowledge and embrace a multiliteracies framework within their classroom. Included in this philosophy is the fact that people can communicate via a number of modes, signs and symbols and consequently these should be embedded in curriculum pedagogy and assessment for adolescent students.

An effective approach to apply in the classroom is Kalantzis et al.'s Learning by Design model so that students can work through a range of knowledge processes. This allows them to understand how to work from factual, through to procedural and to more critical applications of knowledge within the learning context. Evidence suggests that making learning more student-centred for adolescents, such as via a Learning by Design approach, ensures engagement and motivation and therefore positive achievement overall.

Discussion questions and activities

 Questions

1 How do diverse and multi-literate practices impact on learning and teaching for adolescent students?
2 What are design elements and why is it important to include these in literacy learning tasks?
3 What are some ways to implement multimodal approaches to designing assessment tasks?
4 Think about all of the activities you do in a day that involve some kind of text. List the modes included in these texts and create a map to show how diverse they are.
5 What modes are you most effective at communicating with? Are you more able to create a drawing or dance to represent meaning? Or do you prefer to write creatively? Why is it important to know your students' strengths in relation to various ways to represent meaning?
6 Consider your current assessment tasks across the curriculum. Do you set a range of design elements in these tasks for students so that they have the opportunity to display their strengths? Are there any chances for them to select the mode they would prefer in any assessment tasks or is this usually decided for them?

♦♦♦♦ Group activities

1 Explore the Learning by Design model with your colleagues. Consider how you could embed a range of knowledge processes in your curriculum, planning and assessment. Map out where and when these processes are covered in a particular unit of study. Do you notice any gaps?

2   Consider your students – what are they good at? What types of literate practices do they engage in outside of school? How do you include these skills in your assessment tasks?

3   Reflect on how you are preparing your students for an unpredictable future workforce. How are skills like problem solving, creative and critical thinking and design thinking encouraged and developed in your classrooms?

CHAPTER 7

THE TEACHING OF READING

Chapter objectives

- To understand the reading process including the 'big six'.
- To learn about appropriate strategies for teaching reading for adolescents.
- To develop knowledge around reading in the content areas.

Key questions

1   What makes an effective reader?
2   What are appropriate strategies for teaching reading for adolescents?
3   How can the teaching of reading be improved in the content areas?

Key words: A simple view of reading, teaching and learning approaches for reading, reading and adolescents, reading in the content areas.

Introduction

Reading is a crucial skill for people to engage with, and operate in, the world today. By reading we mean the ability to decode and comprehend a range of text types including those with images, sound and movement as a component of the text's meaning.

A simple view of reading

A simple view of reading by Gough and Tunmer (1986) is a widely accepted view of the complex process of reading, particularly for students with learning difficulties. The simple view of reading is as follows:

> Decoding (D) × Language comprehension (LC) = Reading comprehension (RC)

Decoding refers to the ability to turn a code or coded message into a usable and comprehensible form. Language comprehension involves two elements: understanding language as a form of meaning making in a macro sense and the process of deriving meaning from language including spoken or written words, images, sound, gestures, etc.

If a student is able to both decode and comprehensively understand language as a communicative device, as well as comprehend meaning from a text, then they are able to read effectively and fluently. Farrell et al. (2010: 1) believe that:

> The Simple View formula and supporting studies show that a student's reading comprehension (RC) score can be predicted if decoding (D) skills and language comprehension (LC) abilities are known.

Farrell et al.'s (2010) work shares a number of examples of the formula involving students with reading difficulties.

Understanding the entire reading process is critical for all teachers even in the high school setting where it is often assumed students can already read effectively. Evidence suggests that more and more young adolescents are entering high school with limited reading skills and that this number is predicted to rise. The reasons for this increase are complex and it is important to understand that these may be different for each individual. Therefore, understanding the areas in which students need support is important for planning and improvement across the whole school context.

Further elements to the reading process

The simple view of reading takes into account decoding and language comprehension but these two areas can be broken down into other aspects.

Table 7.1   Scarborough's elements to skilled reading (2001)

Decoding and word recognition	Language comprehension
Phonological awareness – syllables and phonemes	Background knowledge including prior experiences
The alphabetic principle, spelling–sound correspondence	Vocabulary – breadth, precision, links
Sight recognition of familiar words	Language structures – syntax, semantics
NB Visual images, sound and music and moving image can also be included in decoding and sign/symbol recognition	Verbal reasoning including inference and metaphor
	Literacy knowledge such as print concepts, genres, etc.

Scarborough (2001) has clearly identified a number of elements or skills as parts of these two processes. These are listed in Table 7.1.

All of these elements contribute to effective reading and when students have difficulty with reading it may be just one area or a combination of areas that they need support in. The elements represented in Table 7.1 can generally be found in one of six areas related to reading. These are known as the 'big six' of reading instruction (Konza, 2014; 2016):

1. Comprehension
2. Fluency
3. Oral language
4. Phonemic awareness, phonics and word recognition
5. Phonological awareness
6. Vocabulary.

Comprehension

Comprehension involves making meaning from text. When people read they make sense of the text by referring back to prior experiences that they are reminded of; other texts or reading practices; and interactions with others. If students have limited experiences related to the text, limited vocabulary, or difficulty in processing links to prior knowledge then reading can be unenjoyable and making meaning from the text can be interrupted or inadequate. Even though a student may be able to read fluently it may not mean they are able to recall information from the text or think critically about that text.

Fluency

Fluency is about the flow of a student's reading capacity both aloud and in their own minds. As noted above a student may be able to read smoothly but may still not understand what they are reading. If reading is not fluent it is possible students are unable to recognise by sight more unfamiliar words, spell correctly or identify ways in which to decode while they are reading. Fluent readers also consider phrasing and pausing in appropriate places. Students also need to be able to learn how to read for long periods of time to improve their reading stamina and capacity so if the fluency is impeded then sustained reading practices are unlikely.

Oral language

Many educators believe oral language is typically developed in the early years of schooling. It has been noted, however, that oral language may not be fully developed or enhanced for some adolescent learners. Being able to articulate your ideas through oral language is extremely important in the high school context. Many assessment pieces, for example, are oral presentations and require students to present in front of others formally.

Phonemic awareness, phonics and word recognition

Phonemic awareness is about the reader's ability to recognise and manipulate the individual phonemes in spoken language. Phonemic awareness is a specific term that focuses on the smallest units of sound that affect meaning (Hill, 2012), such as the three phonemes in the word cat – c/a/t. There are 41 phonemes of the English language and these are the smallest units that constitute spoken language.

Phonics is the teaching of letter sound relationships used in reading and writing (Hill, 2012). This approach uses a whole–part method to help children identify new words. This means that children or young people can use their knowledge of one word to decode another. For example, students learn about families of words made up of onset and rime such as rhyming words. Similarly, students can learn the blends and digraphs that begin words and create lists of other words with the same beginning sounds by changing the rime.

Sight vocabulary skills such as word recognition includes using the shape of the word, a position in a familiar context and picture clues. Reading experiences, particularly outside of school, contribute to the number of familiar words students can recognise on sight. This is important in terms of high-level vocabulary in the curriculum areas.

Phonological awareness

Phonological awareness is an umbrella term that encompasses a range of skills including awareness of rhyme, rhythm and intonation within words and texts as well as phonemic awareness. It concerns the ability to manipulate words, syllables and sounds in spoken language within the mind (Goldsworthy, 2010).

Vocabulary

Well-developed vocabulary is a good predictor of reading success particularly due to the fact that vocabulary and comprehension are closely linked. In terms of teaching vocabulary, the National Reading Panel (2000) suggests direct and non-direct methods should be used. Further, age and ability should also be considered when planning interventions (Woolley, 2011). Oral vocabulary is regarded as being fundamental to reading, academic growth and school success (Blachowicz et al., 2006). What we do know is that poor vocabulary is a contributing factor to reading difficulties in adolescence. Students with poor vocabularies are often poor readers; poor readers resist reading yet reading builds vocabulary.

Vignette 7.1

David has just entered his first year in high school. He finds comprehending high-level narrative texts, such as novels, as well as content area texts very difficult. When reading David tends to focus most of his efforts on decoding single words rather than remembering and making meaning from whole sentences.

Questions

1   What would be the first task you would do in order to support David's reading development?
2   How would you go about finding out what parts of the reading process David has difficulty with?
3   Who could you ask to assist in supporting David's reading?

Appropriate strategies for the teaching of reading for adolescents

There are a range of strategies that support the success of adolescent readers. Many researchers note that explicit instruction allows learners to fully understand the reading task expected of them as well as receive the required scaffolding in completing this task. It is also important, however, to include a balanced approach to reading instruction as students develop self-regulation, a critical approach to, and enjoyment for, reading. Telling students directly what to do through a formulaic method all the time means they have limited opportunities to make meaning from texts via more innovative and creative approaches. Also purchasing commercial phonics and/or comprehension programmes to implement for readers who need extra support may not necessarily be the best approach either. The best approach is to find out more about your students, their families and the community in which your school is situated. What are the strengths you find? What areas need improvement? And how can this information help you in creating a conducive environment for the enjoyment of, and engagement in, reading? Developing programmes that acknowledge these strengths, address areas for improvement but also embrace diversity and offer a range of learning activities that students also have a choice in will lead to students becoming *active readers*.

Who are active readers?

Active readers read texts with a critical lens in identifying the text's purpose and also the relevance for the reader themselves. When students are active readers they are proactive and able to engage with the meaning of the text in a number of ways.

A number of practical strategies assist students in being active readers. These include: reading aloud with their peers and/or parents; scanning the text and identifying the most important information; summarising the text in their own words; being able to predict what might happen or in regard to non-literary texts what the cause and effect might be; and being able to construct questions about the text that enable further information to be gained.

Before, during and after reading activities

When you are planning for reading with your classes it is important to consider before, during and after reading activities. Before reading or pre-reading activities have the potential for students to connect their prior knowledge to the task at hand. This means that they can create a mental framework that sets them up for success with a new experience or topic. Then when the actual reading of a text occurs (during or reading and re-reading) the before reading connections will be activated and assist students in reflecting back on prior experiences when making meaning from the text. After reading or post-reading activities ensure further understanding but also engagement with the text on deeper and more critical levels.

According to Hill (2012: 84) a range of strategies when using literature in the classroom allow for more effective reading instruction, particularly when using shared texts. These approaches are displayed in Figure 7.1.

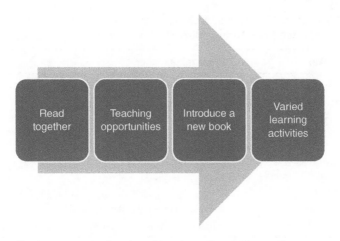

Figure 7.1 Effective strategies for shared book reading (Hill, 2012)

Other approaches can also engage adolescent students in active reading. One such model is known as the Four Roles model by Peter Freebody and Alan Luke (Freebody and Luke, 1990; Luke and Freebody, 1999).

A critical approach to reading: the Four Roles model

The Four Roles model was created in response to the development and diversity of texts and consequently the 'complexity of reading and the changing and challenging demands in order to be a successful reader in today's world' (myread.org/what.htm).

The Four Roles are as follows:

1. Code breaker
2. Text user
3. Text participant or meaning maker
4. Text analyst.

Code breaker is about decoding any signs or symbols, codes or conventions within a text. This begins with sound–letter correspondence for early years readers right through to a senior science student reading a chemistry elements table.

Text user involves a process whereby students understand the variety of purposes of texts. For example, students would be able to discern the difference between advertising materials as persuasive texts as compared to a newspaper report, which aims to inform the reader about an event or particular topic.

Table 7.2   Sample questions for scaffolding students' reading drawing on the Four Roles of the reader (adapted from Anstey, 2002: 30–36)

The code breaker	The meaning maker
How do I crack this text?	How are the ideas in the text sequenced?
What language(s) is it using?	Do they connect with one another?
How many semiotic systems are operating here? What are they?	Is the text linear or non-linear; interactive or non-interactive? How does this affect the way I make meaning?
	Is there anything familiar here?
How do the parts relate singly and in combination? (Letters–phonemes–words)	What prior knowledge and experiences might help me make meaning of this text?
	How will my purpose for reading, and the context in which I am reading, influence my meaning making?
	Are there other possible meanings and readings of this text?

The text user	The text analyst
What is the purpose of this text and what is my purpose in using this text?	What kind of person, with what interests and values, produced this text?
	What are the origins of this text?
How have the uses of this text shaped its composition?	What is the text trying to make me think/believe/do?
	What might be some alternative or resistant readings of this text?
What should I do with this text in this context?	Whose values, attitudes and beliefs might be being privileged by this text?
What might others do with this text?	Whose values, attitudes and beliefs might be being silenced/marginalised?
What are my options or alternatives after reading it?	Having critically examined this text, what action am I going to take?

Text participant or meaning maker is when students draw on their prior knowledge about a topic or their own personal experiences in making meaning from a text. This could include referring to other texts that they have been exposed to.

Finally, text analyst is when students have an understanding of the intent behind the text including the author's personal, social and cultural position or ideologies. Students are able to identify particular language choices that put across these ideologies or biases.

Each of these roles can be used in conjunction with each other, or separately, and have different importance depending on both the text being read as well as the purpose of the reading task. Table 7.2 outlines some key prompting questions that assist students in undertaking each of the roles of an active reader.

Context-to-Text model

Another effective model of reading is called the Context-to-Text model by Michael Halliday (1973).

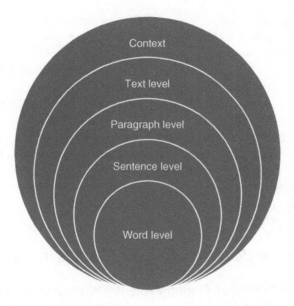

Figure 7.2   The Context-to-Text model

The Context-to-Text model is a functional model of language learning that acknowledges the social and cultural context in which a text is constructed but also comprehended. The model moves between these bigger ideologies down to the text, paragraph, sentence and word levels in order for students to make meaning from the text (see Figure 7.2). This is often referred to as a 'top-down' model. Working from the letter and word level up to explore the social and cultural context in which the text was written is known as a 'bottom-up' approach to reading, of which phonics or learning about sound–letter correspondence first, features greatly. The Context-to-Text model can be both a top-down and a bottom-up approach working in conjunction with each other.

Figure 7.3 shows how we use the socio-cultural context in which we live in when making meaning from the text.

How do high school students make meaning of texts? They can do this through a range of ways including: relating texts with other texts; relating a text to themselves; and making connections between a text and the world

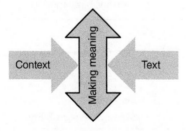

Figure 7.3   Making meaning with texts

through prior knowledge. If a reader's experiences, knowledge and emotions are limited it makes it difficult to make meaning. Therefore, it is important to provide students with a range of rich literacy resources such as literature and other texts including multimodal texts. It is also critical that students can begin to not only comprehend a text literally but also make inferences about the text's meaning – that is, question its meaning, the intent of the author, and unpack the influences upon the author's choices including social and cultural influences. At the same time high school students will decode, recognise sentence form through syntactical features as well as note the structure of a text type, including paragraphs, headings, etc. Cognitive processing from both a bottom-up and top-down approach to reading enables fluency and greater comprehension and therefore effective reading.

The Gradual Release of Responsibility model

The Gradual Release of Responsibility (GRR) model (Pearson and Gallagher, 1983) is one approach that can assist students through a scaffolded method leading towards independence. The GRR model has been used to improve reading comprehension (Lloyd, 2004) and writing (Fisher and Frey, 2003).

There are a number of phases in a GRR model, which are interchangeable and move back and forth fluidly (see Table 7.3). The first, often referred to as the 'I do' phase involves focused lessons where teachers model their 'own meta-cognitive processes as active readers' (Fisher and Frey, 2003: 2). These lessons establish a strong purpose for the reading activity and clearly highlight the learning objectives for students.

The second stage, 'We do', involves guided instruction where teachers support and facilitate students' learning. Through effective prompting and questioning the teacher leads tasks that aid deeper understanding of a text or task.

Then, students work collaboratively, 'You do it together', to create a range of texts or carry out shared reading by solving problems through discussions and negotiation through working with peers.

These phases work in combination and back and forth leading to independent learning, 'You do'. The previous steps allow students to practise and

Table 7.3 The Gradual Release of Responsibility model

Teacher responsibility		
Focus lesson		'I do it'
Guided instruction		'We do it'
	Collaborative	'You do it together'
	Independent	'You do it alone'
	Student responsibility	

learn skills to work towards presentation of information in new ways. Students 'synthesise information, transform ideas and solidify their understanding' (Fisher and Frey, 2003: 2).

It is important to take a balanced approach to the teaching of reading for adolescents as students learn differently, tasks have different purposes, and a balanced and varied approach improves students' engagement and motivation to read. A balanced approach means that both explicit and implicit instructional methods are employed when improving literacy learning.

Strategies to improve comprehension (see also Chapter 8)

Schema theory

Schema theory organises information into units of knowledge, which is important when learning about particular disciplines or content areas. A schema according to CSUS is 'a generalized description or a conceptual system for understanding knowledge – how knowledge is represented and how it is used' (CSUS, n.d.). Reading theorists argue that all readers develop specific schemata in their heads when reading a text. These schemata could be represented as a mind map or graphic organiser. If a student struggles with understanding and remembering the content of a text then their mental processing around schematas may need improvement.

Three level reading guide

A three level reading guide is a teaching strategy that supports students' comprehension of text by allowing them to read texts closely and deeply. Suominen and Wilson (2002) explain these levels as statements, literal, and interpretative and applied.

- Level 1 or statements have the reader locating relevant information exactly in the text. The words are 'right there' or 'as the author has said it'.
- Level 2 or literal has students see the relationships between the statements in level 1. This means they might 'read between the lines' or what 'the author has intended'.
- Level 3 or interpretative and applied requires a student to develop an opinion or evaluate a text.

Morris and Stewart-Dore (1984) state that a three level reading guide can:

- take students beyond the text to explore real-world issues
- encourage students to bring their background knowledge to the reading of the text

- engage students in discussion around the text
- use peer support to scaffold student reading of challenging texts
- scaffold reading with a variety of texts in all curriculum areas.

The ROWAC model

Developed by Betty Roe, the ROWAC model refers to the reading–writing connection and supports the organisation and process of reading via an active model of pre-reading, during reading and after reading activities. The following outlines the model (as cited in Roe et al., 2011: 234).

> *R – Read.* Students read each of the headings present in a text or scan the text by reading the first sentence in each paragraph. This provides students with a brief of the content of the text.

> *O – Organise.* Students then list the headings or topics as a graphic organiser such as a mind map, web or outline. The students will then have a framework for taking notes.

> *W – Write.* Students write a few paragraphs that display their predictions of the text. Predicting what may happen in the text draws on students' prior knowledge about the text. This engages them as active pre-readers.

> *A – Actively read.* Students now read the text with focus and awareness. As students read through the text they should check their own predictions throughout and note any inconsistencies as well as accuracies. They should also question why there may have been differences in what the text actually says and their own predictions.

> *C – Correct predictions.* As an after reading task, students then correct their original predictions. This does not mean they need to rewrite their ideas but rather add words to correct or delete other ideas that were incorrect. In this way new material is integrated into the original work.

QAR model

The Question-Answer-Relationship model (Raphael and Au, 2005) is a strategy to use for after reading activities. The QAR model presents a three-way relationship between quality questioning, the content of texts and the readers' prior knowledge. A number of resources that explore the QAR model highlight the types of questions students can ask after reading. These are:

- *In the book* questions:
  - *Right there* – these are literal and basic questions where the answers can be found directly in the text.

- o   *Think and search questions* – these answers are also found in the text but require deeper thinking. For example, these may be compare and contrast questions, expecting students to draw inferences, and descriptions of emotions or settings (activities include: simple lists, sequencing, describing and explaining).

- *In your head* questions:

  - o   *Author and me* – this is when students need to consider the author's intent and is about what they have learnt as a result of reading the text. Questions beginning with Why? usually feature here (activities include: text to self, text to world and text to theme connections).
  - o   *On my own* – these questions are answered by students relying on their own prior knowledge and experiences.

Vignette 7.2

Treetops High School realised that more of their students were entering their first year of high school with poor reading fluency and comprehension skills. They therefore developed a community Reading Project (see more in Chapter 5) that involved a number of partners including the local feeder primary schools. A strong feature of the reading project was targeted support lessons led by the learning support teacher and head of department.

The first area identified as needing improvement was the students' decoding skills. Consequently, the school employed an expert who had developed a commercial phonics programme, expecting all students in the learning support unit to participate. In addition, a commercial programme that aimed to improve comprehension for adolescent students via an adaptive release online programme was implemented. Students also were provided with the opportunity to support each other through peer-assisted learning.

This multi-pronged approach aimed to improve students' reading capacities so that they could engage more effectively with the 'mainstream' curriculum classes (Barton and McKay, 2016a; 2016b). Treetops High School was committed to providing positive pathways after school for all of their students. After some time, the school realised that other 'risks' needed to be taken as students were starting to plateau with their learning and achievements yet were not quite ready to re-enter their 'mainstream' classes. As such, an English bridging programme/class was introduced. While not usually listed in the curriculum this extra class gave the students more time to develop confidence, particularly when presenting orally to their peers. The following comments highlight the positive impact of these strategies.

> When I was in primary I couldn't read or spell at all, so when I came here it was just like a big jump saying I can do this now and … come to school every day and learn everything and like they helped me.

(Continued)

(Continued)

I help [other students] with their word list if they're under the level that I am. I help them write, I help them read and do their book. I help them on the computer. I really help wherever they need help really. Yeah. I've learnt a lot since I've been – took over tutoring other people. So I reckon that's an easier way for me to learn as well, like at the same time.

Recommendations for further improvement at Treetops High

A number of recommendations are provided for the staff at Treetops High (see Barton and McKay, 2016a). These include:

1   *All* staff in the school, including teaching staff and school leaders, undergoing professional development on the teaching of reading. The professional development should be focused on the 'big six' in reading instruction: phonological awareness, phonics and phonemic awareness, oral language, fluency, vocabulary and comprehension and should also extend into the teaching of reading in curriculum areas.
2   A SWOT analysis on each student currently involved in the learning support programme should be carried out in order to identify the strengths, weaknesses, opportunities and threats present in their learning. This will ensure that their individual 'funds of knowledge' are further recognised and valued.
3   Continue to consider what strategies will best suit the students' needs, e.g. the English bridging programme for those students who are not quite ready to enter curriculum or content area focused classrooms.
4   Focus learning on more sustained reading practices, i.e. build reading stamina with students – employ read aloud, shared reading, guided reading and independent reading activities.
5   Provide more opportunities for students to be engaged in peer support and assessment experiences, i.e. have more advanced students teach others to provide more leadership roles. This will ensure variety and choice in learning activities.
6   Consider structures and strategies that will enable sustainability of the above practices regardless of whether or not individual staff are available, e.g. maintain role of the volunteer coordinator.
7   Strengthen partnerships with feeder primary schools and develop common approaches to teaching reading.
8   Provide time and access to coaching sessions from a literacy coach to build confidence and expertise of classroom teachers.

Reading in the content areas

Literacy across the curriculum is not a new concept and in fact many policies on education state that all teachers are 'responsible for teaching the subject-specific literacy of their learning area; and all teachers need a clear understanding of the literacy demands and opportunities of their learning area. Literacy appropriate to each learning area can be embedded in the teaching of the content and processes of that learning area' (ACARA, 2012b). Understanding the literacy demands associated with distinct content area texts is critical for students' success. According to the Australian Curriculum's general capability of literacy, students should know about the text, word, grammar and visual knowledge within each of their curriculum areas. For adolescent students, this is important given their schooling day is usually structured around different content areas with different teachers.

In fact, Christie and Derewianka's work (2008) shows how the texts that children and students are required to read change significantly across the school years. For young children, texts tend to use 'commonsense' knowledge that is expressed in everyday language. A simple grammar that is matched to generalised categories of experience and simple attitudinal expressions is usually employed in these texts. For children aged 9–12 years this 'commonsense' knowledge is reshaped into 'schooled' knowledge. The grammatical resources expand and grammatical metaphor features in expressing knowledge and attitude. By mid-adolescence (13–15 years) Christie and Derewianka (2008) note that 'school knowledge is increasingly differentiated into curriculum areas, becoming more "un-commonsenseical" as demands on grammatical resources are amplified and attitudinal expression expands and by late adolescence (16–18+ years), curriculum-specific knowledge is characterized by non-congruent grammar expressing abstraction, generalization, value judgment and opinion' (Christie and Derewianka, 2008: 218).

Understanding the expansion of, and difference between, texts across the school years and content areas is important for success in the high school classroom. As stated above, knowing aspects such as the structure of the text types being used in each distinct curriculum area as well as the grammatical features of these texts allows students to meet these literacy demands but also replicate these text types in writing tasks (see Chapter 9).

In science, for example, reports are typically procedural texts, expecting students to understand the elements of a hypothesis, method, findings and discussion. In history, text types such as biographies or historical recounts are typical, which require different language features to scientific reports. It is extremely important then, for teachers to unpack the text types or genres that students are expected to read and write in the content areas.

Modelling these text types through a Gradual Release of Responsibility method (see earlier in this chapter) allows students to view effective approaches to constructing such texts. Further, adolescent students enjoy collaborative and more social approaches to learning, so doing a whole class example first and then having students work on examples together shows that the reading and writing process does not have to always be an individual exercise. When students know what the purpose of the text is, who their intended audience is, then they are more able to complete the task successfully (see Chapter 9 on writing in the content areas).

Vignette 7.3

Reading a science text

Mrs Kumar is teaching her Year 8 students about the states of matter. She has found an excellent explanation of how liquids can change into solids and/or gases. On the two-page spread there is some information about how certain matter can change state through chemical reactions involving heat or cold. There are also a number of images to support these explanations. On the second page there is a description of how to carry out a number of procedures in a science lab.

Science texts are often laid out like the page featured in Figure 7.4.

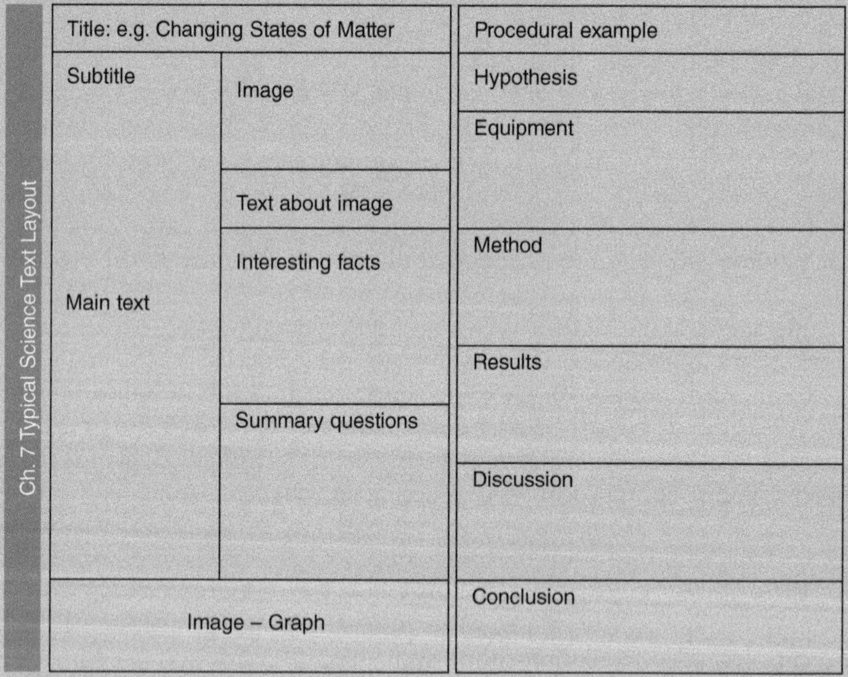

Title: e.g. Changing States of Matter		Procedural example	
Subtitle	Image	Hypothesis	
		Equipment	
Main text	Text about image		
	Interesting facts	Method	
		Results	
	Summary questions		
		Discussion	
Image – Graph		Conclusion	

Ch. 7 Typical Science Text Layout

Figure 7.4 Typical science text layout

If you are expecting students in your science classroom to read a text, consider the ways you will assist students in meeting the literacy demands in the text including text, word, grammar and visual knowledge.

Questions

1   Ask your students where they begin to read this text? Where do their eyes go to next? Is there any information they are skipping? Why?
2   Ask students to identify some features of the text structure, e.g. how many paragraphs? What are the topics of each paragraph? What is the theme/ rheme of each sentence in each paragraph?
3   What are some of the grammatical features? Is nominalisation used? Would you speak like this? If not, what are the differences between written language compared to spoken language?
4   How effective is the procedure? Can you confidently reproduce the procedure in the lab? If not, what is missing?

Reading a history text

On the same day, students from Mrs Kumar's Year 8 science class attend their history class with Mr Potts. They have been learning about how to write biographies and are currently reading through a number of famous figures' biographies. Mr Potts provides the students with an example in their lesson. See Figure 7.5 for a usual template.

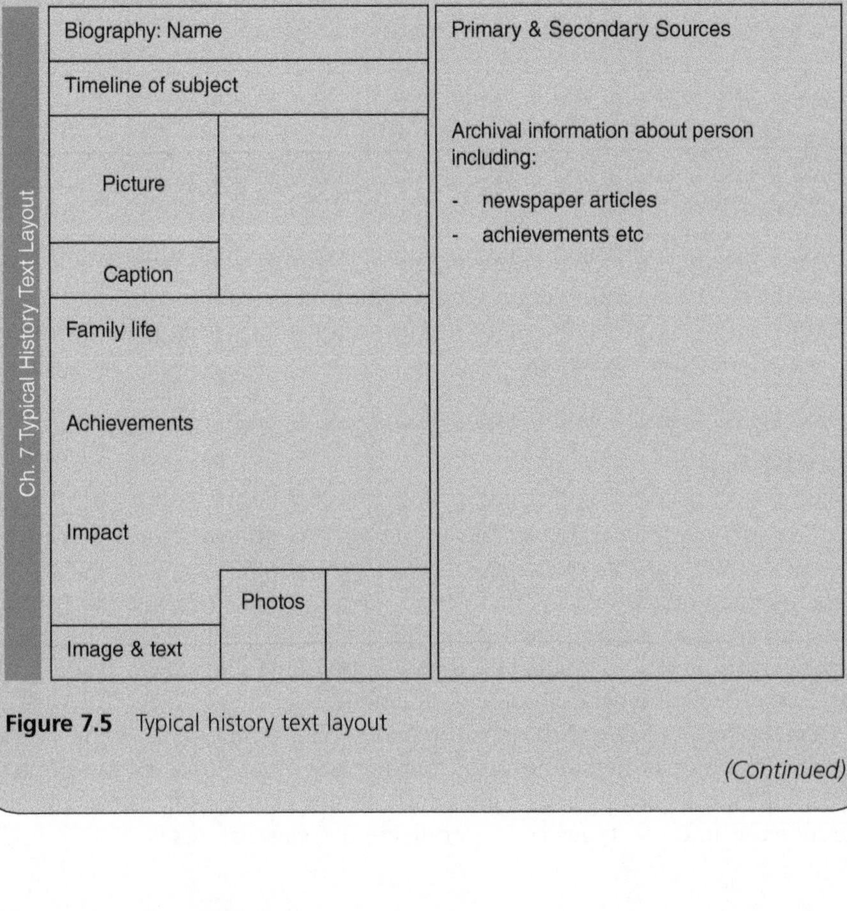

Figure 7.5   Typical history text layout

(Continued)

(Continued)

Questions

1   Ask students how they interpreted the timeline of this particular person's life? Are the dates in proportion with the time indicated along the line?
2   Did they read the caption under the image? What type of images have been selected? Do they show the person in powerful or suppressed positions? Why?
3   From what perspective is the text written? Is the person made out to be a positive or negative figure? What type of language is used and why?
4   When were the primary and secondary sources written? Do they highlight particular social ideologies that are different today? How do you know?

Meeting the literacy demands in texts

It is important to acknowledge that every student may carry out the reading process differently. Explicitly teaching the elements of the text structure, language features and visual images in texts is vital for students to know how texts work in their different curriculum areas of study.

Important concepts for content area teachers include:

- understanding that all teachers are teachers of literacy and reading
- knowing that reading becomes more complex across the school years
- understanding that knowledge of text types and the grammar used in these text types needs to be made explicit
- showing the difference between spoken and written language – use of nominalisation, and encouraging a critical approach to reading
- unpacking the elements of all modes in texts including language, image, sound, gesture, space, etc.

Conclusion

Reading is a complex process and therefore it is important that all teachers understand the various elements of reading for both struggling readers and more competent readers in the content areas. A one size fits all approach does not work as students make meaning from texts differently. It is consequently recommended that a balanced approach to teaching reading, and one that reflects the school context, is embraced.

Developing planning with rich and quality texts is important for adolescent students. So too, is including texts that focus on the students' own interest areas. Further, using diverse, digital and multimodal texts is important given the increase in these types of texts outside the classroom.

Discussion questions and activities

Questions

1   Can you see where the 'big six' of reading could feature in your whole school literacy planning in supporting students?
2   What does a balanced approach to teaching reading look like?
3   How can reading in the content areas be enhanced in your context?
4   What aspects of reading do your adolescent students have difficulty with? List some strategies that could support these students.
5   Scan the types of texts you share with your students to read. As you read these texts note how you go about this task. Where do you first start to read? Where do your eyes go next? Do you read all of the information on the page or skip some? Do you think about how the information being read relates to previous experiences? How does this help you understand the meaning of the text? What are the literacy demands? e.g. text type and structure, challenging vocabulary, concepts, etc.
6   Referring to the same texts you share with your students, are they engaging? Relevant? Varied? Appropriately levelled? Do your students have opportunities to select their own texts?
7   When you have students read texts in the content areas what strategies do you use to support them in meeting the literacy demands of these texts? Do you use a range of models? Are you engaging them as critical readers of these texts?

Group activities

1   If your school is aiming to support adolescent students with reading it is recommended that all teachers be trained in the 'big six' of reading including phonological and phonemic awareness. This would enhance learning for students who struggle with reading and in particular decoding.
2   Carry out an audit of all reading programmes, resources and teaching strategies in your school. Are you using a balanced approach? That is, do you include both explicit and implicit instruction, a range of engaging resources, student choice and community engagement?
3   Explore strategies that could support your content area teachers. How can you implement these and enhance consistent and discipline-appropriate strategies with your students?

CHAPTER 8

READING COMPREHENSION

Chapter objectives

- To understand the thinking processes that occur in reading comprehension.
- To develop appropriate instructional approaches to develop reading comprehension.
- To develop a repertoire of strategies that foster reading engagement and reading independence.

Key questions

1   How do readers process text?
2   How do readers construct and integrate meaning to comprehend text?
3   How do readers use metacognition to regulate their own learning?

Key words: Comprehension, language, memory, vocabulary, fluency, context, questioning, reading, strategies.

Introduction

Reading comprehension is a constructive, cognitive activity influenced by factors within the learner and by other external factors such as text readability, task difficulty, socio-cultural purposes and literacy practices. This chapter explores the notion that readers actively engage in constructing a meaningful interpretation while reading print or electronic text. It is essentially a meaning making process that is enhanced when readers combine what they already know with new text-based information. Comprehension is not only concerned with word forms and meanings but it requires the reader to simultaneously process information at a number of cognitive levels. It is a three-tiered activity comprising of data-driven, conceptually-driven and metacognitive processes whereby learners construct a mental situation model of the text-based ideas. This process requires learners to develop a repertoire of reading engagement strategies to promote self-regulation.

> 'It seems very pretty,' she said when she had finished it, 'but it's rather hard to understand!' (You see she didn't like to confess, even to herself, that she couldn't make it out at all.) 'Somehow it seems to fill my head with ideas – only I don't exactly know what they are! However, somebody killed something: that's clear, at any rate.' (Carroll, 1871)

In this quote by Lewis Carroll in *Through the Looking-Glass* Alice responds after hearing the poem '**Jabberwocky**'. In her statement she sounds somewhat confused. The poem contains a lot of nonsense words but Alice does seem to make some sense out of what appears to be gibberish. For you, the question is where does the meaning lie? Is it in the words, the context or in the head of the reader?

Comprehension is, however, an active process in which learners construct meanings from a range of spoken, written or multimedia forms. Words and combinations of words by themselves do not necessarily convey an entire meaning. There are other contextual and inferential factors that contribute to the overall meaning making process. Often this requires the reader to fill in information gaps with what she or he already knows. This chapter will develop the notion that reading comprehension is a constructive and reconstructive process in which the reader assumes an active role in building meaning rather than being merely a passive receptor of information.

Learner factors

How do readers process text?

Reading comprehension is defined as the process of simultaneously extracting and constructing meaning (Snow and Sweet, 2003). The comprehension

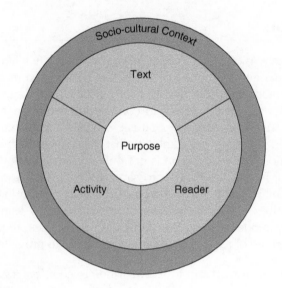

Figure 8.1 Variables that affect reading performance (Woolley, 2011)

of written text is a complex process that depends on multiple and simultaneous cognitive processes (Jenkins et al., 2003; Tiffin-Richards and Schroeder, 2015). Comprehension is not only influenced by text structures and ideas but also by the reading ability and prior knowledge of readers within the socio-cultural context in which they are situated (Vygotsky, 1962). It is also influenced by the purpose for any particular literacy activity. Thus, reading comprehension is shaped by factors within the learner, the text, the learning activity, and within a purposeful socio-cultural context (Snow, 2002) (see Figure 8.1).

The learner: levels of processing

The efficiency of information stored within one's long-term memory is essentially determined by the depth of the initial processing (Craik and Lockhart, 1972). The depth of processing usually takes place at more than one level of cognition. At the surface level of comprehension reading is data driven and is concerned with the verbatim language (Currie and Cain, 2015). Reading at this level requires the reader to focus primarily on decoding by attending to the graphic and phonic features of the text itself. While engaging with printed or electronic texts the reader must not only decode written symbols but also identify the connections between words, phrases and sentences (Dinsmore and Alexander, 2012).

At a deeper level reading is conceptually driven; the reader must go beyond the decoding of the written symbols to build and integrate new meanings from the new text information in combination with the learner's existing prior knowledge. The reader must also integrate local ideas as well as meanings at the paragraph and discourse levels. However, the information in the text is often incomplete and readers are expected to make inferences by filling in the missing information from their own prior knowledge.

Thus, reading comprehension involves a process that is data driven (print directed) while at the same time is conceptually driven (or directed by knowledge that the reader supplies) and requires students to attend to what they think the author intends to say, or what the text means to them (Woolley, 2011). At this deep level, comprehension may be differentiated into two processes: construction and integration of knowledge (Kintsch, 1998). Construction processes are mental processes that activate relevant knowledge from memory as well as information extracted from the text. Integration processes, on the other hand, integrate extracted concepts with information that has been extracted from long-term memory storage (Tiffin-Richards and Schroeder, 2015).

Mental situation models

Contemporary comprehension theories emphasise the role of working memory and background knowledge for generating inferences. For example, in his construction-integration model, Kintsch theorised that reading comprehension involves activating information from both the surface and deep levels and generating a mental situation model, where background knowledge and new knowledge are integrated (Allen et al., 2014; Kintsch, 1998). Situation models do not merely retain the verbatim or exact word-by-word text information but, rather, support more flexible knowledge structures that integrate both visual and verbal content in memory. They are considered to be mental constructions that represent online and ongoing understandings and impressions of the text-base that are largely shaped by the reader's prior knowledge. The quality of the mental situation model will vary depending on the efficiency of an individual's surface-level and deep-level processes that are employed during reading as well as the ability of the reader to utilise working memory efficiently (Tiffin-Richards and Schroeder, 2015).

Surface and deep level processing

Working memory provides the cognitive resources required to drive surface and deep-level comprehension processes during reading (Tiffin-Richards and Schroeder, 2015). Baddeley and Hitch (1994) developed a model of working memory that is compartmentalised into a visual and verbal subsystem under the direction of a central executive (or central processing unit). However, working memory has a limited capacity for holding information while readers process aural or written meanings, particularly when it is necessary to think about or solve problems while mentally processing new information. One factor that limits working memory capacity is the learner's ability to focus attention to information that is central to the reader's learning goals. Obviously, if working memory has a limited storage capacity then it is absolutely imperative that the reader, or listener, or viewer, is able to filter and attend to the most relevant information. One major problem is that many students either attend to unimportant information or mind-wander while reading. Thus, if readers do not have clear goals and are not motivated to achieve those goals they will be more likely to take in superfluous information or develop mind-wandering tendencies while reading. Mind-wandering takes place when the reader, or listener, or viewer, entertains thoughts that are irrelevant to the task at hand. This will often occur in individuals who lack prior experience with the topic of interest and who lack clear task goals.

Visual and verbal working memory

The verbal subsystem of working memory operates in a sequential and linear mode but has a very limited storage capacity. For example, the average adolescent normally only retains and remembers about three to seven separate verbal items at any one time for a short period without decay. Another limitation on the efficiency of verbal memory is how quickly information is presented and retained (Alloway, 2011). The capacity of working memory is presumed to partly determine an individual's ability to maintain and manipulate information, even in the presence of irrelevant or distracting information (Daneman and Carpenter, 1980; Robinson and Unsworth, 2015).

The visual-spatial memory is another subsystem of working memory that complements verbal memory. Its function is to remember patterns, images and spatial relationships. Dual coding theory (Paivio, 1986) posits that all thinking is composed of the activity of two mental codes: a verbal code that uses language and a non-verbal code that uses mental imagery.

When students are encouraged to visualise story content the capacity of their working memory will be augmented. The quality of their situation models can be enhanced by the descriptive quality of the text and the learner's ability to evoke mental imagery. This can be augmented at this deep level through discussion and elaboration by sharing lived experiences around the text content. Mental imagery is often quite motivating because it inherently draws upon the student's own prior knowledge (Sadoski et al., 2000). The sharing of related experiences should enable learners to make the necessary links between verbal and visual memory content in a much more memorable way. Thus, the capacity of working memory will be improved when the two subsystems of working memory are activated and are linked through elaborative classroom discussion.

Metacognition

While there is a clear distinction between surface and deep-level processing there is evidence to suggest a third level of cognition (Biggs, 1978; Woolley, 2014b). This is usually referred to as metacognition. Metacognition refers to a state of awareness of learners' mental processes as they monitor, regulate and direct them according to a purposeful learning goal. Metacognitive theory posits that the process of thinking about thought processes enables comprehension to occur. Thus, reading comprehension is not a passive or merely receptive process but an active one that engages learners in reflective thinking while processing text (Humphries and Ness, 2015; National Reading Panel, 2000). Metacognitive processes operate at an executive cognitive level by organising and directing learning by controlling how surface and deep-level information is processed. Normally, the individual's goals determine how attention is allocated. However, as mentioned earlier, irrelevant and distracting sources of information sometimes can detract from the focus of attention by drawing thoughts away from the individual's goals and stifling learning outcomes. Normally attention control enhances the learner's ability to focus on important detail and avoids mind-wandering (Robinson and Unsworth, 2015). This type of on-task behaviour is an example of metacognition processes leading to self-regulation. Self-regulating learners tend to be active readers who use metacognitive strategies to direct their attention by clarifying, questioning and monitoring their own comprehension in order to construct meaning from read text (Duke and Pearson, 2002; Gersten et al., 2001; National Reading Panel, 2000; Pressley, 2001; also see Table 8.1 below). Self-efficacy, for example, is a metacognitive process that influences reading attention effort, reading engagement, and persistence in the face of distractions. It is related to a person's belief in his or her own ability to perform a task at a desired level. Thus, as students become more self-aware and self-efficacious their self-regulatory learning behaviours will be realised when they develop adequate task goals, persist at attaining those goals and allocate attention effort appropriately.

Table 8.1 Three effective phases of self-questioning (Hattie and Timperley, 2007; Ogle, 1986; Woolley, 2011)

Self-regulation

Goal-setting (Before)	Monitoring (During)	Reflection (After)
What do I know?	How am I going?	What have I learned?
What do I want to know?	What progress is being made towards the learning goal?	Where to next?
Where am I going? (What are the goals?)		What activities need to be undertaken to make better progress?

Learners should be taught to distinguish two sets of self-regulatory procedures: attention to task outcomes (surface level) and strategy implementation regulation (deep level). Self-efficacy (metacognitive activity) is improved when learners focus their efforts at these two levels by self-questioning, hypothesising, predicting and self-reflecting while, at the same time, being provided with ample opportunities to experience further success in reading within a supportive learning environment. Students with ASD, hyperlexia (precocious decoders but poor comprehenders) or those with general comprehension difficulties will also benefit from this self-regulating activity because it enables them to take control of their own strategy use and encourages active reading engagement and risk-taking (Westwood, 2015; Woolley, 2016; Zimmerman, 2002).

In recent times there has been a much greater focus on multiple strategy instruction and cooperative learning and students' comprehension development (National Reading Panel, 2000; Pressley, 2002). Comprehension is a complex activity and skills and strategies are seldom used effectively in isolation. Moreover, basic and higher-order skills develop simultaneously and interdependently rather than sequentially (Tannenbaum et al., 2006). Thus, when considering what skills and strategies should be taught to facilitate students' comprehension, the National Reading Panel Report (2000) highlighted the teaching of a combination of techniques. It identified eight instructional strategies that were deemed most effective in helping students. These included:

1. comprehension monitoring
2. cooperative learning
3. use of graphic organisers
4. focusing on text structure
5. question answering
6. question generating
7. summarisation
8. multiple strategy use.

Students become more independent learners when teachers use a teaching method that includes: modelling (including think-alouds), guided practice, independent practice and repetition using real-life contexts (Westwood, 2015).

Poor comprehenders, in particular, will need specific training in self-regulation in order to develop independent learning and deep engagement in reading. A large body of research has demonstrated that self-regulatory processes lead to better academic success and higher reading self-concepts (Cox and Guthrie, 2001; Westwood, 2015). Few teachers are adequately equipped to assist students in becoming self-regulating learners. However, you will be a more effective teacher of adolescents by placing an emphasis on motivation, effort and developing independence by strategically encouraging self-monitoring reading comprehension strategies. Self-regulating readers are, therefore, considered to be active constructors of meaning who integrate their existing knowledge structures to incorporate the new information. You should encourage all your students to generate their own learning goals and model the reflective thought processes needed to attain these learning goals. Students should also be shown how to monitor and regulate their own comprehension before, during and after reading.

Thus, comprehension uses three cognitive resources: (1) a surface level resource that involves the sensory decoding of words, phrases and analysis of the syntactic language structures of sentences; (2) a deep level resource utilising language comprehension that seeks semantic coherence, construction of inferences and situation modelling; and (3) a metacognitive level that utilises an executive (controlling) function that operates in the background and determines the reader's goals, monitors understanding and reflects on learning at both the surface and deep levels of cognition (Woolley, 2014a).

Vignette 8.1

Mr Sanders is a science teacher who began a series of lessons based on developing an understanding of the structure of the atom. He began with a lesson based on a story about Madame Curie and her discovery of radiation. To guide the students thinking processes he used a KWHL chart. The KWHL chart is a modified version of the KWL strategy (Ogle, 1986; see also Szabo, 2006; Woolley, 2008) that uses a brainstorming method to identify what the students already **know**, what they **want** to know, and what they have **learned**. The 'H' is for hard words and seeks to identify new vocabulary. The chart was made into three columns: column 1 was the 'before reading' column that was used for the students to brainstorm about what they know about the atom and also what they want to know about the topic in general. The K was also placed in the first column and signified what the students wanted to find out. The second column was for the 'hard' words and was used to list and discuss the hard words encountered *during* the reading. After the reading the students contributed what they had learned at the end of the lesson.

Questions

1 How would the KWHL chart assist the students in reading comprehension at the surface level?
2 At the deep level of comprehension how would group dialogue help with background knowledge, making inferences and developing a situation model of the text?
3 How would the KWHL chart contribute to metacognition?

Text factors

Local and global integration

Most texts have rhetorical devices (linguistic cues and discourse markers) that help readers make appropriate inferences in order to understand text. Local inferences typically involve the integration of separate propositions within the text. Propositions are often linked using cohesive ties such as pronouns and synonyms, for example, 'She finished eating the piece of bacon. It was very tasty'. Thus, the cohesive tie 'it' links 'tasty' in the second sentence to 'bacon' in the first sentence (Garcia et al., 2015).

In contrast global coherence relies on inferences that connect with actions, themes and characters or topics that may be implicit and not specifically stated but can be signalled by connected ideas (Currie and Cain, 2015). The global structure of a narrative, for example, uses signalling devices that often include markers that allude to the overall plot and organisation of the story, the development of the plot and the resolution of the conflict. Readers who have a clear knowledge of narrative story schema and other types of genre are also more likely to understand the global structure (Pearson and Raphael, 1990). This is because various genres such as an adventure novel, a detective story, or play carry with them predictable language and text structures that make reading more negotiable. Introductory paragraphs, for example, may introduce themes, characters and story lines. This enables the reader to relate the text information to their own prior knowledge, making it easier to form links with pre-existing ideas. Within the narrative framework there may also be several sub-plots or vignettes that form the foundations of the larger story. The inter-relationships of the main characters may also provide coherence by providing a story thread.

Coherence within the text and the theme of the story are, therefore, critical factors in the readability of narrative and non-narrative texts (Harris and Pressley, 1991; Zhang and Hoosain, 2001). For inference generation a reader or listener needs to keep active previously processed information in working memory while relating it to the new information that is currently being processed. Normally, readers make more global inferences, possibly because these tend to be thematic in nature and as such there are more links to the central characters and to the setting of the story. Thus, the overall story meaning is more likely to be remembered than information at the periphery (Currie and Cain, 2015).

The QAR (Question-Answer-Relationship) strategy (Raphael, 1984) is a particularly good method to demonstrate to students that not all the answers can be found in the text, whether they are literal or inferential. It requires students to generate their own inferences by generating appropriate questions in order to connect text information to prior knowledge and experience. To generate appropriate inferences your students will need to be shown how to ask strategic questions such as:

1. Is the answer right there in the text? *Answers to literal questions can be found there in the text.*
2. Do I need to think and search the text? *The answer is in the text but the reader must tie it together from two or more sentences in the text.*
3. Is the answer found in my head? *The answer is not in the text. The reader needs to use their own background experiences to answer the question.*

   - Is there a part of this text that reminds me of something else I have read?
   - Is there a part of the text that reminds me of something else?

4. Is the answer a combination of the author and me? *The answer is not in the text. It is found in the reader's own prior knowledge and also from the text.*

Self-generated questioning is a metacognitive strategy that aids memory and recall and identification and integration of main ideas. In particular, question generation will contribute to an active reading comprehension process by helping students to initiate a number of cognitive processes (Taboada and Guthrie, 2006).

It has been demonstrated that students who generate their own questions when reading exhibit improved reading comprehension scores (Humphries and Ness, 2015; National Reading Panel, 2000). However, left alone most students favour memory-based and convergent questions but rarely generate divergent thinking or evaluative thinking questions (Woolley, 2014a). While reading narratives they tend to focus mainly on the story line or text plot; they generate questions about the title, author and pictures in the book, and to main characters, events and the setting, but seldom stray from the topic or plot (Humphries and Ness, 2015). Consequently, students often need to be shown when and how to draw on their background knowledge during text comprehension and this ability might improve with age (Currie and Cain, 2015). When you, as their teacher, demonstrate knowledge-based questions you demonstrate to students how to integrate their prior knowledge with new learned information (Humphries and Ness, 2015). For example, questions such as, 'Why did the king banish the prince?' will encourage causal connections between actions and events in the historical narrative (Laing and Kambi, 2002). Furthermore, Kintsch (2005) argued that the use of open-ended 'WH' questions (who, when, where, why and how) assisted adolescents in comprehending text by enabling them to elaborate and enhance their recall and processing of the words and to connect to themes within the text. 'Why' questions are particularly good in helping with the organisation and consolidation of relations at the discourse levels (Trabasso, 1981).

Cloze

Cloze activities are strategic because they help adolescents develop, predict and use contextual strategies. A cloze activity can be made from any reading passage by deleting every nth word. It derives its name from the ability to close the gaps by focusing on the whole. Typically, adolescents are presented with a reading passage with a number of words deleted so that the adolescents can use the context to predict what the missing word should be. Cloze exercises can be easily developed from any printed material that they are currently working with (by using white-out to delete words). However, commercially developed cloze activities are not always helpful in many classroom situations, particularly when they are merely used for testing or for filling in time.

When introducing a new learning strategy, such as 'prediction' (used in cloze), it is important that you explain exactly what the strategy can be used for and why the strategy is important together with when and how to use it with different genres and contexts (Duke and Pearson, 2002; McNamara and Kendeou, 2011). You should model the strategy by using think-alouds to demonstrate the types of self-talk and self-questions the students should employ when performing such a task (Gambrell et al., 1987; Woolley, 2011). After teachers model reading strategies, students practise the skills while the teacher guides them by giving corrective feedback which is timely and specific. You can do this in a systematic way by gradually withdrawing support and providing ample opportunities for the students to practise taught strategies using a variety of texts and genres (Afflerbach et al., 2008; also see Chapter 7).

Pedagogical practices such as cloze activities can be used to develop cognitive processing at all three levels. For example, at the surface level students could be asked to look for cues that will help predict the missing word. After inserting a word they could be asked to justify their inclusion. This also requires a metacognitive process that monitors thinking. At a deep level students could be asked to focus on meaning by suggesting other words that could be used instead. After the insertion of the substitute word the students could be asked whether or not there has been a shift in meaning. Once again the question becomes a metacognitive activity. Thus, the three levels are interactive and interdependent and should be taught together in concert.

Cloze activities based on materials that adolescents are using in the classroom are more relevant to their needs. They should be used in the context of classroom discussion so that the adolescents can learn from each other and consider the various clues that are embedded in the text. Often adolescents will have adequate background knowledge but are unsure as to how to link their experiences to the particular topic or story (Catts, 2009). Normally, skilled readers fill in missing information from their background knowledge by making the closest match from their own life experiences. You should, therefore, take every opportunity to discuss familiar and unfamiliar text-based content as well as any new or unfamiliar vocabulary before the students undertake a reading activity such as cloze. Rich talk can activate and develop the students' background knowledge so that they can make appropriate inferences, ask strategic questions, and develop detailed situation models as they read.

Images and diagrams

Images used in information and multimodal texts may vary quite considerably from simple photographs or drawings to quite complex diagrams and flowcharts containing labels, boxes, circles and other devices. Images in texts are used to give visual representations of topic material, classify ideas, depict events, show part/whole relationships, show topographical accuracy, develop timelines and use symbolic images to portray interaction of one kind or another. They can not only inform the viewer by providing more information but can be used very effectively as a memory device particularly when combined with group or whole class discussion. Graphs and diagrams have their own unique visual conventions and students should be made aware as to how the data should be analysed. They use different semiotic systems that provide distinct codes and conventions through which meaning is conveyed. Multimodal information texts also use linguistic, visual, audio, gestural and spatial conventions (see Chapter 6).

Dialogic interaction incorporated during a literacy lesson tends to integrate verbal and imaginal information while forging links with information stored in long-term memory. Many of the visual codings will be similar to those presented in narrative picture books or graphic novels (see Chapter 10). On-screen diagrams and illustrations may have some interactivity through hyperlinks. The problem is that unless readers are provided with an opportunity to engage in discussion they will often have difficulty knowing how and when to make appropriate inferences (Pearson et al., 2007).

A concept map is a graphic device used to organise words and to graphically represent word relationships. It is a network in which the nodes signify concepts, the lines linking the nodes denote relationships, and the labels on the lines (or style of the lines) represent the nature of the relationships. Making a concept map enables learners to become aware of their own understandings because it facilitates their meaning making and metacognitive thinking skills. Moreover, group concept mapping can also encourage discussion and negotiation of meanings at deeper levels. This negotiation process should be characterised by asking and answering questions, resolving disagreements and co-constructing meanings through discussion. Thus, adolescents can develop an awareness of their new vocabulary, knowledge gaps and inconsistent reasoning through focused dialogue in cooperative group settings.

Genre

An author's purpose for writing, the targeted audience and the mode of delivery will largely determine the type of genre used (Kress, 2003). Genre is not just about how content is arranged but also about the form and the way in which it should be navigated. Information is presented differently according to whether the text content is dealing with: cause and effect, problem/solution, compare/contrast, or is simply a list. Narratives and recounts can also convey information, as can newspaper articles, cooking recipes and timetables of various kinds. Top-level structuring is a teaching strategy that makes the structural elements that are embedded within information text genres more explicit by utilising a graphic organiser.

Task factors

Comprehending the written form of a language is significantly related to the students' vocabulary knowledge (Ricketts et al., 2007). Moreover, successful comprehension of a read text is not only dependent on vocabulary but also on fluent and automatic word recognition skills and the reader's knowledge of word meanings (Kintsch, 1998; Stanovich, 1986). Normally, as readers become more skilled they tend to learn new words from the context as they read, and with greater efficiency than do less able readers (Stanovich, 1986). The frequent exposure to volumes of print facilitates their ability to decode and derive meanings from unknown words.

Vocabulary instruction should ideally occur within the framework of a passage or text being studied (Hay et al., 2007). One effective way to develop intentional word learning during a literacy activity is when teachers expose learners to new words around a theme or content area. This may include the explicit teaching of selected words as well as providing background information associated with the text being explored. The emphasis should be on the promotion of word awareness and intentional lexical encoding (word learning). Other words may also be taught incidentally as they are encountered during whole class or group sessions.

Although frequent reading provides momentum for vocabulary development, if the text contains too many unfamiliar words it will place heavy demands on the reader's memory during a slow and tedious word decoding process that requires the reader to decode each succeeding word (Nation and Norbury, 2005). However, it is more efficient for this new incoming reading information to be linked with other prior information (or experiences) relevant to the topic being read. Unless the teacher is able to adapt their teaching approach and encourage the students to read words fluently, comprehension of any text will be adversely affected when a reader's memory capacity is overextended. Typically, by the time such readers reach the end of a sentence or passage they have little or no understanding of the text information that they recognised earlier and are unable to answer correctly the comprehension questions that may have been related to that text.

Explicit instruction

Explicit instruction and modelling of comprehension strategies such as inference-making and self-monitoring have been found to be very effective (National Reading Panel, 2000; Troegger, 2011). This involves the transfer of three types of knowledge: declarative knowledge referring to what it is;

procedural knowledge of how; and conditional knowledge of when and why to apply a particular strategy in different contexts.

Vignette 8.2

Mrs Flynn used a jigsaw arrangement with her middle school science group to discover and learn about ecosystems. She chose to look at the reintroduction of wolves into Yellowstone National Park in the USA. Before giving the class two articles to read about the impact of their reintroduction she decided to have the students do some research using their laptops and smartphones during their double period.

She used a jigsaw teaching method by dividing the class into several focus groups whereby each member of the group would become an expert on one aspect related to wolves, such as habitat, food, hunting, living in packs, etc. After each group had done their research and discussed their findings she formed new groupings composed of one member from each of the previous groups to become a research 'expert' and share the knowledge they had gained from their original groups. The new groups had roles assigned such as time-keeper, facilitator, note-taker, and questioner and clarifier (to clarify ideas presented). The ideas were written in note form on coloured card and placed on a wall chart. Each group reported back to the whole class and compared their charts so that each could fill in any missing information.

In the next lesson they would read one newspaper article for the reintroduction and one article against the proposition and discuss the pros and cons by listing them on a brainstorming wall chart.

Questions

1   How would the jigsaw groupings enhance the three levels of comprehension?
2   How could you differentiate the groupings?
3   Why would you assign roles to the groups and what other issues need to be addressed when conducting small group discussions.

Pedagogy

Bloom's taxonomy is an example of pedagogy that has been highly esteemed by educators and used extensively in many different learning contexts, usually in the form of a hierarchy of thinking skills. However, while comprehending print, sound, video or multimedia text types learners usually use both lower and higher order thinking skills in combination. For example, rather than conceptualising 'remembering' as being merely a lower order skill you should realise that higher order processes such as 'evaluating' and 'creating' require remembering, understanding, applying and analysing as prerequisite skills. Thus, the thinking skills of Bloom's taxonomy will operate at the three levels of cognition and will function more effectively as interdependent operators (see Table 8.2).

Table 8.2 Levels of cognition and Bloom's taxonomy

Levels of cognition	Blooms taxonomy	
Surface level	1.	Remember
Deep level	2.	Understand
	3.	Apply
	4.	Analyse
Metacognitive level	5.	Evaluate
	6.	Create

Traditionally comprehension skills have been taught in isolation but contemporary methods teach comprehension skills as sets of procedures. Procedures such as 'WHL' (Ogle, 1986), 'WHoL' (Woolley, 2008) and 'reciprocal teaching' (Palincsar and Brown, 1984) are examples of other effective comprehension multiple strategy treatments that require students to use a combination of comprehension strategies in concert.

Conclusion

Reading comprehension is a three-tiered cognitive process. Readers use their own prior knowledge together with their understanding of the message conveyed by the print to develop an interpretation. Reading instruction should engage learners as active constructors rather than passive receivers of information. Reading comprehension is not only influenced by the characteristics of the learner but also by the nature of the reading material and by instructional and task purposes. All of this is influenced by the socio-cultural context that gives meaning and relevance to any literacy activity.

For students to efficiently construct meaning from text they will often need to be shown explicitly how strategies can operate at each level. Comprehension skills should not be taught in isolation but should be taught in combination with other skills. Learners will become more independent when they employ metacognitive processes by setting learning goals, monitoring progress and reflecting upon their learning.

 Discussion questions and activities

 Questions

1   What are the thinking processes that occur in reading comprehension?
2   What instructional approaches are needed to enhance reading comprehension?
3   How do you foster reading engagement and reading independence?

♈♈♈♈ Group activities

1   Discuss the importance of setting a purpose for a reading activity.
2   Go to www.readabilityformulas.com/fry-graph-readability-formula.php and assess the readability of a reading passage that adolescents are likely to read. Discuss the pros and cons in using the formula to grade a book or article.
3   Use a black bag in which to place an unseen object. One participant is asked to place their hand in the bag and to feel the object without looking and describe it in such a way that others have to guess what it is. Discuss, 'How does this develop language?' and 'How does this develop visualising skills?' Then discuss, 'How are they linked?'
4   Divide into groups of two. Provide each group with a picture so that one student cannot see the picture (you may need to place a barrier between them so that one participant can see the picture while the other one is blocked from seeing it). Have the participant with the picture describe it as best they can so that the other person can imagine and draw the picture.

▦ Whole class activity

1   Read a descriptive passage from a typical novel used at school by adolescents and ask them to close their eyes and imagine the scene.
2   Ask, 'What do you think about asking adolescents to read a passage and then giving them ten questions at the end? Make a chart of pros and cons as it applies to effective reading comprehension.
3   In groups of two make up a cloze activity using a photocopied page from a story and join with another group to fill in the gaps. As a whole group discuss the pros and cons.
4   In groups use your mobile technology to investigate a different reading comprehension strategy from the following list:

- Reciprocal teaching
- Cloze
- Concept mapping
- Brainstorming etc.

   i   Discuss enhanced reading comprehension in terms of text processing, learner engagement and fostering metacognition.
   ii Report your findings back to the whole class group (use a graphic organiser on butcher's paper to illustrate your ideas).

CHAPTER 9

THE TEACHING OF WRITING

Chapter objectives

- To understand the writing process as an engaging and creative endeavour.
- To learn about a range of text types and writing approaches for adolescents.
- To develop knowledge around literacy and writing in the content areas.

Key questions

1 How do people attend to writing and what is its purpose?
2 What are appropriate strategies for teaching writing for adolescents?
3 How can students understand writing in the content areas?

Key words: Writing as a process, text types, six discourses of writing, teaching and learning approaches for writing, writing in the content areas.

Introduction

Writing is a complex process and it often takes time to produce a quality product (Ryan and Barton, 2014). In order to have success with writing students need a strong understanding of the task including its purpose and also the audience for which the task is aimed at. Writing is carried out for many different reasons including to tell stories, to entertain, to persuade, to inform and to report on certain phenomena. If students do not have an in-depth understanding of the text type or purpose of the task they are composing, as well as the targeted audience, then the process can be meaningless, leading to students disengaging and being unmotivated to write (Myhill, 2009; Myhill and Fisher, 2010).

Writing, however, can be engaging if appropriate activities and processes take place such as working within students' interest areas (Graves, 1983). Evidence suggests that practices tend to provide students with knowledge about the genre and content to write about rather than explicit and effective modelling of writing as well as engaging tasks for skill development that lead to the final product. Tasks such as quick or free writes, responses to language rich materials, journaling, peer assisted and assessed tasks can all contribute to greater motivation towards writing.

This chapter aims to share detailed information about the process of writing. In addition, six discourses of writing (Ivanic, 2004) will be unpacked with the aim of viewing writing as a balanced process. These discourses will help students become familiar with a range of writing purposes as well as assist teachers to uncover these in their own work. The chapter will also present some strategies that support some micro-elements of the writing process such as sentence structure and effective paragraph construction. This includes a range of text types in different content areas. A number of varying approaches to teaching writing for high school students will also be offered.

The process of writing

Writing as a process means how writing happens (Walshe, 2015). Walshe (2015: 13) explains further that:

> While the final writing *is* linear – that is, flowing along smoothly in lines on the page – the 'process' is far from linear. Rather, it is recursive, in the sense that writers read back and write forward again and again as they work towards the end. The extent of this careful, recursive back-and-forth and the amount of re-drafting will of course depend on the purpose of the writing – very little, if any, for the writing of a shopping list, for instance, but a good deal for the writing of a letter to a Senator.

Also people tend to approach writing differently. Some need a substantial amount of time thinking about their writing before putting pen to paper, others need to chat about their ideas with others, and then there are those that get straight into the task without much planning. Research shows, however, that good writing takes time and that effective planning, drafting and editing makes all the difference.

Process writing involves a five-step approach to writing – pre-writing, drafting, revising, editing, proofreading (see also Woolley, 2014a and Chapter 11 on podcasting). Of course publishing or presenting and evaluating one's writing, via a reflective process, are also important. A process writing approach values writing as a creative endeavour. In order for effective writing to happen students need quality time to write as well as critical feedback throughout the five or more stages.

Pre-writing

Pre-writing can involve a number of exciting and fun activities including:

- on the spot characterisations – e.g. drawing characters after being provided some initial descriptions from the teacher or peers; writing one sentence about a particular character when viewing an image
- mind mapping prior knowledge about the topic at hand
- graphic organisers that may address who, what, when, where, why and how
- drawing or moving about to represent meaning or ideas
- journaling that could include not only writing but drawings and collages
- writing prompts such as using stimuli to encourage a response.

There are many more activities that could be used in the pre-writing phase when working towards completing a formal writing task.

Drafting

Drafting requires more specific skill development related to planning a task. This means students need to be clear about the purpose of the writing tasks as well as who they are writing for. Without an identified audience, writing can become a meaningless exercise. For adolescent students sharing work throughout this phase is vital as it encourages a socially supportive approach to writing. It also ensures students are less self-conscious of their writing but rather, provides a more open and iterative approach to the writing process. Further, peers are often more honest with their opinion and can assist each other through the writing process (see Cope and Kalantzis' website for example, http://newlearningonline.com/scholar/projects, where students share their work with each other online). During the drafting phase research on the topic should continue so that knowledge can be enhanced.

Revising

Revising involves an iterative process that moves between drafting, revising and redrafting. The writer needs to look at the text as a whole and revisit the main points they want to make throughout the text. This stage also involves receiving feedback, usually from the teacher or the person responsible for setting the task. This could also include, however, the audience for which the writing is intended (Ryan and Barton, 2014). Peer feedback is also important for adolescent students as sharing their work improves their confidence and also ensures students understand writing as a process rather than just a product (Graham and Perin, 2007). Quality feedback needs to provide specific examples of evidence for improvement as well as information related to the particular text type the student is writing.

Editing and proofreading

Editing and proofreading are critical to improve and perfect a writing task. This stage of the writing process ensures that students check the conventions of print and other modes such as use of images, audio and/or movement. Language conventions such as spelling, punctuation and grammar are corrected and students can update their use of vocabulary to express their ideas more effectively (Woolley, 2014a).

Publishing and evaluating

Publishing and evaluating the writing product is crucial for writing to be as effective as possible. Publishing requires certain skills outside of the technical aspects of writing such as design thinking and creativity in relation to presentation of one's work. Evaluation should include both summative feedback from the teacher but also from peers or other readers of students' texts and even artificial intelligence (Crossley et al., 2013). This ensures that students receive authentic advice on how to improve for next time.

Vignette 9.1

Mr Jones is planning writing tasks for Years 7 and 8 across a whole term. He has backward mapped from the assessment items students are expected to complete by the end of term. He includes activities in the planning such as research about the topics students will need to write about; some lessons where students can start their writing tasks as well as the final submission dates. He has, however, not included any pre-writing, drafting, proofreading or evaluating activities.

Questions

1   How do you think this approach will impact on students' writing?
2   Think about how you plan for writing tasks for your students. Do you include some exciting activities for pre-writing activities? Do you draw on students' prior knowledge?
3   How do you go about proofreading the students' work? Are you the only person who provides feedback? Or do you include peer feedback/assessment within the task?
4   When will the students get the chance to evaluate their final product?

Six discourses of writing

If we are to improve writing, including creative writing, in schools for middle years students then it is important to explore the evidence base of what works. A lot of research on the teaching of writing acknowledges the increased pressures on teachers to focus on both 'genre' and 'skills' approaches (Comber, 2012; Ryan and Barton, 2014). These involve teachers working with whole classes by modelling a particular text type and then expecting students to complete the same task in a formulaic and de-contextualised way (similar to NAPLAN (the National Assessment Programme: Literacy and Numeracy (in Australia) or high-stakes testing quick writing tasks).

In her seminal work titled 'Discourses of writing and learning to write', Ivanic shares a framework that can analyse a range of writing examples by looking for 'evidence of the underlying beliefs of those from whom it originated' (2004: 220). She argues that six different discourses of writing display sets of beliefs evident in not only the writing but consequently, teaching and assessment practices. These discourses are:

- skills
- creativity
- process

- genre
- social practices and
- social-political.

A skills discourse involves certain beliefs about the written text such as applying knowledge of sound–symbol relationships and syntax. A creativity discourse relates to the author's level of creativity and often relates to writing about topics of interest. Pedagogical practices include rich language experiences related to narrative and the inclusion of the senses. A process discourse involves the mental processes of writing such as how writers compose the text in their mind as well as the practical realisation of the text's meaning. Explicit teaching about these processes is critical for success for middle years students. Similarly, a genre discourse explores different text types that are shaped by social context as well as the purpose of the text. Ivanic (2004: 225) notes that 'learning to write involves learning the characteristics of different types of writing which serve specific purposes in specific contexts'. Social practices discourse is purpose-driven and studies how to communicate in a particular real-life social context. And socio-political discourse is about the socio-cultural and political nature of writing and identities that accompany writing tasks and products. This approach takes a critical literacy lens to the social and cultural purpose and responsibility of writers and writing.

Ivanic (2004) explains that considering each of these six discourses ensures a comprehensive pedagogy towards teaching writing. Each discourse is 'constituted by particular views of the nature of writing and of learning to write, specific ways of talking about writing, and specific pedagogic and assessment practices' (2004: 240). Understanding and consequently unpacking each of the discourses throughout the writing process leads students towards a critical approach to literacy learning.

Writing multimodal texts

Literacy in the twenty-first century presents a range of demands on students in schools including technological and digital considerations when undertaking writing tasks. In fact, the National Council of Teachers of English (NCTE) prepared a Belief Statement for the Teaching of Writing, which notes:

> Just as the nature of and expectation for literacy has changed in the past century and a half, so has the nature of writing. Much of that change has been due to technological developments, from pen and paper, to typewriter, to word processor, to networked computer, to design software capable of composing words, images, and sounds. These developments not only expanded the types

of texts that writers produce, they also expanded immediate access to a wider variety of readers. (https://writing.wisc.edu/wac/node/117)

Not only have writing tools exponentially increased, but it is the ways in which writers use a range of modes to communicate and make meaning that is important in today's classrooms (Jewitt, 2006). Being faced with more and more complex technologies requires us to consider how we use these with our students, particularly through their adolescent years.

Writing multimodal texts – texts that use more than one mode including gesture, image, language, sound and space – features in many curriculum documents. It is therefore important that as teachers we are able to support our students in composing effective work. The following vignettes show how two schools set the writing of multimodal texts and how the students' work could be improved overall (see also Barton et al., 2015).

Vignette 9.2a

At Wattle Seed Primary the middle years students were required to compose a simple multimodal text: a short narrative about a particular historical event that

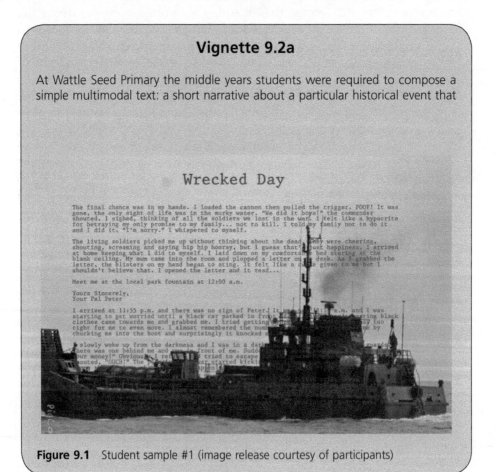

Figure 9.1   Student sample #1 (image release courtesy of participants)

included a relevant image. In order to carry out this task the teacher utilised the twenty-first-century learning design model (https://www.sri.com/work/projects/21st-century-learning-design-21cld) which highlights a number of skills for young people to become more active in and responsible for their own learning. The following skills are proposed:

- collaboration
- knowledge construction
- self-regulation
- real-world problem solving and innovation
- use of ICT for learning and
- skills communications.

The example in Figure 9.1 shows a student's final product. It can be seen that this student has positioned both the title and the text in an appropriate position; however, the size and colour of the font throughout the text is, at times, unreadable. The narrative, presented in a letter format, explores a soldier's experience during conflict while on a warship. The image, again appropriate for the task and meaning, is well positioned but hinders the visibility of the language used. Overall, the student has done some effective work here but with further knowledge about graphic design including compositional layout, the work could be more effective.

Vignette 9.2b

At Riverview High students were encouraged to develop their 'writer's voice' by using imagery and literary devices such as alliteration, personification and figurative language. The following sample (Figure 9.2) shows a student's work – an example inspired by *Mao's Last Dancer* by Li Cunxin. While the student uses language and image well there are a few areas in need of improvement, largely related to layout and design. The drawn manga-style images on the page could be used more effectively by manipulating the size of each image, through the use of software programs such as Photoshop, or by merging the background with the Powerpoint design. For a young adolescent student, however, they have begun their creative and multimodal text writing at a high standard with good understanding of the ways in which visual image can, and does, interact with written text (see also Barton et al., 2015).

(Continued)

(Continued)

The student has selected an appropriate background design for their Powerpoint to depict 'Victorian London'.

While the first page after the title is text heavy the student has chosen a 'mist-filled' image of London by the light of the moon to support the imagery of their story's setting.

To highlight the 'enraged and screaming figures' the student's drawing shows two up-close faces – appropriate for louder volume in the word descriptions. The eyes are not shown so that the focus is on the sound from the mouths.

The next image shows a great deal of movement with the wispy lines coming off the back of the body. It is a mid-shot of the upper body with the character displaying a strong intent to move forward – always on the run as a thief. The facial expression shows us she is not necessarily a nice person.

This image is a long shot with the two characters being positioned on different levels. The standing character is in a power position over the 'beggar on the street'. The framing of the drawing is effective as the brick wall provides a supportive break for the lower character and still maintains a London setting.

In the final two images the student has chosen to have limited text on one page 'the beggar stuttered after Violet' to an image of only the compassionate eyes of Violet. This is a command.

Figure 9.2 Student sample #2 (images release courtesy of participants)

Writing in the content areas

If we take into account curriculum or content-specific literacies, we are faced with a complex process in literacy practices. This is particularly prominent in adolescent learning where a shift in pedagogy occurs from learning fundamental skills, such as reading and writing in the early years, to learning that is structured around specific knowledge areas from the age of 9–10 years.

> Schooling in the middle years challenges students to develop control of the literacy demands and learning expectations of increasingly sophisticated and specialised areas of knowledge represented in the curriculum. As knowledge becomes more specialised within these areas, so too the literacies associated with the ways this knowledge is constructed and represented become more complex. (Culican et al., 2001: 4)

Once children enter the phase of middle years, teachers often assume that the literacy capabilities of students, that is reading and writing, have been safely achieved and supported within their early years of learning. What schools often fail to recognise is that subject-specific texts are often new to middle years students and their ability to decode such texts is limited.

> A great deal of the academic curriculum from middle primary school onwards required that children could not only read and write, but also that they could learn new concepts and information (and display such learning) through their textual practices. (Comber et al., 2002: 15)

Such textual practices include various modalities and literacies and the use of these literacies contributes to knowledge being built in specific content areas.

According to Freebody et al. (2008: 8) each discipline has its own take on literacy and Moje et al. (2000: 38) agree stating, 'discourses, and texts throughout a single day in a secondary school require sophisticated uses of language and literacy by teachers and students'. Intertwined into literacy practices in specific discipline or content areas are the ways in which knowledge is built up through the teaching and learning. The difference between taking a discipline-specific approach to learning rather than a trans- or inter-disciplinary approach is that students gain an understanding and appreciation of particular forms of evidence and truth and in a sense assist in providing increasingly powerful, profound and distinctive answers to recurring questions about human experience.

Freebody and Muspratt (2007: 17) argue that disciplinary approaches to teaching and learning enable students to value 'what counts as evidence, about how an enquirer moves from experience of a phenomenon to a set of speculations to knowledge, and about what it is ... intellectually and socially, that the enquirer is trying to accomplish'. In this sense 'disciplines can be understood as social fields of practice comprising both relatively formal struc-tures of knowledge and practices' (Freebody et al., 2008: 5).

> In classrooms that adopt the collaborative knowledge-building approach, the basic job to be done shifts from learning in the conventional sense to the con-struction of collective knowledge. The nature of the work is essentially the same as that of a professional research group, with the students being the principal

doers of the work. Thus, in the ideal case, there is a complete shift from students as clients to students as participants in a learning organization. (Scardamalia and Bereiter, 1999: 275–276).

What is distinct about middle to senior years of learning is the introduction of discipline-specific teachers and classroom environments and as such it is important for each of these contexts to be familiar with and appreciative of what literacies are used and useful in conveying knowledge. It is also important to understand these aspects when students write texts in the content areas.

In music, for example, it is necessary to acknowledge that a number of ways are used to communicate musical concepts including traditional music notation as well as more recent developments that have matched technological advances (Hoos et al., 2001). If we explore traditional music notation as a textual form, we notice it has developed and changed over time according to social place and space originally beginning with four lines and the use of symbolic neumes around the eighth century and extending to five lines to accommodate musical style and genre as well as development in the production of instruments. Similarly, musical elements such as melody, rhythm, harmony and other expressive aspects are applied differently through the compositional process. Therefore, if one is to be literate in music or write in music this can mean multiple concepts in multiple contexts (Barton, 2003).

Another example is in the teaching and learning of history. Although there is great debate on the content, approach and purpose of teaching history we can deduce that the study of history 'enable[s] students to acquire the habits of mind that characterise what it means to think historically' (Greene, 1994: 89). Admittedly reaching this goal can be achieved very differently. Wineburg and Wilson's study (1991) compared two expert history teachers resulting in distinct pedagogical differences yet they had underlying similarities in their philosophical approach.

> Each thought of history as both fact and interpretation, each strove to create educational opportunities that capture those aspects of historical knowledge … treating the textbook as an intellectual companion. (Wineburg and Wilson, 1991: 531)

Wilson continues by highlighting what is 'good' history teaching focusing on desirable skills of both teacher and student as discovered by Newmann et al. (1990). These skills led to six minimal criteria for effective history lessons:

1. sustained examination of a few topics rather than superficial coverage of many
2. substantive coherence and continuity
3. appropriate amount of time given to students to think and respond
4. challenging questions or tasks presented by teacher

5. thoughtfulness modelled by teacher
6. explanations and reason for their conclusions offered by students.

Otto (1992: 51) presents a more academic view advocating for history students to view history as a humanity and highlights the importance of improving the literacy skills of students so that they can better interact and respond with a variety of written texts. Shanahan and Shanahan (2008) discuss content area differences and found that historians hold a particular epistemological view when reading:

> Their purpose during the reading seemed to be to figure out what story a particular author wanted to tell; in other words, they were keenly aware that they were reading an interpretation of historical events and not 'Truth'. (2008: 50)

They compare this to the reading of scientists who were more 'interested in the transformation of information from one form to another' assisting them to understand various representations (Shanahan and Shanahan, 2008: 49). Further, Kress, Jewitt and Lemke have all explored literate features of the science classroom paying particular attention to multimodalities and representations of knowledge. This is also important for writing practices.

Overall there is acknowledgement that 'there are differences in how the disciplines create, disseminate, and evaluate knowledge, and these differences are instantiated in their use of language' (Shanahan and Shanahan, 2008: 48) and to this end pedagogical practice in the middle to senior years needs to respond in a way that student literacy and learning are reflective of these disciplinary differences.

> Most students need explicit teaching of sophisticated genres, specialized language conventions, disciplinary norms of precision and accuracy, and higher-level interpretive processes. Simply put, sound later-reading instruction needs to be built on a solid foundation of sound early-reading instruction if students are going to reach literacy levels that enable them to compete for the most lucrative jobs in the U.S. economy. (Shanahan and Shanahan, 2008: 43)

The following section outlines a genre discourse of texts in the content areas.

Text types in the content areas

Text structure

Text structure is how information is laid out and organised and varies according to the text's purpose and function. For example, a newspaper report is very different from a personal letter. When students have a clear idea as to the structure of the text they are to write it enables them to also understand the

Table 9.1 Text types, purpose and structure

Text type	Main purpose	Typical structure
Responses – reviews and critical analyses	To analyse a text critically through evaluation and author's opinion	Begins with describing the context by giving background information
		The text is then unpacked including various elements such as characters, setting or incidents and events
		Ends with personal opinions or judgements
Description	To describe a thing or place – a factual text	Introductory statement identifying the subject matter
		Body of text that provides an in-depth description or various aspects of the subject matter through a systematic process
		Concluding statement
Information report	To report on and classify a phenomenon, person or animal	Beginning general definition
		Provides a number of descriptions related to the topic, e.g. parts, attributes, behaviours or appearance
		Can end with personal statement
Procedural report	To show how to make or do something through sequence of steps	Starts with a statement or goal
		Provides list of materials required
		Gives sequential steps or instructions that begin with a verb, i.e. command sentence
Recounts – factual and procedural	To retell an event in order of time	Introduction with background information on who, when and where including aim
		Record of events in chronological order
		Results including what happened and limitations or variability
		Evaluation about the aspects of the procedure and outcomes
Narrative	To tell a story and entertain	Exposition of characters and setting
		Complication where something goes wrong
		Climax
		Resolution when things work out or leave the reader asking questions

purpose but also have an idea as to who they are writing for. Students will come to understand whether a text presents main ideas and elaborations or has cause and effect and different views or opinions about a particular topic.

Table 9.1 outlines a range of text types, their main purpose and typical structure.

Paragraph and sentence structure

Understanding the text type and structure as a writing task is important for students but so too is knowing how to write cohesively within paragraphs.

Table 9.2

The destruction of the rainforest	can impact greatly on animal habitats.
theme	rheme

Most students struggle with writing coherence because they haven't planned their writing properly before starting to write. Having a plan that includes the topics of each paragraph can assist in making the writing flow more easily and therefore more readable.

Paragraphs generally begin with a topic sentence and the beginning of a sentence is called the theme. The remaining part of a sentence is rheme which elaborates on the theme.

The remainder of the paragraph is supporting evidence about the topic at hand and usually contains a concluding sentence that often links to the next paragraph:

> The destruction of the rainforest can impact greatly on animal habitat. Loss of trees and other foliage means that native creatures such as the orangutan have no place to live or breed. This impact has a profound effect on the daily life of orangutans, placing them on the endangered animal list.

There are a number of strategies available to assist in effective paragraph writing. The first is known as the PEEL method – point, evidence, explanation and link. Another strategy is known as the TDSC approach – topic sentence, definition, support and conclusion. Whatever the strategy, it is important that students stick to one topic per paragraph and consider ways in which they can make their writing flow or have a sense of cohesion.

Cohesive texts use a range of language devices to create a unified unit of text rather than random ideas that are not linked. Devices such as backward referencing, ellipsis, substitution and repetition are all useful in creating cohesion through texts.

Backward referencing can utilise related words to aspects previously said in the text. The use of pronouns and conjunctions are probably the most useful linguistic devices used when referring back to events or people in texts. For example, if a student wrote:

> Toby went to the shop. Toby bought some batteries. Toby needed the batteries. The batteries were for Toby's calculator.

They could improve this by writing:

> Toby went to the shop *because he* needed to buy some batteries for *his* calculator.

Rather than having four simple sentences which create a disjointed flow the use of a conjunction – *because*, and pronouns – *he* and *his*, create a compound sentence that flows more easily for the reader.

Another technique used in written texts is nominalisation. This textual resource is used to change words that are not typically nouns into nouns. An example would be changing: 'The people *destroyed* the rainforest' to 'The *destruction* of the rainforest'. The verb *destroyed* is changed to the noun *destruction*, which results in the text being unbiased as it no longer blames 'the people' for this destruction. Nominalisation builds abstract nouns in order to change every day spoken language into more formal written language. This is particularly relevant in disciplines such as science, history and geography as it builds specific vocabulary.

Word knowledge

Word knowledge, according to the Australian Curriculum, involves:

> students understanding the increasingly specialised vocabulary and spelling needed to compose and comprehend learning area texts. It includes the development of strategies and skills for acquiring a wide topic vocabulary in the learning areas and the capacity to spell the relevant words accurately. (ACARA, 2012a)

Building vocabulary or comprehensive word banks in each of the students' curriculum areas is critical for success and engagement. As students move through the schooling years more sophisticated use of technical language is required. Strategies such as word walls, dictionary exercises and KWL charts assist in vocabulary development.

Visual knowledge

Knowledge about visual images in texts is important for students, especially when they write texts that include pictures, graphs, tables, maps or other graphic representations. Understanding how these elements contribute to the overall meaning is essential for text construction to be effective (see Chapter 6 for more information on visual literacy).

Conclusion

Writing is an important skill for all adolescent students to acquire throughout their schooling. It is significant for teachers to understand that writing is a complex process and that different students may approach writing in different ways. Allowing the opportunity to undertake these various methods as well as creating new chances to experiment with writing, ensures students are engaged in and motivated by their writing tasks. Balanced and varied approaches to writing ensure all students can succeed at writing. For adolescent students collaborative and social approaches to teaching writing, rather than individualised, closed ones, are effective as it means they can work within a supportive and iterative environment. Using tools such as online blogs, OneNote and wikis allows easy access for students to upload and share their work while receiving quality feedback from teachers and peers.

Students also need to know about the purpose of their writing and who they are writing for. In different content areas this is particularly important as texts tend to be disciplinary-specific and require different and more nuanced approaches to writing. Science can be more procedural than the arts, while history focuses on events rather than the way things work in physics. Further, it is important to consider exciting and creative ways to teach writing; this is critical for adolescent students especially when using a range of technological and digital tools to write. These approaches ensure all students are successful and effective writers.

Discussion questions and activities

 **Questions**

1   What are the stages in the process of writing?
2   What are some effective strategies for teaching writing?
3   How can we make writing engaging for adolescent learners?
4   What are some text types students might write in science and history and other content areas?
5   Reflect on the types of writing tasks you set with your students. Do you discuss the purpose of the writing and provide an authentic audience?
6   Choose one or two of the writing tasks you set and complete the tasks to develop exemplary models for your students.
7   Explore some samples of your students' writing. Identify some areas in need of improvement. What strategies could you use to assist the students in improving their writing?

†††† Group activities

1   Discuss with your colleagues some ways in which you could make writing enjoyable in the school. Some examples would be to invite professional authors to work with the students; do collaborative writing tasks; share writing examples with the intended audience.
2   Share some of the exemplars you have written with your colleagues. Are there ways in which you could improve these or use them with different classes?
3   Create ways in which students across classes could share and comment on each other's work. For example, set up a writing blog where the students can upload their work; invite professional writers to provide feedback to class work, etc.

CHAPTER 10

ADOLESCENT LITERACY AND LITERATURE

Chapter objectives

- To further unpack issues related to literacy, adolescence and adolescents.
- To share a range of strategies to improve literacy learning in school contexts.
- To develop knowledge about embedding quality literature in adolescent literacy planning and programmes.

Key questions

1 What issues do adolescents face in relation to literacy learning and outcomes?
2 How do schools plan for and deliver quality literacy programmes for adolescent learners?
3 What quality literature can be utilised in such programmes?

Key words: Literacy learning and education, achievement gap, literacy outcomes, school contexts, quality literature, adolescents.

Introduction

As we have highlighted earlier in this volume adolescent literacy has received much attention in the research literature over the past few decades (Alvermann, 2001; Goldman and Snow, 2015; Hinchman et al., 2003; Jackson and Davis, 2000; Luke et al., 2002). It is important to acknowledge that literacy education needs to be different in the high school particularly in terms of content area knowledge but also for those students who may experience difficulty at school. Evidence suggests that there is still some improvement needed in terms of achievement levels; more specifically the achievement gap appears to be widening for students who are from disadvantaged backgrounds (Freebody and Muspratt, 2007). Simply attending to these issues with approaches more suited to early years learners will not suffice. Adolescent learners have different needs, learn in different ways and are experiencing a significant time of change.

Therefore, this chapter will explore how adolescence is a time of great change and how understanding this should impact on the ways in which we plan for literacy education in the high school setting. It will also share some examples of quality literacy programmes for adolescents where positive outcomes have resulted. Finally, the chapter will explore the importance of including quality literature in programmes for adolescent students in schools.

Adolescence, adolescents and literacy learning

Adolescence is a time of uncertainty and great change. Young people, between 11 and 15 years of age, experience extreme physical, emotional and cognitive growth at differing rates of change. This time of change means that specific needs are to be met particularly through schooling. Certain maturational changes that occur in the brain during adolescence may help to overcome certain areas of reading difficulty (Watson and Gable, 2013). Further, significant intellectual growth may contribute to adolescents' ability to process information, increase their capacity of short-term memory, and also their ability to reason. For students who have been experiencing ongoing reading difficulties however, certain attitudinal factors resulting from these difficulties may also impact on their success at school.

It can therefore be seen that literacy learning during the adolescent years can be quite complex. In fact, the International Reading Association (2012: 2) states: 'in the 21st century, adolescent literacy is understood as the ability to read, write, understand and interpret, and discuss multiple texts across multiple contexts'. Additionally, it is not only the complex nature of literacy and literate practice that impacts on planning for adolescents in the classroom but also the diverse needs of these students that are important to consider.

An example of addressing these needs was a major reform in high school practices in Queensland, Australia. This educational change saw a new focus for adolescent learners, or what the Department of Education called Junior Secondary. This approach, focusing on middle years or Junior Secondary learners, acknowledged six guiding principles for effective learning and teaching for this age group. These are:

- distinct identity
- quality teaching
- student wellbeing
- parent and community involvement
- leadership and
- local decision-making. (ACER, 2012, cited in Pendergast et al., 2015)

Distinct identity ensures that adolescents are encouraged and supported to develop their own group identity within the wider high school context. A distinct identity can include a dedicated school area and even unique events for these students. Quality teaching means teachers commit to learning new skills through professional development and learning in order to support young people more appropriately. Student wellbeing comprises students' social and emotional needs with a strong focus on pastoral care. Strategies include providing regular support to students, particularly as they enter high school as they adjust to new routines and greater academic demands (Pendergast et al., 2015).

Parent and community involvement is critical for success with adolescent learners (see Chapter 5). It is important that parents are informed about the activities at school and encouraged to participate in school events. Adolescent students appreciate opportunities to show leadership. In Chapter 7 we showed how students who struggled with reading felt empowered when given the opportunity for leadership with and for their peers. And finally, local decision-making means that the community in which the school is a part should influence the ways in which students are involved in learning and teaching more generally (Pendergast et al., 2015).

Whole school literacy planning

In relation to literacy learning these six guiding principles should also influence whole school planning for adolescent students. Positive outcomes will result if students feel connected, feel like they belong to a community of learners, and feel like their opinions and interests are valued and included in decision-making about their future.

Rumble and Aspland (2010) explored how schools can support positive outcomes for adolescent students. They noted four attributes of an effective high school teacher. These are:

- A capacity to forge a middle school identity

  o The presence of a dedicated school space for learning
  o A changed teaching and learning culture
  o New leadership patterns

- A designer of a wholesome curriculum

  o Commitment to the adolescent learner
  o New forms of engagement with colleagues and students
  o Working in teaching teams
  o Engaging in curriculum design
  o Design an integrated curriculum
  o Give students a voice

- A specialist in adolescence

  o Meeting the affective needs of young adolescents
  o Advocate for the adolescent learner
  o Communicator with parents
  o Flexibility
  o Quality pastoral care

- A capacity to sustain the middle years reform

  o Engages in continuous professional learning
  o The middle years teacher is a learner
  o The middle years teacher is a moral motivator
  o Forge a new professional identity. (Rumble and Aspland, 2010: 8–12)

Literacy teaching and learning benefits greatly from such attributes and considerations. If pedagogical approaches are effective and aim to address adolescent needs, then positive literacy learning outcomes will be the ultimate outcome.

Whole school approaches to literacy learning have long been associated with quality student outcomes (Ainscow and Sandhill, 2010; Fullan et al., 2006; Hill and Crévola, 1997). Effective whole school approaches to school improvement are driven by strong leadership as high performing schools report on this as a necessary factor for success (Masters, 2009; Robinson et al., 2009). In fact, Fullan et al.'s (2006) Breakthrough model provides a significant framework by which to base a whole school literacy plan. At the core of this model is *moral purpose*, which Fullan et al. explain as going beyond the skills of the teachers to the beliefs of the school community. There are three elements that support this concept. These are:

1. Personalisation of learning, which places students at the centre of the instruction aimed to improve motivation and engagement.
2. Precision, which is the purposeful planning of learning experiences based on data-driven decision-making, so that learning instruction precisely matches students' needs.

3. Professional learning targets the skills, knowledge and attitudinal growth
    of teachers. A whole school approach targets professional learning for all
    educators in the community.

Each of these aspects contributes to a fully considered methodology to learning
and teaching in a high school context. Personalising learning with precision as
well as providing quality professional development and learning for teachers
will ensure all students achieve. Embedding an evidence-based approach to
improvement is also critical as this bridges theory to practice within an educational environment.

Aside from whole school literacy planning and philosophies as those
above, schools need to consider the classroom environment.

Supportive classroom environments

Creating supportive classroom environments allows students to achieve success among their peers. Within a supportive classroom setting students need
to know clearly what the learning goals are for a lesson as well as how they
will be assessed in relation to their understanding; whether formative or summative. According to Woolley (2014b) good learning intentions are made
explicit at the beginning of learning tasks. Also when students know how
their level of performance will be attained then they will know where to
invest their energy, be able to select appropriate strategies as well as apply
relevant thinking skills, positioning them for success (Hattie, 2012).

Another concept related to supportive classroom environments is inclusion. Gargiulo and Metcalf (2013) show how rich literacy learning activities
can be created for all students. Balanced and authentic literacy programmes
are essential in allowing all students to interact meaningfully with all tasks
including those involving reading, writing, literature and language. Gargiulo
and Metcalf (2013) suggest conducting purposeful reading activities with
interactive texts, ultimately increasing literacy levels. Recommendations such
as beginning learning events with higher order questioning techniques; offering a wide range of experiences related to students' interest areas; and
well-considered interactions with rich language tasks all contribute to raising
standards in the high school classroom.

Social interaction is also important for young adolescents through to late
adolescence. Friends become extremely influential in learning so group work
and social interaction are effective teaching strategies in the classroom. In
terms of institutionalised needs, addressing curriculum expectations is important; however, it is also important to consider ways in which to address the
distinct learning needs of the students. Young adolescents, when they enter
high school, are faced with a period of transition from dependence to
independence, collaborative to individualised, commonsense to specialised

learning. Therefore, arranging learning based on peer assisted or collaborative approaches including joint construction has proven to support students' learning generally (Woolley, 2014b).

Literate practices in the adolescent years

Adolescent students experience a wide variety of literate practices in any one day. Aside from the integral out-of-school literacies that adolescents possess they also participate in a range of literate practices within the school environment. For example, students may start the day with their pastoral care teacher, then move to learning about states of matter in science, to Shakespeare in English, to nutrition in health and physical education, not to mention the debating team or music ensemble at lunchtime. Each of these experiences contributes to a wide bank of knowledge and skills including the distinct literacies inherent in each content area.

In Chapter 9 we explored how literacy becomes more technical and specialised due to discipline-specific literacies across the school years (Freebody et al., 2013; Scardamalia and Bereiter, 1999; Shanahan and Shanahan, 2008). Indeed, Christie and Derewianka's (2008) work unpacks the types of language students face from early childhood through to late adolescence.

In addition to the increasing demands, both in literacy and disciplinary, it is integral to consider the 'knowledges' that students bring to the classroom space (Pearson and Johnson, 1978). This takes into account the contextual surroundings in which literate practices take place. David Barton's (1994) notion that all literacy events are 'socially situated' is important to consider, as the ways in which various communities, and individuals within these communities, interact and engage with text as well as other forms of communication are distinctly diverse. Moll et al. (1992) and Moje et al. (2004) refer to this experience as students' own *funds of knowledge*, or what Thompson (2002) calls *virtual schoolbags* or backpacks. This means that students' prior learning and life experiences are important to know before considering strategies to use in supporting literacy learning.

This has serious implications when considering the teaching of reading but also other factors within the high school context. Young children start school and young people transition to high school with different experiences, having up to five years at home with their families and the community in which they live. There is strong evidence to suggest that if teachers and students have not taken the time to become familiar with each other's funds of knowledge and therefore ways in which they make meaning from the text (Hill, 2012) then this causes potentially deficit models of reading instruction. If this process is overlooked, students who have distinct and different cultural and social ways of making meaning may struggle with reading instruction that privileges some strategies over others. Having an awareness and understanding of these developments and needs is incredibly important when considering adolescents and their literacy learning.

Effective instructional approaches

Many schools access a range of programs or approaches to improve learning across the whole school. One such approach is known as the *Art and Science of Teaching* by Marzano. Marzano (2007) provides nine instructional strategies that aim to improve students' learning outcomes. Many of these methods we have addressed elsewhere in this book but it is worth mentioning them here and relating them to literacy education for adolescent learners. The nine strategies are:

1. Identifying similarities and differences
2. Summarising and note-taking
3. Reinforcing effort and providing recognition
4. Homework and practice
5. Nonlinguistic representations
6. Cooperative learning
7. Setting objectives and providing feedback
8. Generating and testing hypotheses and
9. Cues, questions, and advanced organisers. (Marzano, 2007: 1)

According to Marzano (2007), being able to compare and contrast different phenomena across the curriculum allows students in the high school context to be able to understand complex problems and analyse them in a simpler way. While these methods alone may be approaches you already utilise in the classroom, together they can provide a powerful platform for students to engage with and be motivated by learning. The use of metaphor and analogy assists students understanding of cause and effect as well as in comparative studies. The skill of summarising and taking notes needs to be taught effectively. We cannot assume students know how to do this. Therefore, modelling this practice is key to success and, in fact, providing scaffolds is important for students to be able to build on and improve this skill across the high school years.

Reinforcing effort shows the correlation between a student's individual effort and achievement levels. This is particularly pertinent for adolescent learners who may need extra support. If they are willing to work hard to accomplish set tasks then their self-esteem and self-worth also improve (Barton and McKay, 2016a). One strategy that supports students, particularly those that need extra assistance, is known as Pause, Prompt, Praise. The teacher pauses to discuss the problem, then prompts with specific suggestions for improvement, and praises if the student's performance improves as a result.

Homework and practice does receive some controversial attention; however, if extra learning occurs at home it should have a specific purpose that students understand. Feedback should always be provided about any tasks that have been completed at home. Practising skills and deepening knowledge is beneficial for students; so too, is discussing learning within the home environment. In Chapter 6 we explored the notions of multiliteracies and multimodalities. Offering a range of ways to represent knowledge is important for students whose strengths may lie in modes other than language.

Cooperative and group learning impacts positively on students as they develop social skills and interaction and interdependence. Setting learning objectives means that students have direction about their learning and should focus on individual learning needs. Using strategies such as a KWL chart or explicit methods such as 'We are learning to – WALT', 'What I am looking for – WILF', 'We are learning about – WALA', and 'This is because – TIB' promotes focused learning intentions. Providing feedback needs thoughtful consideration and should be clear and succinct for students in relation to how they can improve for next time. The feedback process should be iterative and engaging and involve both teacher and students.

Generating and testing hypotheses enables students to use both deductive and inductive reasoning across all curriculum areas. Developing hypotheses prior to activating learning aligns with problem-based learning. Finally, cues, questions and advanced organisers assist students to organise their thinking and allows them to be able to discuss relevant issues and concepts with their classmates.

Vignette 10.1

Ms Anderson teaches in a culturally diverse school with over 70 per cent of the students being from an ESL or EAL background. The school has implemented a whole school approach to improve literacy by providing ongoing and regular professional development and collegial discussions for staff. Collaborative meetings have been organised where two staff members from different disciplines work together by discussing student samples of work and strategies for improvement. These occur twice a term throughout the year. The two staff members are also joined by a 'listener', who provides an objective view on the teachers' work.

Questions

1   How do you think this process would work in your own school context?
2   Do you regularly have staff across the content areas converse about student work?
3   What are some ways you think you could assist other staff members in improving literacy learning outcomes for the students at your school?

Adolescents and literature

Quality literature in the classroom has the potential to 'widen our horizons, bring us social and personal insights, set our imaginations aflame and engender linguistic richness' (Hoogstad and Saxby, 1988: viii). In order for this to happen students need to connect with the stories, poems and other literary works presented to them.

When implementing quality literature for teaching and learning purposes the literature itself shapes instruction (see Beach, 1998: 10–16). Strategies such as perspective-taking, constructing social worlds, explaining character's actions, inferring meaning via symbolism and theme, making connections, posing questions and solving problems are important for engagement with literature. Encouraging students to engage in debate and engage with a variety of opinions can also be motivating for students. Of course, not all students will appreciate all examples of literature exposed to them; however, it is important to explain to students the benefits of immersion into the literary world.

Adolescent literature covers many important topics relevant to young people's lives. Topics such as gender and sexuality, race and difference, world politics and economics, disability, the environment, refugees and asylum seekers, religion, etc. are critical in supporting students in understanding the world they live in. Not only should teachers select a range of texts for students to study but there should also be opportunities for students to have a choice in the literature they read.

How to select quality literature

Not all literature is good so it is therefore important for teachers to select quality literature for adolescent students to engage with. Firstly, it is necessary to have an idea as to what literary texts are. According to Ewing et al. (2008) literary texts:

- have real, not controlled language that makes sense beyond sentence level
- will be rich in words and/or images
- will be multi-layered
- will be intellectually challenging
- will be provocative of emotional responses, and
- will represent life in an artistic rather than every day manner.

The importance of stories and storytelling

Stories and storytelling have the capacity to explain a series of events or a way to recount actions of people in a particular setting. The purpose of telling stories varies from entertainment through to conveying important information such as when conserving culture or communicating a particular point of view (Exley, 2010). According to Mills and Exley (2014: 136) 'narrative plays a pivotal role in the socialisation of learners'.

Stories or narratives are central to any culture. Jerome Bruner has written a great deal on the role narrative plays in our lives, and in particular children's development. Bruner (1985) has noted that there are two modes of human thought. These are paradigmatic thought and narrative thought. The difference between these two modes is that paradigmatic thought is about categorising and conceptualising natural phenomena and is therefore objective, whereas narrative thought is subjective and about human actions and interactions.

> Through narrative we develop a deeper understanding of the social world – of how others think, why they behave the way they do, and the implications people's actions hold for others. The stories we share of our life's experiences are shaped, in terms of content and organisation, by the stories others tell to us within our culture. (McKeough et al., 2008: 150)

The importance of storytelling for students from diverse backgrounds should be considered in learning plans in high schools. This can be particularly empowering for students from Indigenous backgrounds as the power of story has been recognised for cultural and historical heritage, communication purposes, learning and immersion in context (Corntassel, 2009). Storytelling is important to Indigenous children because it is fundamental to the way they learn and the way their parents, siblings, other family members and the broader community teach (Harrison, 2011). Indigenous children are immersed in stories and storytelling from an early age and so over time develop a portfolio of stories about themselves, their family and community, and their culture.

Digital storytelling or the creation of digital narratives can be an effective way to empower and engage students who may be marginalised. Being able to use a range of modes including language, image and sound can assist students in expressing themselves. In fact, Thompson (1995: 10) highlights that digital storytelling can be used:

- to encourage students to make links continually between the world of the text and the world of their own personal experiences outside it, between literature and their own lives
- to ensure that students do a great deal of onlooker role writing, sometimes from personal experience, sometimes from imagined experience, and sometimes in response to literature read
- to assist students to find the books that speak to them of their immediate concerns, and try to help them to progress from the kinds of books that merely confirm prejudice and strengthen self-ignorance and self-indulgent emotionalism, to those which promote reflection, understanding and human growth.

Other benefits of employing quality learning based on quality literature include being more aware of language in context; encouraging deep discussions about multiple meanings present in texts; and appreciating the artistic-aesthetic elements including language, image, sound and gesture.

Models for teaching literature

Work by Carter and Long (1991) and Lazar (1993) presents a number of models related to teaching literature in the classroom, and in particular for ESL/EAL learners. The first is known as the cultural model, which understands literature as a product. This means texts are seen as a source of information about specific social, political and historical events. A language model aids students through a process investigating the use of grammar and vocabulary with the purpose of explaining interpretative possibilities. The third is the personal growth model, which is also a process-based approach that promotes an exploration of one's own feelings, experiences and opinions based on the literature being studied (Clandfield, 2003).

Effective strategies when using literature

Similar to other teaching and learning strategies that we have shared in other chapters throughout this book, there are a number of methods that support adolescent students when engaging with new literature. Moore et al. (1999, cited in International Reading Association, 2012: 5), for example, suggest the following activities:

- Activating their prior knowledge of the topic and text
- Predicting and questioning themselves about what they read
- Making connections to their lives and other texts and to their expanding worlds
- Summarising key ideas
- Synthesising information from various sources
- Identifying, understanding, and remembering key vocabulary
- Attending to text cues and features to recognise how a text is organised, then using that text organisation as a tool for learning
- Organising information in notes, graphs and charts, or other representations of key ideas
- Searching the Internet and other resources for related information
- Monitoring and judging their own understanding
- Evaluating authors' ideas and perspectives.

Creating a balanced and critical approach to literature enables students to achieve deep understanding of associated topics, concepts and themes explored by authors.

Other effective approaches in teaching literature are creative and arts-based ways in which to develop deeper understanding of texts as well as opportunities to improve the metalanguage of students about topics and literary devices (Barton and McKay, 2015; Leavy, 2009). Dramatic and artistic methods such as readers' theatre, freeze frames, draw and talk, hot seating, poetic responses, collaging, writing lyrics, soundscores and music as well as embodied experiences all contribute to meaning making.

Vignette 10.2

Riverview High School is a fairly typical high school with a diverse range of students who both live locally and travel some distance to get to school. The school has made a concerted effort to improve reading comprehension with a strong link to Marzano's (2007) instructional framework of the *Art and Science of Teaching*. As a further development, the school has begun to turn their attention to the more systemic and consistent approaches to the teaching of writing which explore productive ways to improve outcomes for students.

A major component of the Riverview High English education programme is based on engagement with quality literature. They plan their English curriculum according to the set syllabus including meeting the demands of incorporating creative and multimodal learning experiences and assessment opportunities at each year level. According to the English head of department, teaching the reading of images across the school, including the reading of multimodal texts, is essential for students' success and much focus is on showing students how meaning appears to be 'layered' using the whole range of textual features available to authors.

Riverview Year 8 students (the second year in high school) explore the understanding of creating voice in a written literary task. The students are required to transform one of the allegories from *Mao's Last Dancer*, a typical biographical text drawn upon in schools, into a realistic short story. The sample in Figure 10.1 demonstrates that this young person can purposefully shape a text that innovates on aspects of another text.

Not only do students at Riverview explore creative fiction and writing tasks related to this learning but they also exploit intertextual possibilities to support students to make meaning and innovate on aspects of another text. This is carried out in conjunction with the development of their creative skills. Students innovate on a parent text by writing an effective introduction to their allegory but can also explain the creative choices they have made and why, as can be seen below.

(Continued)

(Continued)

Shadow Melody

"The Shadow melody" has been inspired by the allegory of "Frog in the well" in Mao's last dancer. It describes a small slice of time, just around 10 hours, in which the main character chris realises if you overcome obstacles you can find a great opportunity. While the character in, toad, in the book faces a truth about the outside world, my central character, Chris, works out for himself that there is a better world out there. I was keen to show that if you put effort into life you get good things out of it. At the beginning of the story I showed that Chris is depressed and angry, but at the end I showed that he's happy that he has found a better life.

The Shadow danced across the room, making Chris feel like he wasn't really alone in the world. The open window was welcoming the moonlight and the shadows of the swaying trees. The small room was a stage for the dancers, who were performing around Chris's bed at the back corner of the room. He looked towards the window and stared right at the moon. The moon: his only friend ever since being left at the orphanage.

The student is able to describe the choices made around characterisation, which in turn improves voice. Chris, the main character, has suffered from prior experiences growing up in an orphanage but can now overcome this sorrow.

Use of figurative language and personification assists the reader in visualising the emotion in this introduction. 'shadow danced', 'window was welcoming', 'The moon: his only friend'.

Figure 10.1 Student sample #3 (image release courtesy of participants)

Predators

Terezi breathed deeply.

The world around her shifted through saccharine waves. Honey glazed the sky, swirling candied skirls into an effervescent, cranberry lace; suspending everything in glossy syrup. An explosion of orange zest and crushed cherry crystals sprinkled the atmosphere as velvety pinks slivered through the grape of evening and the burning, sweet-chilli orb of the sun. Against the fruity juice of the sky, spray of sugar silk pitted their lucidity as they collapsed into a billowing vanilla butter froth.

The girl pauses, flicking her nose upwards to inhale the last whiff of the sun's bite. At last, a sweeping curtain of liquorice ended the cascade with a simple sweetness, and Terezi rose from her perch.

The student uses expanded vocabulary to increase meaning and sophistication in this narrative.

Use of figurative language increases the visual images in the readers' mind. It addresses the senses of taste, sight and smell.

Figure 10.2 Student sample #4 (image release courtesy of participants)

In the following school year students study speculative fiction, moving on from the more directly derivative approach of the Year 8 task. First, students work on a kinaesthetic multimodal task in groups. Having read *The Chrysalids* they work collaboratively to create a two-sided diorama – one that represented the world created by John Wyndham; the other, an alternative reality created by them. Individuals in each group then write their own short story set in this new world.

In the example in Figure 10.2 it can be seen that there is little doubt this student is able to create literary texts that 'innovate on aspects of other texts'. We can see, however, the over-emphasis on sensory imagery. This may seem over emphasised; however, it is serving an important purpose in the development of this student's style. Similarly, and in contrast with the Year 8 piece, this student is testing out the effects of playing with differently constructed paragraphs and sentence structures.

Literature circles

Literature circles are student-directed dialogues about literary works. They are usually carried out in small groups where students can engage critically and collaboratively with each other, discussing certain elements of a text they are learning about. In some literature circles students are assigned explicit roles and prepare notes in alignment with this role. Alyson Simpson (2014) has devised a few roles that you could consider using. These are:

1. Creative connector: find connections between the book and outside world.
2. Literary luminary: select a passage from the text to read aloud with a dramatic voice.
3. Artful artist: think about a section of the story that is effective and represent it artistically.
4. Discussion director: write down some questions about the story your peers can answer.
5. Word wizard: look for interesting vocabulary throughout the text and define the words.
6. Summariser: provide a brief retelling of the story.
7. Investigator: explain how the author makes the reader feel and how they have done this.
8. Profiler: profile a character from the text and present this creatively.

Simpson states that literature circles are a 'pedagogic strategy that supports engagement with literary texts through purposeful dialogue' (2014: 7). Evidence suggests that literature circles can empower students in their own learning through purposeful conversations, working collaboratively and creating supportive learning environments.

Graphic novels

Graphic novels are usually described as a format not a genre. Graphic novels can in fact be any text type where information is represented through the use of sequential art and images and sometimes text. This form of text can be used to support readers who may need less text in order to engage with and comprehend a text more effectively. Graphic novels are often more appealing for adolescent readers as the images assist in making meaning. While similar to comics, graphic novels tend to be longer and are often bound like books. Many graphic novels are based on longer text-based versions of stories, which are also made into movies.

Woolley (2014a) outlines the following elements that are included in graphic novels (see Table 10.1).

It is important to teach students how to read graphic novels as sometimes they can get quite complex with the use of dialogue bubbles and frames and panels on a page. Figure 10.3 highlights the directional and format features of a graphic novel.

Table 10.1 Graphic novel elements (Woolley, 2014a: 96)

Feature	Description
Narrator	The person telling the story within the text
Narrative boxes	Contains the narration text
Directionality	The arrangement of the panels can indicate the direction and time sequence
	Size of the panels can also determine the pace of the viewer/reader
Speech bubbles	The boundaries that contain the words – different shapes to indicate spoken words or thoughts and also show the order of speaking/thinking
Panels	The frames that contain the pictures and words
Layout	The way in which the page is organised
Gutter	The space between the panels
Framing	A device used to separate, connect or confine elements within pictures and helps to interpret meaning
Interpersonal function	Establishing a relationship between the reader and the character
Symbolism	Something that stands for or represents something else
Speech and thought processes	Speech and thinking bubbles
Composition	The arrangement of elements in the picture to give a sense of what is happening
	Salience – the way in which the creator of the picture gives prominence to one element over another
	Left-to-right orientation – a western device to indicate movement or growth, good on the right and evil on the left

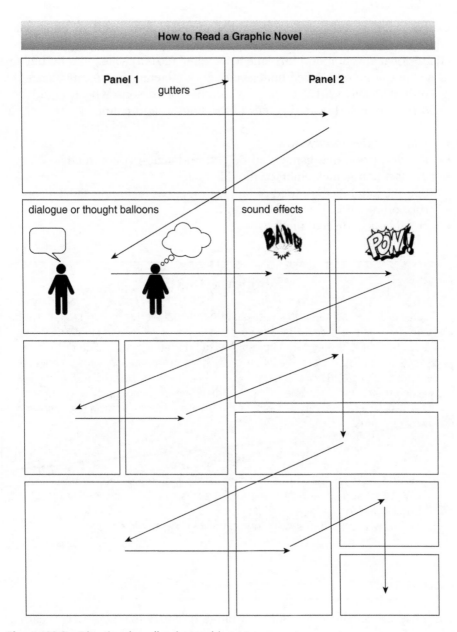

Figure 10.3 Directional reading in graphic texts

Video games as texts

Video games including computer and console games can be viewed as effective narratives where students are directly involved in the co-construction of this narrative. They can act as a creative and innovative form of communicative expression, particularly for adolescent students. Linking students' engagement with these kinds of texts to their everyday learning within school settings is critical for motivation and enjoyment. Woolley (2014a) states that by building these links a more enriched understanding of a literary classroom is enabled.

Further, Beavis (2012) outlines a number of reasons why it could be a good idea to include video games in the English curriculum. These include:

- telling stories in new ways
- the distinction that games can be text and action concurrently
- the fact that games embrace multiliteracies
- that they embrace a range of literacy practices including situated play
- supporting critical perspectives and
- creating texts in real time.

Vignette 10.3

Sophie is a keen gamer who creates her own digital worlds through role-playing games. She likes the fact that she can create stories as she is actually playing a game. It is through her own choices that the narrative is built. She does, however, think that the skills she has learnt through interaction with a range of computer games are not understood by her teachers at school. Sophie has decided to ask if it is possible for her to create a new game for their next assessment task where students are required to create a literary written text involving characters and a setting.

Questions

1   How would you, as Sophie's teacher, be able to support her request?
2   What are some ways you could include this kind of task for all students in your class?
3   What would you have to learn in order to do a task like this?

Conclusion

This chapter has aimed to address a range of issues that adolescent learners face in relation to literacy education including: students' own funds of knowledge or virtual backpacks; the six guiding principles for adolescent learners; the importance of whole school literacy planning; developing supportive classroom environments as well as effective pedagogies for adolescents.

The chapter has also explored the importance of embedding quality literature through English and literacy learning in the high school via engaging and student-led approaches to learning. It is important to ensure that students are engaged and motivated by being active constructors rather than passive receptors of information (Woolley, 2014a: 103). Further, students should comprehend that literature is based on narrative structures or stories that carry important socio-cultural meaning. In fact, storytelling as a peda-gogical method is crucial for students who hail from diverse cultural backgrounds, including Indigenous students, as stories play an integral role in maintaining culture and identity.

Drawing on a range of literary forms is also important for adolescent learn-ers so that literature can be embraced in their learning. Above all quality literature is critical for effective learning.

Discussion questions and activities

 **Questions**

1   What are some important considerations related to adolescence, adolescents and literacy?
2   List a range of strategies that can support adolescents' literacy learning.
3   What makes quality literature? And why is it important to select quality literature for adolescent learners?
4   How can literature learning be made more engaging in the classroom?
5   Reflect on the strategies you use to engage adolescent students in classroom activities. Are these engaging, varied, relevant?
6   Review the literature currently being implemented in your English and literacy programmes. Are they quality texts? Are they relevant for adolescent learners?
7   Consider where you could allow students to self-select the literature being studied in class.

♁♁♁♁ Group activities

1   In a staff meeting discuss with your colleagues how the school is addressing issues related to adolescents, adolescence and literacy learning. What are the strengths of these approaches? Where could the school improve these approaches?
2   Reflect on the whole school approaches to literacy education. Are all teachers aware of these approaches? How can you continue professional learning for your staff in this area?
3   Carry out an audit of the literature being used in each of the classes in the school. Should these be renewed or altered? Do you use a range of literature including graphic novels, games, digital and multimodal texts?
4   Think of ways in which to implement effective literature circles with classes across the school.

CHAPTER 11

DIGITAL LITERACIES

Chapter objectives

- To understand how new technologies change the way people communicate and function in society.
- To discover how digital literacy can be inclusive.
- To analyse how teaching and learning can be flexible, adaptable and empowering.

Key questions

1 How does the shift from consumers of knowledge to creators of knowledge impact learners?
2 What type of skills will students need to become literate in a digital environment?
3 How do you think new technologies will change the way in which you teach?
4 How can you engage learners so that they can be creative and interdependent?

Key words: Digital literacies, new technology, connectivism, digital devices, digital divide, collaboration.

Introduction

New digital technologies are constantly being introduced and are changing the way people work and communicate. In today's advanced economies the workforce is becoming more collaborative and decentralised. Mobile technology, wearable technologies and Cloud-based systems are making information and communication much more accessible and more mobile. The new technologies are transforming not only how people work but also the types of skills that are needed to function in society. Many employees are no longer tied to an office desk but are able to work in other locations with their mobile devices. New technologies such as 3D printing, cyber security, voice recognition, facial recognition and robotics are transforming the types of functions performed, the types of tools used and the types of products created. In health, for example, data analytics and data mining techniques will make the job of diagnosis much easier and more precise, enabling a more personalised approach. 3D printing is on the cusp of being able to reproduce human organs and high-speed broadband will enable diagnosis and even surgery to be performed instantly in remote locations via broadband. Wearable technologies will allow patients to monitor many of their own health issues by keeping an eye on heart rate, blood pressure and blood chemistry.

> Adolescents' inherent capacity to adapt raises questions about the impact of one of the biggest environmental changes in history: the digital revolution. Computers, video games, cell phones and apps have in the past 20 years profoundly affected the way teens learn, play and interact. Voluminous information is available, but the quality varies greatly. The skill of the future will not be to remember facts but to critically evaluate a vast expanse of data, to discern signal from noise, to synthesize content and to apply that synthesis to real-world problem solving. Educators should challenge the adolescent brain with these tasks, to train its plasticity on the demands of the digital age. (Giedd, 2015: 32)

In the above quote Giedd raises the issue of adolescents being able to adapt to the rapid changes of today's society. Education will no longer be driven by the knowledge of facts but knowledge that is enduring and enables learners to determine what is needed to perform a task, to be able to locate relevant information and to know how to synthesise and create new knowledge. In the Australian context the Melbourne Declaration stated that when students leave school they should be 'confident, creative and productive users of new technologies, particularly information and communication technologies, and understand the impact of those technologies on society' (MCEETYA, 2008: 8–9). Such learners need to be resilient, self-motivated and self-reliant. In England, the House of Lords gave this important challenge, 'Having a forward-looking and responsive further education sector is vital if the UK is to have a responsive workforce and remain competitive' (House of Lords Select Committee on Digital Skills, 2015: 50). The challenge for you as a teacher in this ever changing and fluid environment is to equip learners to rise to this challenge.

The definition of ICT literacy adopted by the *Adelaide Declaration on National Goals for Schooling in the Twenty-First Century* (MCEETYA, 1999: goal 1.6) is: 'the ability of individuals to use ICT appropriately to access, manage, integrate and evaluate information, develop new understandings, and communicate with others in order to participate effectively in society'. It emphasises the interaction of information literacy with computer technology. The *Melbourne Declaration on Educational Goals for Young Australians* (MCEETYA, 2008) includes the following statement as part of its preamble. 'Rapid and continuing advances in information and communication technologies (ICT) are changing the ways people share, use, develop and process information and technology. In this digital age, young people need to be highly skilled in the use of ICT. While schools already employ these technologies in learning, there is a need to increase their effectiveness significantly over the next decade'. This goal is reflected in the Australian Curriculum where capability in information and communication technology (ICT) is identified as an important skill that will enable students to live and work successfully in the twenty-first century (ACARA, 2102a).

According to the Ofcom report (2015) 33 per cent of Internet users in the United Kingdom say their smartphone is the most important device for getting online, compared to 30 per cent who cite their laptop. A majority of Internet users aged 16–24 (93 per cent) have a social media profile, such as a Facebook or Twitter account. Over three-fifths of younger adults often use social media to share photos, compared to just over a third of older adults. The impact on society is all encompassing and the skill requirements can be quite multifaceted. Even though there has been a large uptake in mobile technology many users appear to lack basic digital literacy skills. For example, an influential report from the UK requested by the House of Lords Digital Skills Committee estimated that 9.5 million people currently lack a minimum level of digital skills and called for a radical rethink of education. The report warns that the UK risks becoming less prosperous and influential if it doesn't overtly pursue a digital education agenda. *The Guardian* (Weale, 2015) reported that Baroness Morgan of Huyton, chair of the House of Lords Digital Skills Committee and a former chair of Ofcom, added momentum to this notion when she cautioned that 35 per cent of jobs in the UK are expected to be automated within the next 20 years.

Digital (ICT) literacy is concerned not just about keyboard skills and how to use a word processor. 'Digital (ICT) literacy has been defined as the use of digital technology, communication tools, and networks information to function in a knowledge society' (ICT Literacy Panel, 2002).

Both the media and the context related to digital literacies are in a constant state of flux and so also are the social and communicative contexts which students inhabit. Society is continually adapting new and innovative ways to communicate with technology from using keyboards to the use of voice recognition software, gestures or intuitive algorithms to predict what is to be written, said or done. Over the past two decades there have been a number of approaches to digital literacy and with that there have been a variety of terms used to describe these new forms of literacy, including such terms as: digital literacy, information literacy, e-literacy, media literacy, computer literacy, Internet literacy, ICT literacy or just plain literacy (Zylka et al., 2015).

The difficulty is that technological change and societal expectations are outpacing the curriculum and it is difficult for teachers to remain up-to-date. Some enthusiastic teachers misguidedly embrace the new technologies, claiming they offer a panacea for educational problems. The challenge for you, however, will be to learn how to utilise the new technologies appropriately, responsibly and ethically, with a view to tapping the educational potential of all students. You will need to include in your understanding and teaching of literacy the unique digital technological skills that adolescents have already developed outside of school such as: text messaging, Facebook, blogs, video, wikis and emails using mobile technologies – mobile phones, tablets and other devices (New London Group, 2000).

Education and the digital landscape

It is assumed that many students will be 'digital natives' and already have a depth of knowledge and experience with various types of digital platforms and in many aspects of digital literacy they may be more proficient than their teachers. Most of these knowledgeable students will have acquired their digital literacies from practical applications developed incidentally through leisure and social activity (Ting, 2015).

A survey conducted in Australia in 2012 and 2013 of household use of information technology (Australian Bureau of Statistics, 2014), indicated that 83 per cent of households had access to the Internet at home (up from 64 per cent in 2006–7), and 77 per cent of households had broadband access to the Internet (up from 56 per cent in 2006–7). Almost every household with children under 15 years of age had access to the Internet at home (96 per cent, which was up from 81 per cent in 2006–7). In 2012–13, more than four out of five households (81 per cent) accessed the Internet at home every day and a further 16 per cent of households accessed the Internet at home at least weekly. Internet access varied among states and territories (from a low of 78 per cent to a high of 89 per cent) and was associated with household income.

Inclusion and equity

'Digital inclusion' is a term that has been used to highlight the notion that young people will have the digital skills to enable them to use computers and use the Internet in order to do things that benefit them day to day. However, this term implies that some people in modern western societies may be at a disadvantage due to a lack of digital skills. Not having the necessary skills and technology translates into not having the ability to access the Internet and exclusion from functioning as worthwhile and productive citizens of the twenty-first century. Thus, accessibility problems (often referred to as the digital divide) are a barrier for some young people because this excludes them from many essential services that would normally be available to them.

According to the PISA test results (OECD, 2011) the differences in computer access between advantaged and disadvantaged students shrank between 2009 and 2012 in most OECD countries. The percentage of students who reported having at least one computer at home increased from 72 per cent in 2000 to 94 per cent in 2009, while home access to the Internet doubled from 45 per cent to 89 per cent during the same period. There was also an increase in the computer-to-student ratio in schools and the gender gap was reduced showing reading performance as being narrower for digital modes than for print reading. The digital divide is now not so much about having access to technology but about having the necessary digital literacy skills to enable adolescents to access twenty-first-century digital communications, communities and education or information systems. The ability to use communicative tools, assess, analyse, manage, and evaluate, integrate and create information will always be a critical component of a digital literacy environment. The important thing to remember is that you should not assume that your students automatically know how to use a particular digital tool or application. For example, when using Google, you should not presuppose that they all have the basic precursory skills for navigating online text. For example, basic proficiencies such as: how to copy/paste a Web address, bookmark a website, view two windows side by side, and understand the basic layout of a website all play their part in building digital competency (Kingsley, 2015).

In most western countries, governments have spent considerable sums of money on the development of infrastructure (NBN, wireless, devices) but have provided minimal funding for research into developing good pedagogical practices using digital technologies. At present education authorities have largely been concerned with providing the actual devices that are used and the basic skills that are required such as keyboard skills, using word processors, spreadsheets and knowing how to use Google. The risk of focusing too heavily on any particular technological device is that it can be very costly and can quickly be outdated. Some education authorities in a number of countries had introduced programmes to give laptops to students with varied results for classroom learning (White, 2013). However, these devices are increasingly viewed by adolescents as somewhat obsolete due to the increasing popularity of tablets and smartphones. This is because tablets and smartphones are more mobile and have broader applications. For example, they can be used as cameras, audio recorders or note-takers, and can connect users instantly to the Internet allowing communication with others using Facebook or other social networking apps. Teachers often find that, despite having access and positive attitudes towards implementing ICT into their teaching and learning, on-going technical and pedagogical support is necessary.

Educational technologies can improve teaching and learning when they are used judiciously, are user friendly, and support high quality interactions (Lewis-Spector, 2015). They, however, cannot replace the classroom teacher but can be a useful tool to personalise learning by tailoring to the needs and interests of individuals. Within this very complex and fluid landscape it will be important for you as a teacher to find ways for students to become highly engaged, by critically reflecting on the content of texts that they view and read. By blending face-to-face and online learning you will more likely enable students to work at their own pace, be flexible in accommodating according to need, and gain information about how students are doing and what they are struggling with. Students do, however, need to feel excited about their learning. This will often be an outcome of their creative endeavours and their growing confidence in using the new literacies (Beavis, 2012; Beavis et al., 2015).

Theoretical understandings

Siemens (2005) argues that knowledge is diverse and changeable, and that being connected on the Internet means that knowledge resides in networks that need to be constantly sustained. His 'Connectivist' theory maintains that the capacity to learn is more important than what is currently known by an individual learner. This notion represents a fundamental departure from the view that knowledge is an integral part of the individual as opposed to thinking that learning is essentially about knowing how to navigate and interact in online networks.

Several of Siemens' (2005) main principles are listed below:

- Learning and knowledge rests in diversity of ideas
- Learning is a process of connecting specialised nodes/information sources
- Capacity to know more is more critical than what is currently known
- Ability to see connections between fields, ideas, and concepts is an essential skill
- Currency is the intent of all connectivist learning activities
- Decision-making is an integral learning process.

Thus, a connectivist approach to teaching and learning emphasises the role of the student in fashioning personal communicative networks and being a creator of new knowledge. This theory has given impetus to online experimentation in education and new forms of blended learning like 'flipped' classrooms and the use of online learning platforms (Johnson et al., 2015).

Blended learning and flipped classrooms

A fundamental shift is taking place in pedagogical practice in schools in various regions of the world as students across a wide variety of disciplines are moving away from being mere consumers of information to learning by accessing, connecting and creating. Students can now effortlessly produce videos, access 'maker' communities and 'crowd funding' for projects. These trends are causing teachers to rethink: how can they engage students more deeply and how can they drive innovation through student centred approaches like project- and challenge-based learning? Web 2.0 has also changed the possibilities of student writing and text production (Walsh, 2011). Students need to consider and understand design elements, such as layout, composition, use of text and image or graphics, and how these will serve a particular audience (Clary et al., 2013). Perceptions of online learning have changed and blended learning is gaining popularity in schools as educators see it as a viable alternative to some forms of face-to-face learning. Blended learning is flexible, increasingly accessible and enables the integration of sophisticated multimedia and technologies.

The flipped classroom is directly associated with blended learning platforms and is based on the idea that independent learning is expected to take place at home, while the classroom is used for projects and collaborative activities. In the flipped classroom the environment is homelike and relaxed, learners can exercise their autonomy as they access and review online resources at home before formally meeting in the classroom (Johnson et al., 2015). The classroom then becomes a place where groups can discuss the ideas generated from the online environment and work on collaborative activities and group projects. When you blend instruction in this way you shift the focus from delivering content to unpacking content at much deeper levels of learning. This inverted teaching strategy has the benefit of providing richer and more diverse learning opportunities than more traditional pedagogical practices (Moyle, 2010). In a flipped learning environment your students will have more scope for self-directed learning of basic course content through an increased variety of online resources. Your students will enjoy the variety of resources and the flexibility that supports individual learning and group sharing of ideas and online communication.

Vignette 11.1

St Jude's College is an independent co-educational school in a metropolitan area. The college ran a school laptop programme but this was discontinued several years ago. The school decided to replace the laptop programme with a programme that focused on sound pedagogical process at the centre of the learning process. They decided to build a content management system for their online content using a 'WordPress' platform, which is a free open-source blogging tool. The software was installed on the school server for the students to use with a username and password login. The students were able access the platform from anywhere using their own devices. By moving their content to the 'Cloud', the teachers were able to use the 'flipped' classroom model. The model inverted traditional teaching methods by delivering instruction online to encourage consumption of reading articles, video and podcasts to take place at home before face-to-face discussion. The content creation was undertaken in the classroom with the support of the teacher to provide guidance and explanation.

Questions

1   When moving from a laptop programme to one based on open-source blogging what pedagogical practices would need to change?
2   What is a flipped classroom model and what are the advantages?

STEM and STEAM

Technological innovation is shifting how school disciplines are being viewed; many schools are converging subjects that have traditionally been separate such as science, mathematics and art in favour of more integrated learning. This push is largely driven by society's requirement for future advanced technological development and the importance of high-quality science, technology, engineering and mathematics (known as STEM). Added to this is that educators are also pioneering new methods for integrating the arts into STEM activities by imitating the ways in which subjects naturally connect in real life situations. Even though the upsurge of science, technology, engineering, art and mathematics (STEAM) learning is a relatively new learning perspective, there are already indications that the integration of these superficially distinct disciplines is improving student performance at school. Thus, experiencing the full range of STEAM education can enable students to generate more comprehensive skill sets and understandings (Johnson et al., 2015).

These trends generally require higher order and more complex thinking leveraging multiple skill sets, such as problem solving and creativity. Laurillard (2013) has built on the notion that the skill of teachers is about designing appropriate learning experiences for students. She argued that teaching is a design science that builds pedagogical patterns for learning using digital technologies. Her argument advances the strengths of learning using inquiry methods, discussion, practice and collaboration that can be enabled using digital technologies (White, 2013). Even a relatively simple task of making a podcast can be quite complex particularly when done as a group project. However, as with most projects there are a number of production stages that students should be aware of during the process. In the box below this process is explained; it has been taken from the companion book *Developing Literacy in the Primary Classroom* (Woolley, 2014a: 55–57).

Podcasting

Podcasts are an exciting way for children to learn how to use computers and Web 2.0 technologies as well as developing the skills of speaking and listening (Kervin and Mantei, 2009; Richardson, 2010). They tend to be approximately 5 to 15 minutes in length. As a finished product it is a clear example of oral text. However, there is considerable engagement with writing, drawing, talking and listening.

A podcast is essentially an audio file and is usually encoded as an MP3 file. MP3 files are commonly used by iPods and iPads but there are many other devices that use these files. Podcasting is easy to develop as a learning and teaching tool. The term 'podcasting' is made up from 'pod' that comes from the 'iPod' and 'cast', which derives from 'broadcast'. Podcasts are usually audio shows that become part of a series or collection that are published on Internet sites. They can be accessed through iTunes or iPad applications or can be found using a suitable search engine, such as Google. There are a growing number of websites that feature podcasts; many of these are dedicated to particular topics of interest.

For a podcast to be done effectively and for it to be useful and interesting there needs to be considerable planning and developing. However, they can be quite easily produced using everyday equipment that is readily accessible to the children. An iPod, iPad or smartphone is quite adequate for the task. However, an external microphone will be an advantage and a quiet place to record is essential. The important thing for you to realise is that the process is just as important as the product. When children work in pairs or in triads they develop many language and social skills such as negotiating and knowing how to take turns and how to listen to others.

The first stage in developing a podcast is to determine a purpose for the activity and listen to several examples of podcasts that have a similar audience and purpose. The children should then brainstorm to determine what will be similar and what will be different in their own production.

The next stage is the planning stage to determine the length, content and style of presentation. During this time the children could practice using the equipment by adjusting the tone and pitch of their voices, for example. The children will also need to gather the information or data that they will use as their content. This stage will also require the students to do some brainstorming, note-taking, and developing a concept map or storyboard to structure their podcast.

The drafting stage may utilise the concept map or storyboard developed in the previous stage to write a suitable script. On completion of the script the children will need to make one or more podcasts.

The editing stage requires good listening skills and constructive criticism from interested others. It is always a good idea to include the children's peers as much as possible because children often learn from each other. The feedback that is given may also help their peers with their own podcasts.

The creating phase is a polishing phase that may take a number of iterations before the finished product is decided upon. This phase is followed by the dissemination of the podcast. This will require uploading to a suitable hosting site on the Internet such as a blog, wiki or iTunes.

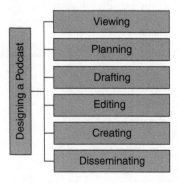

Figure 11.1 A podcast flow chart

Podcasts can be disseminated in a number of ways such as:

- placing them on computers
- putting the audio files into portable MP3 players or iPods
- placing the files in a particular folder on the school intranet
- embedding an RSS feed into an existing website to automatically upload to personal computers.

Podcasts can take many different forms depending upon the purpose and classroom units of work. Such examples are:

- radio talk shows
- news broadcasts
- interviews
- interest articles
- short radio plays
- poems and
- show and tells.

(Also see Chapter 9 on the writing process.)

Personalised learning

Digital stories and video demonstrations can also emulate the same process as with podcasting. What is certain is that you, as a teacher, should understand the use of ICT and the way in which pedagogy interacts to facilitate the development of digital competencies. One way in which to achieve this is to negotiate the learning process. Students should be encouraged as autonomous learners, and as such will need to make many decisions about their own learning as they use the digital literacies. Wherever possible, they should be involved in the decision-making process during curriculum development (Ting, 2015). Thus, individuals will be more engaged in metacognitive learning and self-regulation when they are expected to set their own goals, check how much has been understood and determine future directions.

Digital literacy understandings and skills

Some important questions that students may need to ask themselves as they engage with new literacies:

- Who is the audience?
- What is the message?
- Who is sending this message?
- Why are they sending this message?

These understandings and skills are important characteristics of digital literacies, with particular application to contexts involving collaboration and interaction (Oblinger and Oblinger, 2005).

Getting started

Digital technology also has the potential to enable you to use your time and talents more effectively and to personalise the learning experience to the needs and interests of your students. Online collaboration between teachers has the power to harness digital literacies for learning (Harasim, 2012). Online professional collaboration is particularly appropriate for applications in education in an age when participation is expected and rewarded (Mellor and Seddon, 2013).

With so many new directions and options just where should you, as a teacher, start? Obviously the best place to start is with what you are interested in. If the students see that you are excited about a tool or process then they will be more inclined to respond. Start simply and give structure to the activity and engage in joint goal setting.

Vignette 11.2

Mrs Smith decided to use a tool-based approach to using technology in literacy with her middle school class. QR codes are used in many applications in the environment. QR codes can be generated quite easily using QR code generator apps that can be downloaded for free or cheaply purchased. QR code apps can be installed on the student's own device such as mobile phones and tablets and can be used with Apple, MacOz or Android platforms. Due to the fact that Internet connectivity was a problem in the school Mrs Smith decided to use the QR codes to generate plain text.

The QR codes were placed around the classroom on poster boards to replace written instructions for independent practice. The students found this activity engaging because they could move around the room, use their own technology and it gave an element of mystery when they unlocked the code. They were more focused and were more able to use higher order thinking skills because they seemed to take ownership of the problem.

In another activity they analysed an artwork that was related to an historical event. The QR codes replaced actual written questions and related to graphic elements within the picture and to the interpretation of the artist. The task required the students to work in groups and to answer one question at a time.

Questions

1   Where are QR codes normally found? Why use them in the classroom?
2   Do you think that this would be a motivating activity for the students? Why? Why not?
3   Do you think that students should be able to use their own devices in the classroom? Why? Why not?

Apps

At schools where tablets are used to create content, teachers and tech staff also need to sort out how files created on the tablet will be managed. There are a variety of apps that can be used for students to share files with their teachers and peers such as Dropbox and Edmondo, but these need to be discussed and adopted before students begin creating content on the tablets. It is generally advised that schools develop an overall policy for how this will work, what apps and programs will be suitable for curriculum purposes and safe (protecting student identity etc.) to use.

New directions for education technology

With the use of new technologies learning becomes more fluid, interdisciplinary and student-centred with more time for independent study and flexible schedules. For example, using tools such as YouTube, Twitter, blogs and podcasts enables the learner to have the opportunity to become an independent learner (Brooks, 2015). Another key skill of complex thinking is the ability for students to make complex ideas understandable, using data visualisation, media and other communications techniques.

Some applications that have been identified in the *Horizon Report* (Johnson et al., 2015) as possibly having a major impact in schooling in the near future are:

- mobile technology and bring your own device (BYOD)
- electronic books
- gaming
- makerspaces
- 3D printing
- wearable technologies
- augmented reality
- robotics.

Mobile technology and bring your own devices (BYOD)

Mobile devices continue to expand their capabilities and have increased access to affordable and reliable networks. Many students are now entering the classroom with their own devices, which easily connect to the school's network. BYOD policies have been shown to reduce schools' technology spending and they are gaining more popularity because they reflect contemporary lifestyle and learning (Johnson et al., 2015). However, some schools will resist the use of smartphones in the classroom but a growing number of institutions are finding ways to take advantage of BYOD such as tablets and smartphones because they are extremely useful in using and storing information on a single device. Not all students will have a mobile device of their own and not all devices are equal and so schools will need to find ways to overcome this problem (Hockly and Dudeney, 2014; Hower, 2015).

Electronic books

Electronic books continue to generate strong interest in the consumer sector and are increasingly available in schools. A number of modern electronic readers support note-taking and research activity. They are now beginning to augment basic functions with more sophisticated capabilities that are changing our perception of what it means to read. They are generally moving from immersive experiences to supporting social interaction.

Gaming

Gaming emphasises co-constructed knowledge and places knowledge acquisition in an active, non-decontextualised context; learners may perceive heightened utility and engagement particularly in the formal learning space of the middle years of schooling (Elliott, 2014). Gesture-based computing is gaining more traction due to the recent arrival of interface technologies such as Kinect, SixthSense and Tamper, which make interactions with digital devices far more embodied and intuitive. Games-based education has the potential to engage learners at all age levels and range from single users to small-groups and involve online communities. Some of the greatest benefits of games for learning is in their ability to integrate with course work and foster collaborative, problem solving and procedural thinking skills.

Makerspaces

Makerspaces are spaces where anyone, regardless of age or experience, can exercise their ingenuity to construct tangible products. For this reason, many schools are seeing their potential to engage learners in hands-on learning activities (Johnson et al., 2015). Makerspaces, developed by the Maker movement, have a following comprised of artists, tech enthusiasts, engineers, builders, tinkerers and anyone else who has an interest in making things. In this space educational considerations, creativity, design and engineering using tools such as 3D printers, robotics and 3D modelling can be exhibited and demonstrated.

3D printing

3D printing enables users to construct physical objects from three-dimensional digital content such as 3D modelling software, computer-aided design (CAD) tools and computer-aided tomography (CAT). A 3D printer builds a tangible object one layer at a time in a similar way that an inkjet printer works from an electronic file; it deposits a bonding agent onto a very thin layer of fixable powder to build an object from the bottom up, layer by layer (Johnson et al., 2015).

Wearable technology

Wearable technology refers to devices that can be worn by users in the form of accessories such as jewelry, glasses, backpacks or even actual items of clothing such as shoes or a jacket. Wearable technology has many benefits to the user as it can conveniently track sleep, movement and location. Smart watches, for example, are becoming more widely used and enable users to check emails and perform other functions while on the go (Johnson et al., 2015).

Augmented reality

Augmented reality refers to the layering of information over a view or representation of the normal world. It is an intuitive way to access place-based information in ways that are compelling. Augmented reality brings a significant potential to supplement information delivered via computers, mobile devices, video and even the printed book. Much simpler to create and use now than in the past, augmented reality feels at once fresh and new, yet an easy extension of existing expectations and practices.

Robotics

Robotics enables users to solve problems and to design cross-curricula connections with mathematics and science (Chandra, 2014). It is a tremendous platform that can demonstrate student problem solving, creativity and technological literacy skills. The project-based learning pedagogy can be a useful device in fostering literacy across a variety of modes, for example, using oral and written communication with peers in problem solving and with others to present and justify project solutions (Chandra, 2014).

Issues and concerns with digital technologies

Those in charge of educating today's 'connected' learners are confronted with a number of new (or newly relevant) issues, from information overload to plagiarism, from protecting children from online risks (fraud, violations of privacy, online bullying, pornography) to setting an adequate and appropriate media diet. In addition, many parents and teachers will not be surprised to find that some students spend more than six hours online per day and are at risk of feeling lonely in and out of school. You can educate students to become critical consumers of Internet services and electronic media by helping them make informed choices and avoid harmful behaviours (ACARA, 2015). You can also raise awareness in families about the risks that adolescents face online and how to avoid them. Schools and parents can help students balance the use of ICT for entertainment and leisure with time for other recreational activities that do not involve digital screens, such as sports and other recreational activities.

The rapid expansion of the World Wide Web and other multimedia technologies demands a complex skill-set for children to function appropriately in the age of the Internet. Many teachers posit that Web-based texts are more complex than traditional print media and students must now acquire added literacy skills to critically and effectively evaluate the quality of materials and consider any potential bias of that material. Students should be formally introduced to the concepts of copyright theft, intellectual property and plagiarism in an age-appropriate manner as early as possible.

As there are many ethical considerations you should consider developing a device code of conduct for your class such as the one below:

1. Follow all teacher directions including when to use the device.
2. Access only the information related to the learning task.
3. Inform the teacher or others when using the camera and audio recording functions.
4. Ensure that your device is password locked.
5. You should not appropriate other people's intellectual output.
6. You should not use information about others without their permission.
7. You should always show consideration and respect for others in your endeavours.
8. It is not ethical to copy other people's work.

Your code of conduct may have to be revised periodically as future technologies are developed and digital literacies change.

Conclusion

Digital technologies are changing society and the types of literacies that enable people of the twenty-first century to communicate, create and function as responsible citizens. In a globalised world it is imperative that adolescents develop the necessary literacy skills so that they can develop as autonomous and interdependent learners. As a teacher you will need to stay up-to-date with new and emerging technologies to ensure that the literacies that you access are relevant and have the power to engage your students productively.

Discussion questions and activities

 Questions

1 Using your own device use a search engine such as Google to find out about MOOCS and blended learning. Make up a Y chart with the following questions: What do they look like? What do they sound like? What do they feel like?
2 Do you think that paper books have been superseded? Why? Why not?
3 How will your role as a teacher change by using digital technologies?

†††† Group activities

1 In a small group discuss the problems that are likely to be experienced when using social media. Make up an Internet code of conduct chart for developing a podcast.

(Continued)

(Continued)

2 Search the Internet and sign up to 'Today's meet' and pose the question, 'What app is most useful in the classroom and why?' Cut and paste the answers into 'Wordle' to make a word cloud.

3 What are other ways to use word clouds (such as Wordle) in the classroom?

4 In small groups share ideas that you have observed in classrooms that you have visited. What has worked and what has not worked?

5 Sign up to Pinterest and search for ways in which to use social media in the classroom. What do you think it means to become a curator of ideas using Pinterest?

6 What are some ways that teachers can use YouTube, TED talks and Khan Academy? How can the students be creators of content?

7 Look up Bloom's taxonomy and search for Bloom's digital technology. Would you find this useful in the classroom? How? Why?

CHAPTER 12

ASSESSMENT

Chapter objectives

- To understand the purposes of assessment for teaching and learning.
- To develop a repertoire of dynamic and flexible assessment strategies.
- To develop strategic approaches to inform effective instruction.

Key questions

1 What should teachers assess?
2 How is assessment linked to learning and instruction?
3 Why is it important to involve adolescents in the assessment process?

Key words: Assessment, testing, formative assessment, summative assessment, dynamic assessment, self-assessment, process, product.

Introduction

Chapter 12 considers assessment as an integrated and essential aspect of teaching. It discusses the dynamic application of formal assessment along with other more informal assessment procedures. It will focus on the learner within the learning context rather than assuming that all of the problems are situated within the learner. A balanced approach to assessment can be the means by which you will be able to develop high-quality evidence-based teaching and literacy programmes that enhance student achievement. To enable this you need a range of assessment procedures or activities that are capable of measuring and describing student learning while fostering appropriate literacy skills and strategies. Effectual assessment should also consider affective aspects such as: motivation, perseverance, academic self-concept and attribution beliefs necessary for literacy success or failure (Afflerbach, 2007).

> The student assessment process produces evidence of learning. That evidence is critical information for informing the learning process for both the student and teacher and for informing decision makers about the quality of the educational program and the accountability of the personnel who are responsible. But there must be a balance in the system between these two uses of the evidence. The need for accountability using large-scale, high-stakes, summative assessments should not overshadow assessment's primary purpose of providing timely feedback to the teachers and learners engaged in the instructional process. (Darling-Hammond, 2010: 4)

The above quote by Darling-Hammond raises a number of issues related to a balanced approach to assessment. This chapter addresses these concerns and explores this crucial notion of feedback and learning engagement.

A changing view of assessment

Educators generally agree that quality assessment is key to the design of effective curriculum and the teaching of literacy (Coccamise and Snyder, 2005). However, most literacy assessment procedures currently being used in schools today are based on limited theoretical models of learning and tend to give the impression that all difficulties are found solely within the learner (Joshi and Aaron, 2000). Reading is a good example: some theoretical viewpoints place more emphasis on internal student factors such as word decoding while neglecting context or purpose (Freebody and Freiberg, 2001; Joshi and Aaron, 2000; Woolley, 2011). The reality is that successful learning requires a complex interaction of language, sensory perception, memory, motivation and environmental and contextual factors (Pikulski and Chard,

2005). There are factors within the learner and factors outside the learner such as context, purpose, task and teaching that have an impact on learning.

During the 1960s until the late 1980s structured reading programmes and criterion-referenced tests (CRT) became popular in classroom assessment. Mastery learning and teaching was the driving force behind CRT with its emphasis on precision learning. The notion behind mastery learning was that if the essential elements within the domain of learning could be identified and mastered students would be able to achieve high levels with confidence as they learnt the prerequisite lower-level skills (Paris and Stahl, 2005). This process tended to operate from an outside-in perspective.

During the 1970s and 1980s there were two different perspectives that emerged. The first perspective focused on schema theory, which provided an internal framework to account for how knowledge is understood in terms of what is already known by the learner. This emphasised an inside-out model whereby learners can have differing understandings using very diverse background experiences and prior knowledge. This notion motivated educators to examine texts from the student's own perspective that included prior knowledge and cultural understandings when comprehending new information. During this time another group of theorists focused on a different perspective: an outside-in model that emphasised the role of external story grammar or genre (Kintsch, 1974). From this perspective educationalists were interested in how socially constructed structures impede or enhance texts and guide the learner's memory and comprehension.

These two trends have been very influential in supporting a constructivist view of learning, whereby learners are seen to actively construct the most coherent model of meaning according to what they understand and know. In other words the learner builds a model of meaning, which is unique to their own experience of the world guided by the conventions of language and other socio-cultural norms (Paris and Stahl, 2005). By the late 1980s, a social constructivist approach to literacy assessment emerged which emphasised the need for assessment to reflect resources such as prior knowledge, environmental factors, the text itself and the social interaction involved in the learning process. In particular, it emphasised metacognition as a reflective element in literacy processes.

These theoretical trends, along with others, have added to our collective understanding of assessment and educational practice. It is obvious that any one inside-out or outside-in approach has its limitations according to the particular theoretical perspective. Consequently, some researchers have called for better assessment tools and more appropriate intervention programmes to reflect the complexity of learning in contemporary learning contexts (Pressley, 2001; Schunk, 2004). However, to overcome the limitations of any one approach you will need to use a range of assessment strategies and instruments that robustly reflect the dynamic, developmental nature of adolescent literacy learning contexts (Duke and Pearson, 2002; National Reading Panel, 2000; Snow, 2003).

Summative and high-stakes testing

In recent times there has been an emphasis on the value of competition among students and schools and on formal high-stakes international and national testing. Governments now have a greater determination to know how their education systems 'stack up' against others. For example, in recent years the PISA tests have been used to test some 510,000 15-year-old school students across 65 countries and economic regions in the academic domains of reading, science and mathematical skills.

Many western governments have made the shift to national testing in order to determine how their education systems are functioning. It is important for governments to monitor and allocate funding where it is most needed. This is also part of a general trend to have more central control of curriculum and teacher quality by maintaining 'standards' and demonstrating accountability and professional integrity. Education authorities seek to provide parents and caregivers with assurance that their schools are consistently applying national standards and making progress according to expectations (Hayward and Hutchinson, 2013). The results are made available to parents and caregivers who tend to value this process because the information provided is viewed as comprehensible and trustworthy. Hence, they are more able to evaluate the progress of their children and the overall performance of the school in meeting educational objectives (Curry et al., 2016).

A whole range of educational, public and political beliefs concerning the role of education influences the choices various states and education author- ities make about national tests and assessments and how they interpret and use those results. For example, Australia's national testing is motivated by a desire to maintain public confidence in the nation's education institutions by demonstrating accountability and transparency, and maintaining national education standards. The concern for educators is whether this drive will result in the improvement of teaching and learning without compromising equity (Klenowski and Wyatt-Smith, 2012). In Scotland, newspapers have been encouraged to publish the results of the tests with the view to compar- ing schools in the form of what has become known as 'league tables'. As a consequence, schools have often been judged unfairly due to the fact that results can be misrepresented in the media. However, it is difficult to compare schools as they are resourced differently. For example, some schools may have an overabundance of students from lower socio-economic backgrounds or from migrant backgrounds.

In contrast, the New Zealand Ministry of Education (2010) claimed that the publishing of raw and highly aggravated assessment data without quantitative contextual information undercuts the collegial teaching environment and undermines the reliability of assessment data (Hayward and Hutchinson, 2013). Different understandings of 'standards' often cause confusion and frustration, especially when it is related to putting the learner at the centre of education.

Another negative aspect of national testing is that it may cause students and teachers to lose motivation: accountability-driven testing regimes that focus on rote learning of a narrow range of 'basic' knowledge sets may decrease intrinsic student motivation while teachers may suffer from a perceived lack of professionalism.

The drive towards perceived higher school achievement has a disadvantageous effect upon students with diverse educational needs, by inadvertently labelling them as failures and increasing their levels of stress. Many schools, in an attempt to lift their overall standards, ask low performing students to stay at home during testing or alternatively they may provide an aide to help them with the examination questions (Hayward and Hutchinson, 2013).

Many schools conduct regular practice sessions using questions similar to those anticipated in the examinations. With this in mind, a whole new industry has developed to support this trend. For example, publishers are providing testing and other practice materials so that students can prepare for the tests. As a consequence of the pressure to increase a school's performance the curriculum has, in many instances, become narrower by ignoring content that is not directly associated with the high-stakes testing. This narrowing of the content has a somewhat dumbing down effect on the tests as higher order thinking skills are usually neglected because they are difficult to assess on most standardised tests. Furthermore, the omitted aspects of the curriculum generally include skills that are regarded as essential for the twenty-first century such as collaborative decision-making, creativity and innovation.

Recent trends in education in most western countries focus on the identification of 'standards' that students should attain throughout their schooling. However, you should understand that standards are not fixed entities but are constructs negotiated within a particular learning community that outline expectations of the quality of learning as measured by an analysis of actual examples of student work. Thus, assessment and moderation practices have become important elements as they enable practitioners to identify, evaluate, and communicate appropriate 'standards'. A process of review and revision ensures consistency of expectations so that learners know what to expect and are appropriately challenged. However, in the drive for consistency, standardisation and quality control, innovation may be in danger of being sidelined. This may be because many teachers are reluctant to take risks by avoiding experimentation with new pedagogy (Hayward and Hutchinson, 2013).

External examinations were thought to eliminate subjectivity and provide some degree of standardisation by developing a 'universal' measure of achievement, thereby making schools more accountable. However, all tests have some limitations, and validity becomes an important issue. For example, concerns about the construction of the tests include aspects such as focus, reliability, validity, application and purpose (Stobart and Eggen, 2012). What is certain is that high-stakes testing does have an important place in providing valuable information but will not tell you everything about the quality of education. Therefore, you should not rely solely on high-stakes testing as a single indicator of achievement. It should be noted that the teacher, and not the test, is the change agent and there is no such thing as a values free assessment (Klenowski and Wyatt-Smith, 2012). Furthermore, deeper learning combines the goals of standardised or high-stakes testing with soft skills that usually require an element of teacher judgement. Thus, assessment should be based on a wide range of sampling that includes not only high-stakes testing and standardised tests but should also include a repertoire of formative and summative teacher-made tests and observations.

In classrooms, summative assessment routinely takes the form of formal teacher-made tests that are implemented at the end of a unit or school term. This type of assessment is important, as it will help you, as the teacher, to understand whether students have reached grade-level benchmarks, unit and lesson goals, and standards in classrooms, systems and states (Afflerbach, 2007). Classroom assessments usually occur over an extended period of time and usually mirror what actually occurs in the day-to-day learning activities. A typical criticism of today's testing methods is that the focus is too often weighted towards what can be managed rather than towards broader formative and diagnostic perspectives (Kalantzis et al., 2016). The risk is that teachers will focus on attainment levels rather than on the quality of their assessment practices (Klenowski and Wyatt-Smith, 2012).

Formal or informal tests

Formal assessment typically samples students' learning behaviours using uniform or standardised procedures for administering and scoring tests. Formal tests can be either norm referenced or criterion referenced. Norm-referenced tests compare the performance of an individual student with large samplings of a wide population of individuals. Comparisons are made between individual students and standardised measures of the larger group, usually in the form of percentile score rankings. For example, a student attaining a percentile score of 72 would be regarded as performing better than 71 per cent of the same aged population at a particular grade level. Criteria-referenced tests, on the other hand, are a measure of attainment in relation to certain learning outcomes. Informal assessment may also involve students doing self-assessment activities (Lipson and Wixson, 2009). This form of assessment can provide valuable information on the usefulness of instructional approaches or curricular materials and provide an indication of an individual student's achievement over a fixed period of time. It can also provide teachers with feedback on the effect of classroom settings and instructional approaches.

Formative assessment

Formative assessment is the process of evaluating learning as it occurs and is reflective upon student performance, pedagogy and teaching in the regular classroom. It is ongoing and evaluates the actual learning tasks and products that students generate in their classrooms and gives teachers valuable and ongoing appraisal of students' performance and learning task relevance. Usually, this involves regular teacher-made tests of learning outcomes of particular activities that students may be engaged in. In contrast, informal assessment usually involves observation of real-life or hands-on tasks and sometimes utilises incidental learning activities and experiences. Thus, routine and frequent assessment will provide you with the necessary information for effective literacy instruction and enable you to identify teachable moments for each student. It is imperative to know where students are individually placed in terms of their literacy skills and strategy development, motivation, literacy engagement, prior knowledge of the texts they read, and their self-perception as literacy learners (Afflerbach, 2007; Afflerbach et al., 2011).

Diagnostic assessment

Most classrooms will have quite diverse communities of learners: a number of students may need to have a more intensive diagnostic assessment with the assistance of a specialist learning support teacher. Diagnostic assessment is used to identify what the learner is capable of doing, what the learner knows and what the learner needs to know. Generally, it needs to happen before learning takes place so that the curriculum can be adjusted to cater for the developmental needs and interests of the individual. This can be achieved using a combination of formal and informal tests. Time spent getting to know the students at the beginning of the year will be time well spent and can save time at a later date. School records and interviews with parents and previous teachers can also be very informative. Thorough data gathering and research contributing to discussions with colleagues will also provide more reliable information in order to make the necessary changes and modifications for curriculum development and inclusion of students with diverse learning needs (Gambrell et al., 2007; Gunning, 2006).

Diagnostic assessment, in some cases, may require the input of other allied professionals such as educational psychologists, speech therapists, occupational therapists or paediatricians. The important thing is that diagnostic assessment should examine three levels of functioning: biological, cognitive and metacognitive. Assessment at the biological level is mainly concerned with the sensory aspects such as hearing and vision. It stands to reason that if you can't see or hear what is presented then any form of teaching will not be adequate unless the sensory input is rectified and this often requires medical advice and remediation. Many students with a learning difficulty may be able to see and hear quite well but have a difficulty with cognition. They often have difficulties interpreting the information or knowing when and how to apply prior knowledge when assimilating new information. The third level is the metacognitive level and this is concerned with the ability of the student to set appropriate goals, monitor progress, reflect and make decisions about their own learning (see Chapter 8).

Dynamic assessment

Dynamic assessment is a term that is often used to describe a more interactive form of diagnostic and formative assessment. It is based on Vygotsky's notion of learning, which views student learning as being mediated by interactions with adults and peers (Vygotsky, 1978). In essence dynamic assessment provides information about an individual's potential learning ability (Gunning, 2006). Essentially, this type of assessment should not only inform about how a student is learning on his or her own at any particular point in time but should also identify what an individual can do with the assistance of a peer or adult. Teachers will be more able to apply reflective teaching when data is used to inform instruction rather than just evaluate instruction (Curry et al., 2016).

Some key questions that you should ask to promote dynamic assessment:

1. What can the student already do unaided for this subject area?
2. What can the student do if given a little guidance or prompting?
3. Are there any important gaps in the student's prior learning?
4. What does the student need to be taught next in order to make progress? (Westwood, 2001)

Teacher-designed assessments

Almost any teaching technique or learning task can be used to inform you about the students' performance and the appropriateness and delivery of the curriculum content. How students perform on any given task will reveal much about their competency. What is important is that your assessment is methodical and that you use a variety of ways to gather your data. Data gathering can utilise direct observations, anecdotal notes, work samples, portfolios, inventories, conferences, rubrics, regular formal or informal tests and quizzes (Lipson and Wixson, 2009). Informal gathering of student performance data, such as inventories, anecdotal notes and observations should supplement formal or standardised test scores and broaden the focus by providing more authentic evaluative data. Teacher-designed instruments will often be more informative than standardised tests but will be more subjective and vary with the content, test conditions and assessor attributes. What is certain is that your judgements and ratings can become less subjective when measured against specific criteria and teacher moderation (August and Shanahan, 2006).

Validity

You should be aware that assessments, whether formal or informal, are never completely error free due to the fact that there are a number of factors that impact upon validity. Different reading tests, for example, may give different age equivalent scores for reading. Test scores can be expected to fluctuate when administered to the same child on different occasions. It is likely that the same test administered a second time will give a higher score or possibly a depressed score if administered while the child is tired, unwell or feeling uncomfortable. Tests should be conducted in a professional manner and balanced against other sources of information such as observations, checklists and anecdotal notes etc. (Witt et al., 1994). Overall, assessment involves deciding what information is important, how it should be collected and what educational decisions are most appropriate.

A metacognitive perspective

Is educational assessment a process or a product? It can be used as a process to measure student progress and attainment of certain standards or it can be used as a product of that process, e.g. a teacher's assessment of a student's abilities and a set of judgements about their progress. In general, assessment of processes will focus on the students' skills, strategies and work as they unfold. In contrast, product assessments focus on what students produce as a result of a literacy activity. Often most attention is given to product assessments, especially with answers to test items, and this creates an imbalance that favours content knowledge assessment at the expense of informing about actual learning processes (Afflerbach, 2007). In contrast, a process-oriented literacy assessment focuses more on thinking skills and strategies that students use to construct meaning in real-world literacy activities. Thus, some assessment procedures should involve a metacognitive perspective by focusing on the literacy learner's own thinking processes (Isreal et al., 2005).

Feedback

Feedback from students is habitually a neglected source of information: they are often the best ones to ask about how they are thinking and usually have surprising insights about their own learning abilities. For example, when you observe a student re-reading a sentence to clarify meaning, you are observing a metacognitive process. Asking the student to explain their thinking reveals the particular skills and strategies that work or do not work as your student attempts to construct meanings. Consequently, a metacognitive focus will highlight the process of learning rather than the learning products or learning artefacts. Assessment examples that focus on metacognitive processes are reading inventories and conferences (Afflerbach, 2007; Clay, 1993). The use of think-aloud protocols is also an effective metacognitive assessment tool popularised by Ericsson and Simon (1984) (see also Beck et al., 2015). It involves students articulating their thought processes at particular points in time during a learning activity so that the thinking processes become more explicit.

A metacognitive assessment should determine how learners use declarative and procedural knowledge as well as conditional (Borkowski and Muthukrishna, 1992; Manset-Williamson and Nelson, 2005). Reflective knowledge generated through various types of self-evaluation is a form of self-assessment. Finally, it is important for the learner to demonstrate adaptive knowledge: does the student know how to combine or adapt practices or techniques to realise a learning need or goal (Gambrell et al., 2007)?

You can support literacy learning by providing timely and effective feedback. Effective performance feedback contributes to the student's sense of security, self-efficacy and confidence, which then encourages the learner to take more risks and to attempt unfamiliar tasks (Hattie and Timperley, 2007). Of course, the aim of performance feedback is to guide the student and eventually reduce the dependence on external feedback as they become more capable, confident and self-regulatory. It is important to focus on student strengths when providing performance feedback rather than on their weaknesses. For example what strategies did they use effectively? How did they successfully negotiate a difficulty? Negative feedback combined with low expectations can be quite damaging to the student's academic and social development. On the other hand, expectations that are too high or unattainable can be frustrating and will often stifle academic performance.

Feedback in the form of nebulous praise can often be problematic. For example, 'Good boy!' or 'Well done!' does not provide adequate feedback but may actually be counterproductive because the student may perceive it as being condescending, meaningless or manipulative. The message that is given to the student may be perceived as, 'Oh, she says that to everyone' or 'She just expects me to do what she wants'. Rather, feedback should be immediate, specific and be related to the student's own performance. In particular, you should avoid comparing the learner's performance with that of their peers. Specific feedback is much more effective when it provides information about a student's actual performance (Hattie and Timperley, 2007).

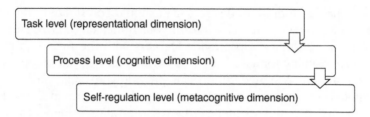

Figure 12.1 Levels of feedback (see also Chapter 3)

Hattie and Timperley (2007) have identified three levels of effective feedback: task level, process level and self-regulation level (see Figure 12.1). Firstly, feedback can be directed at the task or product and can be directed at acquiring more, different or correct information. Process feedback is aimed at the actual processing of information or the understandings and skills needed to learn from the task. The third level of feedback is directed at the self-regulatory process.

Frequent feedback will enable you to adapt your instruction to target students' learning needs, while providing your students with information to develop their skills. What's more, by emphasising the process, effort and strategies involved in accomplishing a task, as opposed to focusing solely on the final product, students come to understand that learning is the result of cumulative effort. This, in turn, improves their resilience, self-regulated learning and academic achievement (Dweck, 1975).

A broader view

What is certain is that progress in literacy involves an interaction between the learner, the task and the learning activity. The implication for educators is to shift the focus of their assessment activities away from sole emphasis on deficits within the learner in favour of a much broader examination of the learner within his/her learning and social contexts. This broader focus should lead to the incorporation of assessment activities tailored to the child's individual learning strengths and needs. What is important is the realisation that progress in literacy may be the result of a combination of factors that include reader proficiency, problems within the text and heavy task demands. Thus, assessment should consider all of these factors filtered within the broader socio-cultural context. Although assessment of adolescent learners is a complex issue, teacher ratings have been shown to be a cost-effective and relatively efficient method for early identification of students who are at high risk of literacy failure (Gresham and MacMillan, 1997; Hecht and Greenfield, 2001; Quay and Steele, 1998).

While your classroom-based assessment should contribute to the gathering of valuable information that can inform your understanding of students and your instruction, it must also provide learners with the means to eventually assume responsibility for assessing their own literacy development. A teacher or teacher/student-designed rubric can provide the means for students to check their own progress towards a particular performance level and to routinely practice self-assessment. When you require students to self-assess you do not give up your responsibility to conduct valuable classroom-based literacy assessments, rather, you look for opportunities to help students learn to become self-supporting learners (Afflerbach, 2007).

You could make a rubric using similar questions to the ones below so that the students have a tangible guide as to how they can self-assess while doing a reading activity.

- Have I checked to see if what I have read/written/designed makes sense?
- Did I remind myself why I am reading/writing/designing?
- Did I focus on the goal of my endeavours while I was reading/writing/designing?
- Did I check to see if I could identify the main ideas?
- Did I ask myself if there are any problems if the reading/writing/designing becomes difficult?
- Did I try to identify the problem?
- Did I try to fix the problem?
- When the problem was fixed, did I get back to the task and make sure I understood what I read/wrote/designed?

Assessment of teaching and pedagogical practices

What is increasingly clear from research is that the teacher is the most crucial factor in the classroom. The teacher who is knowledgeable and able to combine and adjust various methods, practices and strategies to meet the needs of a particular group of students with a differentiated set of needs is most likely to lead students to higher levels of literacy engagement and achievement. Effective teachers are empowered when they identify and select evidence-based literacy practices to create integrated instructional approaches that adapt to the diversity of needs of their students. As a professional teacher you should routinely and systematically assess your teaching (Lipson and Wixson, 2009). However, for assessment of teaching to be effective, evidence-based best teaching practices should be strategically implemented and evaluated (Gambrell et al., 2007).

In Table 12.1 is a practitioner-designed rubric to be used as an instrument to evaluate teaching. A rubric such as this can easily be made into a checklist to be used by yourself or a colleague. It is often a good idea to ask a colleague to use the rubric while observing one of each other's lessons from time to time.

Table 12.1 Teacher self-assessment rubric (Woolley, 2014a)

Participation	Attention	Are all students focused on the literacy activities?
	Engagement	Are the students deeply absorbed in the literacy lesson/task?
	Stimulation	Do I motivate interest in literacy tasks, concepts and learning?
	Pleasure	Do I create an enthusiastic and energetic literacy classroom?
	Consistency	Do I use strong literacy routines that are recognised and understood by the students?
	Environment	Do I use a literate physical environment as a teaching resource?
	Purpose	Do the students' responses indicate tacit or explicit understanding of the purpose of the literacy task?
	Substance	Does the lesson/task lead to substantial literacy engagement?
Knowledge	Explanations	Are explanations of literacy concepts and skills clear and at an appropriate level?
	Modelling	Do the demonstrations of literacy tasks include metacognitive explanations?
	Metalanguage	Are students provided with language for talking about and exemplifying literacy concepts?
	Awareness	Do I show a high level of awareness of literacy activities and participation by students?
Orchestration	Structure	Have I made the environment predictable and orderly?
	Flexibility	Do I respond to learning opportunities that arise in the flow of literacy lessons?
	Pace	Do I provide strong forward momentum in literacy lessons?
	Transition	Is there a productive use of transitions?
	Assessment	Do I show the use of fine-grained knowledge of the student's performance in planning and teaching?
Support	Scaffolding	Do I extend student's literacy learning through modelling, modifying, correcting?
	Feedback	Do I give timely, focused and explicit literacy feedback to students?
	Responsiveness	Do I share and build on students' literacy contributions?
	Explicitness	Word-level – Do I direct students' attention to explicit word and sound strategies?
	Explicitness	Text-level – Do I make explicit specific attributes of a text?
	Persistence	Do I provide many opportunities to practise and master new literacy learning?

(Continued)

Table 12.1 (Continued)

Differentiation	Challenge	Do I extend and promote higher levels of thinking in literacy learning?
	Individualisation	Do I differentiate literacy instruction and show recognition of individual differences?
	Inclusion	Do I facilitate the inclusion of all students in the literacy lessons?
	Variation	Is my literacy teaching often structured around groups or individuals?
	Connection	Are connections often made between class and community literacy-related knowledge?
	Warmth	Am I welcoming and positive and is my classroom inviting and focused on literacy learning?
	Rapport	Does my relationship with the students support tactful literacy interventions?
	Credibility	Do I elicit respect that enables me to overcome any challenges to order and lesson flow?
	Citizenship	Do I encourage equality, tolerance, inclusivity and awareness of the needs of others?
	Independence	Do I make sure that the students take some responsibility for their own literacy learning?

Vignette 12.1

Ms Ryder was a keen teacher that wanted the very best for her students so she used the above rubric (Table 12.1) to self-assess her teaching.

Questions

1   Why is it a good idea to use something like this rubric?
2   What are the pros and cons about having another teacher use the rubric to observe your teaching? How would you feel about this?
3   How else could you reflect upon your teaching?

Assessment supporting students' success

In Chapter 4 project-based learning was discussed as a pedagogical practice that is gaining in popularity because it utilises many of the skills needed for the twenty-first century. However, many teachers will be unsure as to how to assess this methodology as it gives students the opportunity to answer a problem in more ways than one (Hernandez, 2016). For example, students might write a plan for their PBL research project. As part of this plan they may be required to list the questions they will need to address and sources of information they will need before accessing the library or conducting their Internet search. You could also ask students to help define the assessment criteria to ensure that they thoroughly understand what will be expected.

Students as well as teachers will need clear benchmarks for evaluating success on PBL tasks. Therefore, the criteria should be defined clearly at the start of a project with guidelines for success, and should include multiple opportunities for feedback, reflection and time for students to revise their work. The criteria should also provide a challenge and you could show exemplars from former successful students and use rubrics to demonstrate how the expected learning outcomes were achieved. When students have clear understanding of the indicators for success and spend time discussing and evaluating content it promotes improved learning outcomes. Researchers also recommend that end goals should reflect professional practices, such as public exhibitions, portfolios and presentations, which signal the social value and relevance of their work (Barron and Darling-Hammond, 2008).

Barron and Darling-Hammond (2008) recommend assessing these six items:

1. use of evidence
2. accuracy of information
3. evaluation of competing views
4. development of a clear argument
5. attention to writing conventions
6. collaboration.

Vignette 12.2

Mr Hay and Ms Johnson took a group of Year 9 history and English students on a week-long trip to New Zealand to learn about the country's Indigenous culture and history. The task was to produce a documentary. After the trip the students edited the short documentary and posted it on YouTube. The students posted it publicly to YouTube and received comments from a wide audience including some students from the Maori community in New Zealand. The authentic feedback from the Indigenous population profoundly affected the filmmakers making them aware of what was effective, what was overlooked and what impact the film had.

Questions

1 What skills do you think were needed in this project?
2 How do you think that it could be assessed?
3 Is there a place for peer assessment in high-school education?
4 What other way could a teacher elicit peer feedback in the classroom?

Differentiation through project-based learning

Project-based learning naturally lends itself to differentiated learning and assessment because it is essentially a student-centred and student-driven learning process. Andrew Miller (2016) suggests six ways to differentiate project-based learning:

1. Differentiate through teams. One way to differentiate is by grouping according to readability levels, for developing collaboration skills, academic skill levels or grouping according to interest.
2. Reflection and goal setting. Throughout the project the students are expected to be reflecting on their goals and setting further goals for future learning. The teacher can then set learning activities to support what they want or need to know.
3. Mini-lessons, centres and resources. Some students may benefit from mini-lessons designed to improve skills and knowledge that they need for the project.
4. Voice and choice in products. The teacher should allow choice of how the students are summatively assessed by allowing choice of products.
5. Formative assessments. While students are able to choose the products they can also be assessed on the processes, e.g. collaboration. This can feed forward in that they can identify elements that need improving.
6. Balance teamwork and individual work. Not all work will need to be cooperative or group based – there may be times that students are able to work on their own.

Self-determination theory (SDT) posits that a critical issue in goal pursuit and attainment is the degree to which students are able to satisfy their basic psychological needs as they pursue and attain outcomes (Ryan and Deci, 2000). According to SDT, individuals have a natural tendency towards enhancing their human potential when basic psychological needs of autonomy, competence and relatedness are met (Curry et al., 2016) (see Chapter 4).

Informing and involving parents

Assessment data should be communicated regularly to students to inform them about what they are achieving at school to help them improve their learning. Parents also need to know how their children are progressing and how their child can best be helped.

Conclusion

Assessment is an ongoing and multifaceted process that is essential for good teaching as it informs and drives instruction. It focuses on the learner but also considers the learning context, pedagogy and the instructional processes. It requires you to assess data from many formal and informal measures and observations. Virtually any activity can be used for assessment but should be evaluated in light of a range of other sources of evidence. An important, but often neglected, aspect of assessment is the notion of self-evaluation because it leads to self-supporting behaviours, both for teachers and students. It is important also for you as their teacher, to monitor your own teaching content and methods so you can make the necessary improvements to teaching along with appropriate changes to the curriculum.

Discussion questions and activities

 ## Questions

1 How can teachers access data to assess their students' progress? Make a list and beside each item note the pros and cons.
2 How has assessment changed over time since you started your school life?
3 Use Google to search for 'reciprocal teaching' procedure and discuss how you could design a rubric to assess the student performance.

♱♱♱♱ Group activities

1 Discuss the importance of setting a goal before an assessment activity.
2 Go to www.readabilityformulas.com/fry-graph-readability-formula.php and assess the readability of a reading passage that learners are likely to read. Discuss the pros and cons in using the formula to grade a book or article.
3 In groups design a cloze procedure and discuss its effective use for the purpose of self-evaluation.
4 Why do you think that the think-aloud protocol enables you to gain an understanding of the process of learning?
5 In groups of three discuss how you could use the think-aloud protocol to enhance self-evaluation with the procedure.

Whole class activity

1 Divide into groups of about eight and design a rubric to assess a writing activity (report, exposition, narrative, etc.).
2 Observe a video of a teaching method that could be used in the literacy classroom. Ask the class to brainstorm how the activity can be used as an assessment activity. Design a rubric to guide the teacher as to what data can be obtained from the activity.
3 Simulate a parent/teacher interview and report the progress of the fictitious student to the caregivers using a set of assessment data. This could be conducted as a fishbowl activity with some of the participants role-playing while the rest of the group observe. At the end of the role-play conduct a discussion about how assessment data should be communicated to parents.

REFERENCES

ACARA (Australian Curriculum, Assessment and Reporting Authority) (2012a) *The Australian Curriculum: Information and Communication Technology (ICT) Capability*. Sydney: ACARA. Retrieved from: www.australiancurriculum.edu.au/GeneralCapabilities/Information-and-Communication-Technology-capability/ (accessed 8 December 2016).

ACARA (Australian Curriculum, Assessment and Reporting Authority) (2012b) *Literacy: General Capability*. Sydney: ACARA.

ACARA (Australian Curriculum, Assessment and Reporting Authority) (2014) *Foundation to Year 10 Curriculum: Language, Language for Interaction* (ACELA1428). Retrieved from: www.australiancurriculum.edu.au/english/curriculum/f-10?layout=1 (accessed 8 December 2016).

ACARA (Australian Curriculum, Assessment and Reporting Authority) (2015) *The Australian Curriculum: Information and Communication Technology (ICT) Capability*. Sydney: ACARA.

Addison, J.T. (1992) Urie Bronfenbrenner. *Human Ecology*, 20(2), 16–20.

Afflerbach, P. (2007) Best practices in literacy assessment. In L.B. Gambrell, L.M. Morrow, and M. Pressley (eds), *Best Practices in Literacy Instruction* (3rd edn). New York: The Guilford Press, pp. 264–282.

Afflerbach, P., Pearson, D. and Paris, S.G. (2008) Clarifying differences between reading skills and reading strategies. *The Reading Teacher*, 61(5), 364–373.

Afflerbach, P., Kim, J., Crassas, M.E. and Cho, B. (2011) Best practices in literacy assessment. In L.B. Gambrell and L.M. Morrow (eds), *Best Practices in Literacy Instruction* (4th edn). New York: The Guilford Press, pp. 319–340.

Ainscow, M. and Sandhill, A. (2010) Developing inclusive education systems: The role of organizational cultures and leadership. *International Journal of Inclusive Education*, 14, 410–416.

Alexander, R. (ed.) (2010) *Children, their World, their Education: Final Report and Recommendations of the Cambridge Primary Review.* Oxon: Routledge.

Alfassi, M. (2004) Reading to learn: Effects of combined strategy instruction on high school students. *The Journal of Educational Research*, 97, 171–184.

Allen, L.K., Snow, E.L., Crossley, S.A., Jackson, G.T. and McNamara, D.S. (2014) Reading comprehension components and their relation to writing. *Topics in Cognitive Psychology*, 114, 663–691.

Allender, T. and Freebody, P. (2016) Disciplinary and idiomatic literacy: Re-living and re-working the past in senior school history. *Australian Journal of Language and Literacy*, 39(1), 7–19.

Allington, R.L. (2012) *What Really Matters for Struggling Readers: Designing Research-based Programs* (3rd edn). Boston: Pearson-Allyn-Bacon.

Alloway, T. (2011) *Improving Working Memory: Supporting Students' Learning.* London: Sage.

Alloway, N., Freebody, P., Gilbert, P. and Muspratt, S. (2002) *Boys and Literacy: Expanding the Repertoires of Practice.* Australia: DEST Commonwealth of Australia.

Alvermann, D. (2001) Reading adolescents' reading identities: Looking back to see ahead. *Journal of Adolescent and Adult Literacy*, 44(8), 676–690.

Anastopoulou, S., Baber, C. and Sharples, M. (2001) Multimedia and multimodal systems: Commonalities and differences. In *5th Human Centred Technology Postgraduate Workshop, University of Sussex.* Retrieved from: www.syros. aegean.gr/users/manast/Pubs/Pub_conf/C03/C03.pdf (accessed 8 December 2016).

Anderson, L.W. and Krathwohl, D.R. (2001) *A Taxonomy for Learning, Teaching and Assessing* (abridged edn). Boston, MA: Allyn and Bacon.

Anstey, M. (2002) *Literate Futures: Reading, 2002.* Australia: Education Queensland: AccessEd.

Anstey, M. and Bull, G. (2010) Helping teachers to explore multimodal texts. *Curriculum & Leadership Journal*, 8(16). Retrieved from: www.curriculum.edu. au/leader/helping_teachers_to_explore_multimodal_texts,31522.html?issue ID=12141 (accessed 22 November 2016).

Atweh, B. and Singh, P. (2011) The Australian curriculum: Continuing the national conversation. *Australian Journal of Education*, 55(3), 189–196.

Au, K. (1998) Social constructivism and the school literacy learning of students of diverse backgrounds. *Journal of Literacy Research*, 30(2), 297–319.

August, D. and Shanahan, T. (eds) (2006) *Developing Literacy in Second-Language Learners: Report of the National Literacy Panel on Language Minority Children and Youth.* Malwah, NJ: Lawrence Erlbaum Associates.

Australian Bureau of Statistics (ABS) (2014) *Household Use of Information Technology, Australia, 2012–13* (Catalogue No. 8146.0). Canberra: ABS.

Australian Government (n.d.) *Family–School Partnerships Framework: A Guide for Schools and Families.* Department of Education, Employment and Workplace Relations. Retrieved from: www.familyschool.org.au/files/3013/8451/8364/Family-school_partnerships_framework.pdf (accessed 22 November 2016).

Baddeley, A.D. and Hitch, G. (1994) Developments in the concept of working memory. *Neuropsychology*, 8, 485–493.

Bain, J.D., Ballantyne, R., Mills, C. and Lester, N.C. (2002) *Reflecting on Practice: Student Teachers' Perspectives*. Flaxton: Post Pressed.

Ball, A.F. and Freedman, S.W. (2004) *Bakhtinian Perspectives on Language, Literacy and Learning*. Cambridge: Cambridge University Press.

Barron, B. and Darling-Hammond, L. (2008) *Teaching for Meaningful Learning: A Review of Research on Inquiry-based and Cooperative Learning*. Retrieved from: www.edutopia.org/pdfs/edutopia-teaching-for-meaningful-learning.pdf (accessed 21 November 2016).

Bartlett, F.C. (1932) *Remembering: A Study in Experimental and Social Psychology*. New York: Cambridge University Press.

Barton, D. (1994) *Literacy: An Introduction to the Ecology of Written Language*. Oxford: Blackwell Publishing.

Barton, D. and Hamilton, M. (1998) *Local Literacies: Reading and Writing in One Community*. London: Routledge.

Barton, D., Hamilton, M. and Ivanic, R. (eds) (2000) *Situated Literacies: Reading and Writing in Context*. London and New York: Routledge.

Barton, G.M. (2003) Student preference for learning: Investigating the notion of music literacy. In K. Hartwig and G. Barton (eds), *Artistic Practice as Research: Proceedings of the XXVth Annual Conference*. Brisbane: Australian Association for Research in Music Education, pp. 15–24.

Barton, G.M. (2014) The arts and literacy: Interpretation and expression of symbolic form. In G.M. Barton (ed.), *Literacy in the Arts: Retheorising Learning and Teaching*. Switzerland: Springer International Publishing, pp. 3–20.

Barton, G.M. and Bahr, N. (2013) Perspectives on schooling from early adolescent video diaries. *The International Journal of Technologies in Learning*, 19(4), 63–75.

Barton, G.M. and McKay, L. (2015) *Using Arts-based Methods to Improve Adolescent Literacy Learning*. Fremantle: Australian Association for Research in Education.

Barton, G.M. and McKay, L. (2016a) An effective model of reading instruction for adolescent learners: A collaborative approach. *Australian Journal of Language and Literacy*, 39(2), 162–175.

Barton, G.M. and McKay, L. (2016b) Conceptualising a literacy education model for Junior Secondary students: The spatial practices of an Australian school. *English in Australia*, 51(1), 37–45.

Barton, G.M. and Unsworth, L. (2014) Music, multiliteracies and multimodality: Exploring the book and movie versions of Shaun Tan's *The Lost Thing*. *Australian Journal of Language and Literacy*, 37(1), 3–20.

Barton, G.M., Arnold, J. and Trimble-Roles, R. (2015) Writing practices today and in the future: Multimodal and creative text composition in the 21st century. In J. Turbill, G.M. Barton and C. Brock (eds), *Teaching Writing in Today's Classrooms: Looking Back to Look Forward*. ALEA occasional publication.

Bayliss, D.M., Jarrold, C., Baddeley, A.D. and Leigh, E. (2005) Differential constraints on the working memory and reading abilities of individuals with learning difficulties and typically developing children. *Journal of Experimental Child Psychology*, 92, 76–99.

Beach, R. (1998) Constructing real and text worlds in responding to literature. *Theory into Practice*, 37(3), 176–185.

Beavis, C. (2012) Video games in the classroom: Developing digital literacies. *Practically Primary*, 17(1), 17–20.

Beavis, C., Muspratt, S. and Thompson, R. (2015) 'Computer games can get your brain working': Student experience and perceptions of digital games in the classroom. *Learning, Media and Technology*, 40(1), 21–42.

Beck, S.W., Llosa, L., Black, K. and Trzeszkowski-Giese, A. (2015) Beyond the rubric: Think-alouds as a diagnostic assessment tool for high school writing teachers. *Journal of Adolescent and Adult Literacy*, 58(8), 670–681.

Bender, W.N. (2002) Supporting students through performance monitoring. In *Differentiating Instruction for Students with Learning Disabilities*. Thousand Oaks, CA: Corwin, pp. 115–139.

Benware, C.A. and Deci, E.L. (1984) Quality of learning with an active versus passive motivational set. *American Educational Research Journal*, 21(4), 755–765.

Biggs, J. (1978) Individual and group differences in study processes. *British Journal of Educational Psychology*, 48(3), 266–279.

Blachowicz, C.L.Z., Fisher, P.J.L., Ogle, D. and Watts-Taffe, S. (2006) Vocabulary: Questions from the classroom. *Reading Research Quarterly*, 41, 524–539.

Black, A. and Bannan, S. (2010) Functional grammar: A change in writer's self-perception. *Practically Primary*, 15(3), 12–17.

Bong, M. (2004) Academic motivation in self-efficacy, task value, achievement goal orientations, and attributional beliefs. *The Journal of Educational Research*, 97, 287–297.

Borkowski, J.G. and Muthukrishna, N. (1992) Moving metacognition into the classroom: 'Working models' and effective strategy teaching. In M. Pressley, K.R. Harris and J.T. Guthrie (eds), *Promoting Academic Competence and Literacy in School*. Toronto: Academic Press, pp. 477–501.

Boss, S. (2015) *Implementing Project-based Learning*. Bloomington: Solution Tree Press.

Braden, S., Wassell, B.A., Scantlebury, K. and Grover, A. (2016) Supporting language learners in science classrooms: Insights from middle school English language learner students. *Language and Education*, 30(5), 438–458.

Brinthaupt, T.M. and Lipka, R.P. (2002) *Understanding Early Adolescent Self and Identity: Applications and Interventions*. New York: State University of New York Press.

Bronfenbrenner, U. (1990) Discovering what families do. In D. Blankenhorn, S. Bayme and J. Bethke Elshtain (eds), *Rebuilding the Nest: A New Commitment to the American Family*. Milwaukee, WI: Family Service America.

Bronfenbrenner, U. (1992) *Ecological Systems Theory*. London: Jessica Kingsley Publishers.

Bronfenbrenner, U. (1994) Ecological models of human development. In *International Encyclopedia of Education*, Vol. 3 (2nd edn). Oxford: Elsevier.

Brooks, A.W. (2015) Using connectivism to guide information literacy instruction with tablets. *Journal of Information Literacy*, 9(2), 27–36.

Bruner, J. (1985) Narrative and paradigmatic modes of thought. *Teachers College Record*, 86(6), 97–115.

Cain, K. and Oakhill, J. (2006) Assessment matters: Issues in the measurement of reading comprehension. *British Journal of Educational Psychology*, 76, 697–708.

Cain, K. and Oakhill, J. (2007) Reading comprehension difficulties: Correlates, causes, and consequences. In K. Cain and J. Oakhill (eds), *Children's Comprehension Problems in Oral and Written Language: A Cognitive Perspective*. London: The Guilford Press, pp. 41–75.

Cairney, T. (2000) The construction of literacy and literacy learners. *Language Arts*, 77(6), 496–505.

Cairney, T.H. (2002) Bridging home and school literacy: In search of transformative approaches to curriculum. *Early Child Development and Care*, 172(2), 153–172.

Cairney, T. (2016) Building effective relationships between home, school and communities. In J. Scull and B. Raban (eds), *Growing Up Literate: Australian Literacy Research for Practice*. Australia: Eleanor Curtain Publishers, pp. 239–255.

Carroll, L. (1871) *Alice's Adventures in Wonderland and Through the Looking-Glass*. London: Macmillan and Co.

Carter, R. and Long, M. (eds) (1991) *Teaching Literature*. London: Longman.

Catts, H.W. (2009) The narrow view of reading promotes a broad view of comprehension. *Language, Speech & Hearing Services in Schools*, 40(2), 178–183.

Chandra, V. (2014) Developing students' technological literacy through robotics activities. *Literacy Learning: The Middle Years*, 22(3), 24–29.

Christie, F. and Derewianka, B. (2008) *School Discourse: Learning to Write Across the School Years*. London: Continuum.

Clandfield, L. (2003) Teaching materials: Using literature in the EFL/ESL classroom. *One Stop English*. Retrieved from: www.onestopenglish.com/methodology/methodology/teaching-materials/teaching-materials-using-literature-in-the-efl/-esl-classroom/146508.article (accessed 24 November 2016).

Clary, D., Kigotho, M. and Barros-Torning, M. (2013) Harnessing mobile technologies to enrich adolescents' multimodal literacy practices in middle years classrooms. *Literacy Learning: The Middle Years*, 21(3), 49.

Clay, M.M. (1993) *Reading Recovery*. Portsmouth: Heinemann.

Clerke, S. (2013) *Partnering for School Improvement: Case Studies of School–Community Partnerships in Australia*. Victoria, Australia: Australian Council for Educational Research.

Cloeren, H. (1988) *Language and Thought*. Berlin: Walter de Gruyter.

Cloonan, A. (2011) Creating multimodal metalanguage with teachers. *English Teaching*, 10(4), 23–40. Retrieved from: http://files.eric.ed.gov/fulltext/EJ962603.pdf (accessed 22 November 2016).

Coccamise, D. and Snyder, L. (2005) Theory and pedagogical practices of text comprehension. *Topics in Language Disorders*, 25, 5–20.

Cole, J.E. (2002) What motivates students to read? Four literacy personalities. *The Reading Teacher*, 56, 326–336.

Comber, B. (2012) Mandated literacy assessment and the reorganization of teachers' work: Federal policy, local effects. *Critical Studies in Education*, 53(2), 119–136.

Comber, B., Badger, L., Barnett, J. and Nixon, H. (2002) Literacy after the early years: A longitudinal study. *Australian Journal of Language and Literacy*, 25(2), 9–23.

Cope, B. and Kalantzis, M. (eds) (2000) *Multiliteracies: Literacy Learning and the Design of Social Futures*. London and New York: Routledge.

Corntassel, J. (2009) Indigenous storytelling, truth-telling, and community approaches to reconciliation. *ESC*, 35(1), 137–159.

Cortiella, C. and Horowitz, S.H. (2014) *The State of Learning Disabilities: Facts, Trends and Emerging Issues*. New York: National Center for Learning Disabilities.

Cox, K. and Guthrie, J.T. (2001) Motivational and cognitive contributions to students' amount of reading. *Contemporary Educational Psychology*, 26, 116–131.

Craik, F.I.M. and Lockhart, R.S. (1972) Levels of processing: A framework for memory research. *Journal of Verbal Learning and Verbal Behaviour*, 11, 671–684.

Cremin, T., Mottram, M., Collins, F., Powell, S. and Drury, R. (2015) *Researching Literacy Lives: Building Communities Between Home and School*. Oxon and New York: Routledge Publishers.

Crossley, S., Roscoe, R. and McNamara, D. (2013) Using automatic scoring models to detect changes in student writing in an intelligent tutoring system. *Proceedings of the Twenty-Sixth International Florida Artificial Intelligence Research Society Conference*. Florida: Florida Artificial Intelligence Research Society.

Csikszentmihalyi, M. (1997) *Creativity: Flow and the Psychology of Discovery and Invention*. New York: Harpers Collins.

CSUS (n.d.) *Schema Theory*. Retrieved from: www.csus.edu/indiv/g/gipej/teaparty.pdf (accessed 8 December 2016).

Culican, S., Emmitt, M. and Oakley, C. (2001) *Literacy and Learning in the Middle Years: Major Report of the Middle Years Literacy Research Project*. Melbourne: Deakin University (commissioned through DETYA by DEET, CECV, AISV, Victoria).

Cunningham, A.E. and Stanovich, K. (2001) What reading does for the mind. *Journal of Direct Instruction*, 1(2), 137–149.

Currie, N.K. and Cain, K. (2015) Children's inference generation: The role of vocabulary and working memory. *Journal of Experimental Child Psychology*, 137, 57–75.

Curry, K.A., Mwavvita, M., Holter, A. and Harris, E. (2016) Getting assessment right at the classroom level: Using formative assessment for decision making. *Educational Assessment, Evaluation and Accountability*, 28, 89–104.

Dael, N., Goudbeek, M. and Scherer, K.R. (2013) Perceived gesture dynamics in nonverbal expression of emotion. *Perception*, 42, 642–657.

Daneman, M. and Carpenter, P.A. (1980) Individual differences in working memory and reading. *Journal of Verbal Learning and Verbal Behaviour*, 19, 450–466.

Darling-Hammond, L. (2010) *Performance Counts: Assessment Systems that Support High-quality Learning*. Washington, DC: Council of Chief State School Officers. Retrieved from: www.ccsso.org/Documents/2010/Performance_Counts_Assessment_Systems_2010.pdf (accessed 24 November 2016).

De Bono, E. (1976) *Teaching Thinking*. London: Temple Smith.

Department of Education and Science (1975) *A Language for Life* (The Bullock Report). London: HMSO.

Derewianka, B. (2012) Knowledge about language in the Australian curriculum: English. *Australian Journal of Language and Literacy*, 35(2), 127–146.

Derewianka, B. (2015) The contribution of genre theory to literacy education in Australia. In J. Turbill, G. Barton and C. Brock (eds), *Teaching Writing in Today's Classrooms: Looking Back to Looking Forward*. Norwood, Australia: Australian Literary Educators' Association, pp. 69–86.

Dinsmore, D. and Alexander, P.A. (2012) A critical discussion of deep and surface processing: What it means, how it is measured, the role of context, and model specification. *Educational Psychology Review*, 24, 499–567.

Droop, M. and Verhoeven, L. (2003) Language proficiency and reading ability in first- and second-language learners. *Reading Research Quarterly*, 38(1), 78–103.

Duke, N.K. and Pearson, P.D. (2002) Effective practices for developing reading comprehension. In A.E. Farstrup and S.J. Samuels (eds), *What Research Has to Say About Reading Instruction* (3rd edn). Newark, DE: International Reading Association, pp. 205–242.

Dweck, C.S. (1975) The role of expectations and attributions in the alleviation of learned helplessness. *Journal of Personality and Social Psychology*, 31, 674–685.

Elliott, D. (2014) Levelling the playing field: Engaging disadvantaged students through game-based pedagogy. *Literacy Learning: The Middle Years*, 22(2), 34–40.

Ellis, R. and Simons, R.F. (2005) The impact of music on subjective and psychological indices of emotion while viewing films. *Psychomusicology*, 19, 15–40.

Epstein, J.L., Sanders, M.G., Simon, B.S., Salinas, K.C., Jansorn, N.R. and Van Voorhis, F.L. (2002) *School, Family, and Community Partnerships: Your Handbook for Action* (2nd edn). Thousand Oaks, CA: Corwin.

Ericsson, K.A. and Simon, H.A. (1984) *Protocol Analysis: Verbal Reports as Data*. Cambridge, MA: MIT Press.

Ewing, R., Miller, C. and Saxton, J. (2008) Drama and contemporary picture books in the middle years. In J. Hughes, M. Anderson and J. Manuel (eds), *Drama Teaching in English: Imagination, Action and Engagement*. Melbourne: Oxford University Press, pp. 121–135.

Exley, B. (2010) Edgy texts in edgy communities: Social and narrative genres. *Practically Primary*, 15(3), 3–6.

Fairclough, N. (1989) *Language and Power*. London: Longman.

Farrell, L., Davidson, M., Hunter, M. and Osenga, T. (2010) The simple view of reading. Centre for Development and Learning. Retrieved from: www.cdl.org/articles/the-simple-view-of-reading/ (accessed 22 November 2016).

Fielding-Barnsley, R., Hay, I. and Ashman, A. (2005) Phonological awareness: Necessary but not sufficient. National Conference of the Australian Association of Special Education, Brisbane, Australia, 23–25 September.

Fisher, D. and Frey, N. (2003) *Better Learning Through Structured Teaching: A Framework for the Gradual Release of Responsibility*. Alexandria, VA: ASCD.

Freebody, P. (2007) *Literacy Education in School: Research Perspectives from the Past, for the Future*. Canberra, Australia: Australian Council for Educational Research.

Freebody, P. (2015) Ignorance killed the cat: What's left out of literacy research and policy: Implications for teachers' knowledge and practice. Keynote presentation at the *Australian Literacy Educators' Association Annual Conference*, Canberra, July, 2015.

Freebody, P. and Freiberg, J. (2001) Re-discovering practical reading activities in homes and schools. *Journal of Research in Reading*, 24, 222–234.

Freebody, P. and Luke, A. (1990) Literacies programs: Debates and demands in cultural context. *Prospect*, 5, 7–16.

Freebody, P. and Muspratt, S. (2007) Beyond generic knowledge in pedagogy and disciplinarity: The case of science textbooks. *Pedagogies: An International Journal*, 2(1), 35–48.

Freebody, P., Chan, E. and Barton, G.M. (2013) Literacy and curriculum: Language and knowledge in the classroom. In Cremin, T., Comber, B., Hall, K. and Moll, L. (eds), *International Handbook of Research in Children's Literacy, Learning and Culture*. Malden, MA: Wiley-Blackwell, pp. 304–318.

Freebody, P., Maton, K. and Martin, J.R. (2008) Talk, text and knowledge in cumulative, integrated learning. *Australian Journal of Language and Literacy*, 31, 188–201.

Fullan, M.G. (1993) Why teachers must become change agents. *The Professional Teacher*, 50(6), 12–17.

Fullan, M., Hill, P. and Crévola, C. (2006) *Breakthrough*. Thousand Oaks, CA: Corwin.

Gambrell, L.B., Kapinus, B.A. and Wilson, R.M. (1987) Using mental imagery and summarization to achieve independence in comprehension. *Journal of Reading*, 30, 638–642.

Gambrell, L.B., Malloy, J.A. and Mazzoni, S.A. (2007) Evidence-based best practice for comprehensive literacy instruction. In L.B. Gambrell, L.M. Morrow and M. Pressley (eds), *Best Practices in Literacy Instruction* (3rd edn). New York: The Guilford Press, pp. 11–29.

Gambrell, L.B., Mazzoni, S.A. and Almasi, J.F. (2000) Promoting collaboration, social interaction, and engagement. In L. Baker, M.J. Dreher and J.T. Guthrie (eds), *Engaging Young Readers: Promoting Achievement and Motivation*. New York: Guilford Press, pp. 119–139.

Garcia, J.R., Bustos, A. and Sanches, E. (2015) The contribution of knowledge about anaphors, organisational signals and refutations to reading comprehension. *Journal of Research in Reading*, 38(4), 405–427.

Gargiulo, R.M. and Metcalf, D. (2013) *Teaching in Today's Classrooms: A Universal Design for Learning Approach* (2nd edn). Belmont, CA: Wadsworth, Cengage Learning.

Gee, J.P. (1996) *Social Linguistics and Literacies: Ideology in Discourses*. London and Bristol, PA: Taylor & Francis.

Gee, J.P. (1999) *An Introduction to Discourse Analysis: Theory and Method*. London: Routledge.

Gersten, R., Fuchs, L.S., Williams, J.P. and Baker, S. (2001) Teaching reading comprehension strategies to students with learning disabilities: A review of research. *Review of Educational Research*, 71, 279–320.

Giedd, J.N. (2015) The amazing teen brain: A mismatch in the maturation of brain networks leaves adolescents open to risky behaviour but also allows for leaps in cognition and adaptability. *Scientific American*, 312(6), 32–37.

Goldman, S.R. and Snow, C.E. (2015) Adolescent literacy: Development and instruction. In A. Pollatsek and R. Treiman (eds), *The Oxford Handbook of Reading*. Oxford: Oxford University Press, pp. 463–478.

Goldsworthy, C. (2010) *Linking the Strands of Language and Literacy: A Resource Manual*. San Diego: Plural Publishing.

Gough, P. and Tunmer, W. (1986) Decoding, reading, and reading disability. *Remedial and Special Education*, 7, 6–10.

Graham, S. and Perin, D. (2007) *Writing Next: Effective Strategies to Improve Writing of Adolescents in Middle and High Schools*. A report to Carnegie Corporation of New York. Washington, DC: Alliance for Excellent Education.

Graves, D. (1983) *Writing: Teachers and Children at Work*. Exeter, NH: Heinemann.

Greene, S. (1994) The problems of learning to think like a historian: Writing history in the culture of the classroom. *Educational Psychologist*, 29(2), 89–96.

Gresham, F.M. and MacMillan, D.L. (1997) Teachers as 'tests': Differential validity of teacher judgments in identifying students at risk. *School Psychology Review*, 26, 47–61.

Gundlach, R.H. (1935) Factors determining the characterisation of musical phrases. *The American Journal of Psychology*, 47(4), 624–643.

Gunning, T.G. (2003) The role of readability in today's classrooms. *Topics in Language Disorders*, 23, 175–200.

Gunning, T.G. (2006) *Assessing and Correcting Reading and Writing Difficulties* (4th edn). Boston: Allyn and Bacon.

Guthrie, J.T. and Davis, M.H. (2003) Motivating the struggling readers in middle school through an engagement model of classroom practice. *Reading and Writing Quarterly*, 19, 59–85.

Guthrie, J.T., Cox, K.E., Knowles, K.T., Buehl, M., Mazzoni, S.A. and Fasulo, L. (2000) Building toward coherent instruction. In L. Baker, M.J. Dreher and J.T. Guthrie (eds), *Engaging Young Readers: Promoting Achievement and Motivation*. New York: Guilford Press, pp. 209–236.

Halliday, M. (1973) *Explorations in the Functions of Language*. London: Edward Arnold Publishers.

Halliday, M.A.K. (1978) *Language as Social Semiotic: The Social Interpretation of Language and Meaning*. London: Edward Arnold.

Halliday, M.A.K. (2009) Language and education: Implications for practice. In J.J. Webster (ed.), *The Essential Halliday*. London and New York: Continuum, pp. 216–218.

Hammond, J. (2001) *Scaffolding: Teaching and Learning in Language and Literacy Education*. Newtown, Australia: PETA.

Harasim, L. (2012) *Learning Theory and Online Technologies*. London: Routledge.

Hareli, S. and Weiner, B. (2002) Social emotions and personality inferences: A scaffold for a new direction in the study of achievement motivation. *Educational Psychologist*, 37, 183–193.

Harper, H. and Rennie, J. (2009) I had to go out and get myself a book on grammar: A study of pre-service teachers' knowledge about language. *Australian Journal of Language and Literacy*, 33(1), 22–37.

Harris, K.R. and Pressley, M. (1991) The nature of cognitive strategy instruction: interactive strategy instruction. *Exceptional Adolescents*, 57, 392–404.

Harrison, N. (2011) *Teaching and Learning in Aboriginal Education* (2nd edn). Melbourne: Oxford University Press.

Hartman, G. (1990) Peer learning and support via audio-teleconferencing in continuing education for nurses. *Distance Education*, 11(2), 308–319.

Hattie, J. (2012) *Visible Learning for Teachers*. London: Routledge.

Hattie, J. and Timperley, H. (2007) The power of feedback. *Review of Educational Research*, 77(1), 81–112.

Hay, I., Elias, G., Fielding-Barnsley, R., Homel, R. and Frieberg, K. (2007) Language delays, reading delays and learning difficulties: Interactive elements requiring multidimensional programming. *Journal of Learning Disabilities*, 40, 400–409.

Hayward, E.L. and Hutchinson, C. (2013) 'Exactly what do you mean by consistency?' Exploring concepts of consistency and standards in curriculum for excellence in Scotland. *Assessment in Education: Principles, Policy & Practice*, 20(1), 53–68.

Heath, S.B. (1999) Literacy and social practice. In Wagner, D.A., Venezky, R.L. and Street, B.V. (eds), *Literacy: An International Handbook*. Boulder, CO: Westview Press, pp. 102–106.

Hecht, S.A. and Greenfield, D.B. (2001) Comparing the predictive validity of first grade teacher ratings and reading-related tests on third grade levels of reading skills in young children exposed to poverty. *School Psychology Review*, 30, 50–70.

Hernandez, M. (2016) Evaluating project-based learning. *Edutopia*, June 6. Retrieved from: www.edutopia.org/blog/evaluating-pbl-michael-hernandez (accessed 24 November 2016).

Hill, P. and Crévola, C. (1997) *Key Features of a Whole-School, Design Approach to Literacy Teaching in Schools*. Australia: University of Melbourne.

Hill, S. (2012) *Developing Early Literacy: Teaching and Assessment* (2nd edn). Victoria, Australia: Eleanor Curtain Publishers.

Hinchman, K., Alvermann, D., Boyd, F., Brozo, W. and Vacca, R. (2003) Supporting older students' in- and out-of-school literacies. *Journal of Adolescent and Adult Literacy*, 47(4), 304–310.

Hockly, N. and Dudeney, G. (2014) *Going Mobile: Teaching with Hand-held Devices*. Surrey: Delta Publishing.

Hoogstad, V. and Saxby, M. (1988) *Teaching Literature to Adolescents*. Melbourne: Nelson.

Hoos, H., Renz, K. and Görg, M. (2001) GUIDO/MIR: An experimental musical information retrieval system based on GUIDO music notation. *Proceedings of the 2nd Annual International Symposium on Music Information Retrieval*

(ISMIR 2001), 41–50. Retrieved from: http://ismir2001.indiana.edu/pdf/hoos. pdf (accessed 13 June 2011).

House of Commons (2015) Ofsted Report: *The Annual Report of Her Majesty's Chief Inspector of Education, Children's Services and Skills 2014/15*. London: House of Commons, Crown copyright.

House of Lords Select Committee on Digital Skills (2015) *Make or Break: The UK's Digital Future*. Retrieved from: www.publications.parliament.uk/pa/ld201415/ ldselect/lddigital/111/111.pdf (accessed 24 November 2016).

Hower, A. (2015) To BYOD or not to BYOD? *Reading Today*, 32(4), 16–17.

Hudson, R. and J. Walmsley (2005) The English Patient: English grammar and teaching in the twentieth century, *Journal of Linguistics*, 43(3), 593–622.

Hull, G. and Schultz, K. (eds) (2002) *School's Out: Bridging Out-of-school Literacies with Classroom Practice*. New York: Teachers' College Press.

Humphrey, S., Droga, L. and Feez, S. (2012) *Grammar and Meaning*. Marrickville, NSW: PETAA.

Humphries, J. and Ness, M. (2015) Beyond who, what, where, when, why, and how: Preparing students to generate questions in the age of Common Core Standards. *Journal of Research in Childhood Education*, 29, 551–564.

Hung, W. (2008) The 9-step problem design process for problem-based learning: Application of the 3C3R model. *Educational Research Review*, 4(2), 118–141.

Ibbotson, P. and Tomasello, M. (2016) Evidence rebuts Chomsky's theory of language learning. *Scientific American*, September 7. Retrieved from: www. scientificamerican.com/article/evidence-rebuts-chomsky-s-theory-of-language-learning/ (accessed 22 November 2016).

ICT Literacy Panel (2002) *Digital Transformation: A Framework for ICT Literacy*. Princeton, NJ: Educational Testing Service. Retrieved from: www.ets.org/ Media/Tests/Information_and_Communication_Technology_Literacy/ictreport. pdf (accessed 24 November 2016).

International Reading Association (2012) *Adolescent Literacy: A Position Statement of the International Reading Association*. Newark, DE: International Reading Association. Retrieved from: www.literacyworldwide.org/docs/default-source/ where-we-stand/adolescent-literacy-position-statement.pdf?sfvrsn=8 (accessed 14 November 2016).

Isreal, S.E., Bauserman, K.L. and Block, C.C. (2005) Metacognitive assessment strategies. *Thinking Classroom*, 6(2), 21–28.

Ivanic, R. (2004) Discourses of writing and learning to write. *Language and Education*, 18(3), 220–245.

Jackson, A. and Davis, G. (2000) *Turning Points 2000: Educating Adolescents in the 21st Century*. New York: Teachers' College Press.

Jenkins, J.R., Fuchs, L.S., van den Broek, P., Espin, C. and Deno, S.L. (2003) Sources of individual differences in reading comprehension and reading fluency. *Journal of Educational Psychology*, 95(4), 719–729.

Jewitt, C. (2006) *Technology, Literacy and Learning: A Multimodal Approach*. London: Routledge.

Jewitt, C. (2008) Multimodality and literacy in school classrooms. *Review of Research in Education*, 32(1), 241–267.

Johnson, D.W. and Johnson, R.T. (2014) Cooperative learning in the 21st century. *Anales de Psicologia*, 30(3), 841–851.

Johnson, D.W., Johnson, R.T. and Stanne, M.E. (2000) *Cooperative Learning Methods: A Meta-Analysis*. Minneapolis, MN: University of Minnesota Press.

Johnson, L., Adams Becker, S., Estrada, V. and Freeman, A. (2015) *NMC Horizon Report: 2015 K-12 Edition*. Austin, Texas: The New Media Consortium.

Jones, P. and Chen, H. (2012) Teachers' knowledge about language: Issues of pedagogy and expertise. *Australian Journal of Language and Literacy*, 35(1), 147–168.

Joshi, M. and Aaron, P.G. (2000) The component model of reading: Simple view of reading made a little more complex. *Reading Psychology*, 21, 85–97.

Kalantzis, M. and Cope, B. (2012) *Literacies*. Cambridge: Cambridge University Press.

Kalantzis, M., Cope, B. and The Learning by Design Group (2005) *Learning by Design*. Victoria, Australia: Common Group Publishing Pty. Ltd.

Kalantzis, M., Cope, B., Chan, E. and Dalley-Trim, L. (2016) *Literacies* (2nd edn) Melbourne: Cambridge University Press.

Kena, G., Musu-Gillette, L., Robinson, J., Wang, X., Rathbun, A., Zhang, J., Wilkinson-Flicker, S., Barmer, A. and Dunlop Velez, E. (2015) *The Condition of Education 2015* (NCES 2015-144). Washington, DC: US Department of Education, National Center for Education Statistics.

Kendeou, P., Savage, R. and van den Broek, P. (2009) Revising the simple view of reading. *British Journal of Educational Psychology*, 79, 353–370.

Kervin, L. and Mantei, J. (2009) Collaborative gathering, evaluating and communicating 'wisdom' using iPods. Retrieved from: http://ro.uow.edu.au/edupapers/85/ (accessed 8 December 2016).

Killen, R. (2013) *Effective Teaching Strategies: Lessons from Research and Practice*. (6th edn). South Melbourne: Cengage Learning Australia.

Kingsley, T. (2015) How to speak in Google. *Reading Today*, 32(4), 18–19.

Kintsch, E. (2005) Comprehension theory as a guide for the design of thoughtful questions. *Topics in Language Disorders*, 25(1), 51–64.

Kintsch, W. (1974) *The Representation of Meaning in Memory*. Hillsdale, NJ: Lawrence Erlbaum Associates.

Kintsch, W. (1998) *Comprehension: A Paradigm for Cognition*. New York: Cambridge University Press.

Kirby, J.R. and Savage, J.S. (2008) Can the simple view deal with the complexities of reading? *Literacy*, 42(2), 75–82.

Klenowski, V. and Wyatt-Smith, C. (2012) The impact of high stakes testing: The Australian story. *Assessment in Education: Principles Policy and Practice*, 19(1), 65–79.

Konza, D. (2014) Why the 'fab five' should be the 'big six'. *Australian Journal of Teacher Education*, 39(12). Retrieved from: http://ro.ecu.edu.au/ajte/vol39/iss12/10/ (accessed 22 November 2016).

Konza, D. (2016) Understanding the process of reading: The Big Six. In J. Scull and B. Raban (eds), *Growing Up Literate: Australian Literacy Research for Practice*. Victoria, Australia: Eleanor Curtain Publishing, pp. 149–176.

Krathwohl, D.R. (2002) A revision of Bloom's taxonomy: An overview. *Theory into Practice*, 41(4), 212–218.

Kress, G. (2003) *Literacy in the New Media Age*. London: Routledge.

Kurki, S.E.B. (2015) Investigating youth critical literacy engagement. *Language and Literacy*, 17(3), 13–33.

Laing, A.P. and Kambi, A.G. (2002) The use of think-aloud protocols to compare inferencing abilities in average and below-average readers. *Journal of Learning Disabilities*, 35, 436–447.

Laurillard, D. (2013) *Teaching as a Design Science: Building Pedagogical Patterns for Learning and Technology*. New York: Routledge.

Lazar, G. (1993) *Literature and Language Teaching*. Cambridge: Cambridge University Press.

Leavy, P. (2009) Arts-based research as a pedagogical tool for teaching media literacy: Reflections from an undergraduate classroom. *Learning Landscapes*, 3(1), 225–242.

Leu, D., Kinzer, C., Coiro, J. and Cammack, D. (2004) Toward a theory of new literacies emerging from the Internet and other information and communication technologies. In R. Ruddell and N. Unrau (eds), *Theoretical Models and Processes of Reading* (5th edn). Newark, DE: International Reading Association, pp. 1570–1613.

Lewis-Spector, J. (2015) Precautions with educational technology. *Reading Today*, 32(4), 12–13.

Linnenbrink, E.A. and Pintrich, P.R. (2002) Achievement goal theory and affect: An asymmetrical bi-directional model. *Educational Psychologist*, 37, 69–78.

Lipson, M.Y. and Wixson, K.K. (2009) *Assessment and Instruction of Reading and Writing Difficulties: An Interactive Approach* (4th edn). Boston: Pearson.

Lloyd, S.L. (2004) Using comprehension strategies as a springboard for student talk. *Journal of Adolescent and Adult Literacy*, 48, 114–124.

Louden, W., Chan, L.K.S., Elkins, J., Greaves, D., House, H., Milton, M., Nichols, S., Rivalland, J., Rohl, M. and van Kraayennoord, C. (2000) *Mapping the Territory, Primary Students with Learning Difficulties: Literacy and Numeracy* (vols 1, 2 and 3). Canberra, ACT: Department of Education, Training and Youth Affairs.

Love, B.L. (2014) Urban storytelling: How storyboarding, moviemaking, and Hip-Hop-based education can promote students' critical voice. *English Journal*, 103(5), 53–58.

Love, K., Macken-Horarik, M. and Horarik, S. (2015) Language and its application: A snapshot of Australian teacher's views. *Australian Journal of Language and Literacy*, 38(3), 171–182.

Luca, J. and Clarkson, B. (2002) Promoting student learning through peer tutoring: A case study. In *Proceedings of the ED-MEDIA 2002 World Conference on Educational Multimedia, Hypermedia & Telecommunications*. Denver, CO, 24–29 June.

Luke, A., Elkins, J., Weir, K. and Stevens, L. (2002) *Beyond the Middle: A Report About Literacy and Numeracy Development of a Target Group Students in the Middle Years of Schooling*. Commonwealth Department of Education, Science and Technology, University of Queensland.

Luke, A. and Freebody, P. (1999) Further notes on the four resources model, reading. Retrieved from: http://kingstonnetworknumandlitteam.wikispaces. com/file/view/Further+Notes+on+the+Four+Resources+Model-Allan+Luke. pdf (accessed 8 December 2016).

Macken-Horarik, M. (2011) Building a knowledge structure for English: Reflections on the challenges of coherence, cumulative learning, portability and face validity. *Australian Journal of Education*, 55(3), 197–213.

Manset-Williamson, G. and Nelson, J.M. (2005) Balanced, strategic reading instruction for upper-elementary and middle school students with reading disabilities: A comparative study of two approaches. *Learning Disability Quarterly*, 28, 59–74.

Marzano, R.J. (2007) *The Art and Science of Teaching: A Comprehensive Framework for Effective Instruction*. Alexandria: Association for Supervision and Curriculum Development.

Masters, G.N. (2009) *A Shared Challenge. Improving Literacy, Numeracy and Science Learning in Queensland Primary Schools*. Camberwell, Australia: Australian Council for Educational Research.

Mastropieri, M.A. and Scruggs, T.E. (2010) *The Inclusive Classroom: Strategies for Effective Differentiated Instruction* (4th edn). Upper Saddle River, NY: Merril.

McCrae, R., Cost, P., Terracciano, A., Parker, W. and Mills, C. (2002) Personality trait development from age 12 to age 18: Longitudinal, cross-sectional, and cross-cultural analyses. *Journal of Personality and Social Psychology in the Public Domain*, 83(6), 1456–1468.

McDonald, L. (2013) *A Literature Companion for Teachers*. Marrickville, NSW: PETAA.

MCEETYA (Ministerial Council on Education, Employment, Training and Youth Affairs) (1999) *Adelaide Declaration on National Goals for Schooling in the Twenty-First Century* (Standing Council on School Education and Early Childhood). Retrieved from: www.scseec.edu.au/archive/Publications/Publications-archive/The-Adelaide-Declaration.aspx (accessed 8 December 2016).

MCEETYA (Ministerial Council on Education, Employment, Training and Youth Affairs) (2008) *Melbourne Declaration on Educational Goals for Young Australians*. Retrieved from: www.curriculum.edu.au/verve/_resources/ National_Declaration_on_the_Educational_Goals_for_Young_Australians.pdf (accessed 24 November 2016).

McKeon, M.G., Beck, I.L. and Blake, R.G.K. (2009) Rethinking reading comprehension instruction: A comparison of instruction for strategies and content approaches. *Reading Research Quarterly*, 44(3), 218–253.

McKeough, A., Bird, S., Tourigny, E., Romaine, A., Graham, S., Ottmann, J. and Jeary, J. (2008) Storytelling as a foundation to literacy development for Aboriginal children: Culturally and developmentally appropriate practices. *Canadian Psychology*, 49(2), 148–154.

McKoon, G. and Ratcliff, R. (1992) Pronoun resolution and discourse models. *Journal of Educational Psychology: Learning, Memory and Cognition*, 18, 440–466.

McNamara, D.S. and Kendeou, P. (2011) Translating advances in reading comprehension to education practice. *International Electronic Journal of Elementary Education*, 4(1), 33–46.

McNaughton, S., Lai, M., MacDonald, S. and Farry, S. (2004) Designing more effective teaching of comprehension in culturally and linguistically diverse classrooms in New Zealand. *The Australian Journal of Language and Literacy*, 27, 184–197.

Mellor, S. and Seddon, T. (2013) Networking young citizens: Learning to be citizens in and with the social web. Retrieved from: http://research.acer.edu.au/civics/21 (accessed 8 December 2016).

Miller, A. (2016) 6 strategies for differentiated instruction in project based learning. *Edutopia*, 8 January. Retrieved from: www.edutopia.org/blog/differentiated-instruction-strategies-pbl-andrew-miller (accessed 8 December 2016).

Mills, K. (2010) 'Filming in progress': New spaces for multimodal designing. *Linguistics and Education*, 21, 14–28.

Mills, K.A. and Exley, B. (2014) Narrative and multimodality in English language arts curricula: A tale of two nations. *Language Arts*, 92(2), 136–143.

Mills, K.A., Comber, B. and Kelly, P. (2013) Sensing place: Embodiment, sensoriality, kinesis, and children behind the camera. *English Teaching*, 12(2), 11–27.

Moffatt, A., Ryan, M.E. and Barton, G.M. (2015) Reflexivity and self-care for creative facilitators: Stepping outside the circle. *Studies in Continuing Education*, 3(1), 29–46.

Moje, E.B. (2002) Re-framing adolescent literacy research for new times: Studying youth as a resource. *Reading Research and Instruction*, 41(3), 211–228.

Moje, E., Young, J., Readence, J. and Moore, D. (2000) Reinventing adolescent literacy for new times: Perennial and millennial issues. *Journal of Adolescent and Adult Literacy*, 43(5), 400–410.

Moje, E., Ciechanowski, K., Kramer, K., Ellis, L., Carrillo, R. and Collazo, T. (2004) Working toward third space in content area literacy: An examination of everyday funds of knowledge and discourse. *Reading Research Quarterly*, 39(1), 38–70.

Moll, L.C. (ed.) (1990) *Vygotsky and Education*. Cambridge: Cambridge University Press.

Moll, L. (1993) Community-mediated educational practices. Paper presented at the American Educational Research Association Annual Conference, Atlanta, GA, April.

Moll, L.C., Amanti, C., Neff, D. and Gonzalez, N. (1992) Funds of knowledge for teaching: Using a qualitative approach to connect homes and classrooms. *Theory Into Practice*, 31(2), 132–141. Special Issue: Qualitative Issues in Educational Research.

Moore, D.W., Bean, T.W., Birdyshaw, D. and Rycik, J.A. (1999) *Adolescent Literacy: A Position Statement for the Commission on Adolescent Literacy of the International Reading Association*. Newark, DE: International Reading Association.

Morris, A. and Stewart-Dore, N. (1984) *Learning to Learn from Text: Effective Reading in the Content Areas*. North Ryde, NSW: Addison-Wesley.

Morrison, R. (2014) Surfing blind: a study into the effects of exposing young adolescents to explicit search engine skills. Unpublished MEd, Brisbane, QLD: Griffith University.

Moyle, K. (2010) *Building Innovation: Learning with Technologies*. Melbourne: ACER.

Myhill, D. (2005) Ways of knowing: Writing with grammar in mind. *English Teaching*, 4(3), 77.

Myhill, D. (2009) Shaping futures: Literacy policy in the twenty-first century. *Research Papers in Education*, 24(2), 129–133.

Myhill, D. and Fisher, R. (2010) Editorial: Writing development: cognitive, socio-cultural, linguistic perspectives. *Journal of Research in Reading*, 33(1), 1–3.

Nagel, M.C. (2005) Understanding the adolescent brain. In D. Pendergast and N. Bahr (eds), *Teaching Middle Years: Rethinking Curriculum, Pedagogy and Assessment*. Crows Nest, NSW: Allen & Unwin, pp. 65–76.

Nation, K. and Norbury, F. (2005) Why reading comprehension fails: Insights from developmental disorders. *Topics in Language Disorders*, 25, 21–32.

NCTE (National Council of Teacher of English) (n.d.) *NCTE Beliefs about the Teaching of Writing*. Retrieved from: www.ncte.org/positions/statements/writingbeliefs (accessed 7 March 2016).

National Reading Panel (US) (2000) *Report of the National Reading Panel: Teaching Children to Read: An Evidence-based Assessment of the Scientific Research Literature on Reading and its Implications for Reading Instruction: Reports of the Subgroups*. Washington, DC: National Institute of Child Health and Human Development, National Institutes of Health.

Needleman, H.L., Schell, A., Bellinger, D., Leviton, A. and Allred, E.N. (1990) The long-term effects of exposure to low doses of lead in childhood: An 11-year follow-up report. *New England Journal of Medicine*, 322 (2), 83–88.

Netcoh, S. (2013) Droppin' knowledge on race: Hip-hop, white adolescents, and anti-racism education. *Radical Teacher*, 97, 10–19. Retrieved from: http://radicalteacher. library.pitt.edu/ojs/index.php/radicalteacher/article/view/39/21 (accessed 22 November 2016).

New London Group (1996) A pedagogy of multiliteracies: Designing social futures. *Harvard Educational Review*, 66, 60–92.

New London Group (2000) A pedagogy of multiliteracies: Designing social futures. In B. Cope and M. Kalantzis (eds), *Multiliteracies: Literacy Learning and the Design of Social Futures*. London and New York: Routledge, pp. 9–36.

New Zealand Ministry of Education (2010) *Position Paper: Assessment [Schooling Sector]*. Retrieved from: http://assessment.tki.org.nz/content/download/5539/49218/file/MOEAssessmentPositionPaper_October11.pdf (accessed 8 December 2016).

Newmann, F., Onosko, J. and Stevenson, R. (1990) Staff development for higher order thinking: A synthesis of practical wisdom. *Journal of Staff Development*, 11(3), 48–55.

Oakley, B., Felder, R.M., Brent, R. and Eljajj, I. (2004) Turning student groups into effective teams. *Journal of Student Centered Learning*, 2(1), 9–31.

Oblinger, D. and Oblinger, J. (2005) Is it age or IT: First steps toward understanding the net generation. *Educating the Net Generation*, 2(1–2), 20.

OECD (2003) (Organisation for Economic Co-operation and Development/ UNESCO Institute for Statistics) *Literacy Skills for the World of Tomorrow: Further Results from PISA 2000: Executive Summary*. Paris: OECD/UNESCO-UIS.

OECD (2009) (Organisation for Economic Co-operation and Development/ UNESCO Institute for Statistics) *PISA Assessment Framework: Key Competencies in Reading, Mathematics and Science*. Paris: OECD/UNESCO-UIS.

OECD (2010) *PISA 2009 Results: Executive Summary*. Paris: OECD. Retrieved from: www.oecd.org/dataoecd/34/60/46619703.pdf (accessed 22 November 2016).

OECD (2011) *PISA 2009 Results: Students on Line: Digital Technologies and Performance* (Volume VI). Retrieved from: http://dx.doi.org/10.1787/9789264112995-en (accessed 24 November 2016).

Ofcom (2015) *The Communications Market Report* (6 August). Retrieved from: www.ofcom.org.uk/research-and-data/cmr/cmr15#CommunicationsMarketRep ort2015 (accessed 8 December 2016).

Ogle, D.M. (1986) K-W-L: A teaching model that develops active reading of expository text. *The Reading Teacher*, 39, 564–570.

Otto, P. (1992) History as humanity: reading and literacy in the classroom. *The History Teacher*, 26(1), 51–60.

Overett, J. and Donald, D. (1998) Paired reading: Effects of a parent involvement program in a disadvantaged community in South Africa. *British Journal of Educational Psychology*, 68, 347–356.

Paivio, A. (1986) *Mental Representations: A Dual-Coding Approach*. New York: Holt, Rinehart & Winston.

Palincsar, A.S. and Brown, A.L. (1984) Reciprocal teaching of comprehension-fostering and comprehension-monitoring activities. *Cognition and Instruction*, 1, 117–175.

Paris, S.G. (2005) Reinterpreting the development of reading skills. *Reading Research Quarterly*, 40(2), 184–202.

Paris, S.G. and Stahl, S.A. (2005) *Children's Reading Comprehension and Assessment*. Mahwah, NJ: Lawrence Erlbaum Associates.

Paris, S.G., Byrnes, J.P. and Paris, A.H. (2001) Constructing theories, identities, and actions of self-regulated learners. In B.J. Zimmerman and D.H. Schunk (eds), *Self-regulated Learning and Academic Achievement*. Mahwah, NJ: Lawrence Erlbaum Associates, pp. 253–287.

Parris, S.R., Fisher, D. and Headley, K. (2009) *Adolescent Literacy Field Tested: Effective Solutions for Every Classroom*. Newark, DE: International Reading Association.

Pearson, P.D. and Johnson, D.D. (1978) *Teaching Reading Comprehension*. New York: Holt, Rinehart and Winston.

Pearson, D.P. and Raphael, T.E. (1990) Reading comprehension as a dimension of thinking. In Jones, B.F. and Idol, L. (eds), *Dimensions of Thinking and Cognitive Instruction*. Hillsdale, NJ: Lawrence Erlbaum Associates, pp. 209–240.

Pearson, P.D. and Gallagher, M.C. (1983) The instruction of reading comprehension. *Contemporary Educational Psychology*, 8(3), 317–344.

Pearson, P.D., Hiebert, E.H. and Kamil, M.L. (2007) Vocabulary assessment: What we know and what we need to learn. *Reading Research Quarterly*, 42(2), 282–296.

Pendergast, D. (2015) Making great teachers: From global education megatrends to Generation Z. Griffith University News. Retrieved from: https://app.secure. griffith.edu.au/news/2015/08/20/making-great-teachers-from-global-education-megatrends-to-generation-z/ (accessed 21 November 2016).

Pendergast, D. and Bahr, N. (2005) *Teaching Middle Years: Rethinking Curriculum, Pedagogy and Assessment.* Crows Nest, NSW: Allen & Unwin.

Pendergast, D., Main, K., Barton, G.M., Kanasa, H., Geelan, D. and Dowden, T. (2015) The educational change model as a vehicle for reform: Shifting Year 7 into high school and implementing junior secondary. *Australian Journal of Middle Schooling*, 15(2), 4–17.

Perfetti, C. (2007) Reading ability: Lexical Quality to Comprehension. *Scientific Studies of Reading*, 11(4), 357–383.

Pikulski, J.J. and Chard, D.J. (2005) Fluency: Bridge between decoding and reading comprehension. *The Reading Teacher*, 58(6), 510–519.

Prensky, M. (2001) Digital natives, digital immigrants. *On the Horizon, 9*(5), NCB University Press.

Pressley, M. (2001) Comprehension instruction: What makes sense now, what might make sense soon. *Reading Online*, 5(2), 1–14.

Pressley, M. (2002) At-risk students: Learning to break through comprehension barriers. In C. Collins Block, L.B. Gambrell and M. Pressley (eds), *Improving Comprehension Instruction*. San Francisco: Jossey-Bass, pp. 354–369.

Prince, M. (2004) Does active learning work? A review of the research. *Journal of Engineering Education*, 93(3), 223–231.

Prinsloo, M. and Breier, M. (1996) *The Social Uses of Literacy: Theory and Practice in Contemporary South Africa*. Amsterdam: John Benjamins.

Prinsloo, M. and Janks, H. (2002) Critical literacy in South Africa: Possibilities and constraints in 2002. *English Teaching: Practice and Critique*, 1(1), 20–38.

Quay, L.C. and Steele, D.C. (1998) Predicting children's achievement from teacher judgements: An alternative to standardized testing. *Early Education and Development*, 9, 207–218.

Rahn, J. (1998) *A Theory for All Music*. Toronto: University of Toronto Press Inc.

Raphael, T.E. (1984) Teaching learners about sources of information for answering questions. *The Reading Teacher*, 28, 303–311.

Raphael, T. and Au, K. (2005) QAR: Enhancing comprehension and test taking across grades and content areas. *International Reading Association*, 206–221.

Reid, G. (2013) *Dyslexia and Inclusion* (2nd edn). London: Routledge.

Rennie, J. (2016) Rethinking reading instruction for adolescent readers: The 6R's. *Australian Journal of Language and Literacy*, 39(1), 42–53.

Renzulli, J.S. (2002) Emerging conceptions of giftedness: Building a bridge to the new century. *Exceptionality*, 10(2), 67–75.

Richardson, W. (2010) *Blogs, Wikis, Podcasts, and Other Powerful Web Tools for Classrooms* (3rd edn). Thousand Oaks, CA: Corwin.

Ricketts, J., Nation, K. and Bishop, V.M. (2007) Vocabulary is important for some, but not all reading skills. *Scientific Study of Reading*, 11(3), 235–257.

Robinson, M.K. and Unsworth, N. (2015) Working memory capacity offers resistance to mind-wandering and external distraction in a context-specific manner. *Applied Cognitive Psychology*, 29, 680–690.

Robinson, V., Hohepa, M. and Lloyd, C. (2009) *School Leadership and Student Outcomes: Identifying What Works and Why Best Evidence Synthesis.* Wellington, NZ: Ministry for Education. Retrieved from: www.educationcounts.govt.nz/__ data/assets/pdf_file/0015/60180/BES-Leadership-Web-updated-foreword-2015. pdf (accessed 24 November 2016).

Roe, B.D., Stoodt-Hill, B.D. and Burns, P.C. (2011) *Secondary School Literacy Instruction: The Content Areas.* Belmont, CA: Wadsworth, Cengage Learning.

Rohl, M. and Rivalland, J. (2002) Literacy learning difficulties in Australian primary schools: Who are the children identified and how do their schools and teachers support them? *The Australian Journal of Language and Literacy,* 25, 19–40.

Rose, J. (2009) *Independent Review of the Primary Curriculum: Final Report.* Nottingham: DCSF Publications.

Rumble, P. and Aspland, T. (2010) The four attributes model of the middle school teacher. *Australian Journal of Middle Schooling,* 10(1), 4–15.

Ryan, M.E. and Barton, G.M. (2014) The spatialized practices of teaching writing: Shaping the discoursal self. *Research in the Teaching of English,* 48(3), 303–329.

Ryan, M.E. and Ryan, M. (2013) Theorising a model for teaching and assessing reflective learning in higher education. *Higher Education Research & Development,* 32(2), 244–257.

Ryan, R.M. and Deci, E.L. (2000) Intrinsic and extrinsic motivations: Classic definitions and new directions. *Contemporary Educational Psychology,* 25, 54–67.

Sadoski, M., Goetz, E.T. and Rodriguez, M. (2000) Engaging texts: Effects of concreteness on comprehensibility, interest, and recall in four text types. *Journal of Educational Psychology,* 92, 85–95.

Saenez, L.M., Fuchs, L.S. and Fuchs, D. (2005) Peer-assisted learning strategies for English language learners with learning disabilities. *Exceptional Children,* 71(3), 231–247.

Scarborough, H. (2001) Connecting early language and literacy to later reading disabilities: Evidence, theory and practice. In S. Neuman and D. Dickinson (eds), *Handbook of Early Literacy Research.* New York: Guilford Press, pp. 97–110.

Scardamalia, M. and Bereiter, C. (1999) Schools as knowledge building organizations. In D. Keating and C. Hertzman (eds), *Today's Children, Tomorrow's Society: The Developmental Health and Wealth of Nations.* New York: Guilford, pp. 274–289.

Schön, D. (1983) *The Reflective Practitioner: How Professionals Think in Action.* London: Temple Smith.

Schunk, D.H. (2000) Coming to terms with motivation constructs. *Contemporary Educational Psychology,* 25, 116–119.

Schunk, D.H. (2004) *Learning Theories: An Educational Perspective* (4th edn). Saddle River, NJ: Pearson.

Schunk, D.H. (2005) Commentary on self-regulation in school contexts. *Learning and Instruction,* 15, 173–177.

Schwartz, D.L., Chase, C.C., Oppezzo, M.A. and Chin, D.B. (2011) Practicing versus inventing with contrasting cases: The effects of telling first on learning and transfer. *American Psychological Association,* 103(4), 759–775.

Scribner, S. and Cole, M. (1981) *The Psychology of Literacy*. Cambridge, MA: Harvard University Press.

Shaddock, A.J., Giorcelli, L. and Smith, S. (2007) *Students with Disabilities in Mainstream Classrooms: A Resource for Teachers*. Canberra: Commonwealth of Australia.

Shanahan, T. and Shanahan, C. (2008) Teaching disciplinary literacy to adolescents: rethinking content-area literacy. *Harvard Educational Review*, 78(1), 40–59.

Sideridis, G.D. and Padeliadu, S. (2001) The motivational determinants of students at risk of having reading difficulties: Planned behaviour theory and goal importance. *Remedial and Special Education*, 22, 268–279.

Siemens, G. (2005) Connectivism: Learning as network-creation. *ASTD Learning News*, 10(1).

Simpson, A. (2014) *Children's Literature*. Retrieved from: www.nlnw.nsw.edu.au/videos10/Simpson/7549/links/simpson.pdf (accessed 24 November 2016).

Simpson, J., Caffery, J. and McConvell, P. (2009) *Gaps in Australia's Indigenous Language Policy: Dismantling Bilingual Education in the Northern Territory*. AIATSIS Discussion Paper Number 24, Australia.

Skerrett, A., Pruitt, A.A. and Warrington, A.S. (2015) Racial and related forms of specialist knowledge on English education blogs. *English Education*, 47(4), 314–346.

Skidmore, D. (2004) *Inclusion: The Dynamic of School Development*. Buckingham: Open University Press.

Skues, J.L. and Cunningham, E.G. (2011) A contemporary review of the definition, prevalence, identification and support of learning disabilities in Australian schools. *Australian Journal of Learning Difficulties*, 16(2), 159–180.

Slavin, R. (1996) Research on cooperative learning: What we know, and what we need to know (Abstract). *Contemporary Educational Psychology*, 21, 43–69.

Snow, C.E. (2002) *Reading for Understanding: Toward a Research and Development Program in Reading Comprehension*. Santa Monica, CA: Rand Corp. Retrieved from: www.rand.org/publications/MR/MR1465/ (accessed 12 December 2002).

Snow, C.E. (2003) Assessment of reading comprehension. In A.P. Sweet and C.E. Snow (eds), *Rethinking Reading Comprehension*. New York: Guilford Press, pp. 191–206.

Snow, C. (2004) What counts as literacy in early childhood? In K. McCartney and D. Phillips (eds), *Handbook of Early Child Development*. Oxford: Blackwell, pp. 274–294.

Snow, C.E. and Sweet, A.P. (2003) Reading for comprehension. In A.P. Sweet and C. E. Snow (eds), *Rethinking Reading Comprehension*. New York: The Guilford Press, pp. 1–11.

Snow, C.E., Burns, M.S. and Griffin, P. (eds) (1998) *Preventing Reading Difficulties in Young Children*. Washington DC: Department of Education.

Stanovich, K.E. (1986) Matthew effects in reading: Some consequences of individual differences in the acquisition of literacy. *Reading Research Quarterly*, 21, 360–407.

Stobart, G. and Eggen, T. (2012) High-stakes testing: Values, fairness and consequences. *Assessment in Education: Principles, Policy and Practice*, 19(1), 1–6.

Street, B.V. (1995) *Social Literacies: Critical Approaches to Literacy in Development, Ethnography, and Education*. London and New York: Longman.

Street, B.V. (2003) What's 'new' in New Literacy Studies? Critical approaches to literacy in theory and practice. *Current Issues in Comparative Education*, 5(2), 77–91.

Stronger Smarter Institute (n.d.) Our mission and our approach. Retrieved from: http://strongersmarter.com.au/about/approach/ (accessed 21 November 2016).

Suominen, K. and Wilson, A. (2002) *Three Level Guide*. Retrieved from: www.myread.org/guide_three.htm (accessed 22 November 2016).

Szabo, S. (2006) KWHHL: A student-driven evolution of the KWL. *American Secondary Education*, 34(3), 57–67.

Taboada, A. and Guthrie, J.T. (2006) Contributions of student questioning and prior knowledge to construction of knowledge from reading information text. *Journal of Literacy Research*, 38(1), 1–35.

Tam, K.Y., Heward, W.L. and Heng, M.A. (2006) A reading instructional intervention program for English-language learners who are struggling readers. *The Journal of Special Education*, 40(2), 79–93.

Tannenbaum, K.R., Torgensen, J. and Wagner, R.K. (2006) Relationships between word knowledge and reading comprehension in third-grade children. *Scientific Studies of Reading*, 14(4), 381–398.

Terenzini, P.T., Cabrera, A.F., Colbeck, C.L., Parente, J.M. and Bjorkland, S.A. (2001) Collaborative learning vs. lecture/discussion: Students' reported learning gains. *Journal of Engineering Education*, 90(1), 123–130.

Thompson, J. (1995) *The Media and Modernity: A Social Theory of the Media*. Cambridge: Polity.

Thompson, P. (2002) *Schooling the Rustbelt Kids: Making the Difference in Changing Times*. Crows Nest, NSW: Allen & Unwin.

Tiffin-Richards, S.P. and Schroeder, S. (2015) The component process of reading comprehension in adolescents. *Learning and Individual Differences*, 42, 1–9.

Ting, Y. (2015) Tapping into students' digital literacy and designing negotiated learning to promote learner autonomy. *Internet and Higher Education*, 26, 25–32.

Topping, K.J. (1996) The effectiveness of peer tutoring in further and higher education: A typology and review of the literature. *Higher Education*, 32, 321–345.

Trabasso, T. (1981) On the making of inferences during reading and their recall. In J.T. Guthrie (ed.), *Comprehension and Teaching: Research Reviews*. Newark, DE: International Reading Association, pp. 56–75.

Troegger, D. (2011) Teaching reading strategies by using a comprehension framework. *Practically Primary*, 16(1), 10–13.

Uhry, J.K. and Ehri, L.C. (1999) *Children's Reading Acquisition*. In D.A. Wagner, R.L. Venezky and B.V. Street (eds), *Literacy: An International Handbook*. Boulder, CO: Westview Press, pp. 43–48.

UNESCO (2012) Statement on literacy. Retrieved from: www.unric.org/en/literacy/27791-the-evolving-definition-of-literacy (accessed 22 November 2016).

United Nations (1948) *Universal Declaration of Human Rights*. UN General Assembly.

Van Leeuwen, A., Janssen, J., Erkens, G. and Brekelmans, M. (2015) Teacher regulation of cognitive activities during student collaboration: Effects of learning analytics. *Computers & Education*, 90, 80–94.

Van Leeuwen, T. (1999) *Speech, Music and Sound*. Basingstoke: Macmillan.

Vellutino, F.R., Fletcher, J.M., Snowling, M.J. and Scanlon, D.M. (2004) Specific reading disability (dyslexia): What have we learned in the past four decades? *Journal of Child Psychiatry*, 45, 2–40.

Vygotsky, L.S. (1962) *Thought and Language*. Cambridge, MA: Harvard University Press.

Vygotsky, L.S. (1978) *Mind in Society: The Development of Higher Mental Processes*. Cambridge, MA: Harvard University Press.

Wagner, D.A. (1999) Indigenous education and literacy learning. In D.A. Wagner, R.L. Venezky and B.V. Street (eds), *Literacy: An International Handbook*. Boulder, CO: Westview Press, pp. 283–287.

Walsh, M. (2011) *Multimodal Literacy: Researching Classroom Practice*. Primary Newtown, NSW: English Teaching Association.

Walshe, R.D. (2015) Writing as process. In J. Turbill, G.M. Barton and C. Brock. (eds), *Teaching Writing in Today's Classrooms: Looking Back to Look Forward*. South Australia: Australian Literacy Educators' Association Ltd, pp. 13–25.

Walton, C. (1993) Aboriginal education in Northern Australia: A case study of literacy policies and practices. In P. Freebody and A.R. Welch (eds), *Knowledge, Culture and Power: International Perspectives on Literacy as Policy and Practice*. Pittsburgh, PA: University of Pittsburgh Press, pp. 55–81.

Warnock, M. (2012) 'Foreword' to L. Peer and G. Reid (eds), *Special Education Needs: A Guide for Inclusive Practice*. London: Sage, pp. xix–xx.

Warnock, M. and Norwich, B. (2010) *Special Educational Needs: A New Look*, ed. L. Terzi. London and New York: Continuum.

Wastiau, P., Blamire, R., Kearney, C., Quittre, V., Van de Gaer, E. and Monseur, C. (2013) The use of ICT in education: A survey of schools in Europe. *European Journal of Education*, 48(1), 11–27.

Watson, S.M. and Gable, R. (2013) Cognitive development of adolescents at risk or with learning and/or emotional problems: Implications for teachers. *Intervention School and Clinic*, 49, 108–112.

Weale, S. (2015) Digital skills teaching in schools needs radical rethink, says report. *The Guardian*, 17 February. Retrieved from: www.theguardian.com/education/2015/feb/17/digital-skills-teaching-in-schools-needs-radical-rethink-says-report (accessed 8 December 2016).

Westwood, P. (2001) *Reading and Learning Difficulties: Approaches to Teaching and Assessment*. Camberwell, Victoria: ACER Press.

Westwood, P. (2015) *Commonsense Methods for Adolescents with Special Education Needs* (7th edn). London and New York: Routledge.

White, G. (2013) Forward thinking: Three forward, two back: what are the next steps? Extended version of a presentation given to the Australian College of Educators National Conference, Melbourne, June. Retrieved from: http://research.acer.edu.au/cgi/viewcontent.cgi?article=1005&context=digital_learning (accessed 8 December 2016).

Whitehurst, G.L. and Lonigan, C.J. (1988) Child development and emergent literacy. *Child Development*, 69, 848–872.

Wigfield, A., Guthrie, J.T., Tonks, S. and Perencevich, C. (2004) Children's motivation for reading: Domain specificity and instructional influences. *The Journal of Educational Research*, 97, 299–310.

Wineburg, S. and Wilson, S. (1991) Subject matter knowledge in the teaching of history. In J. Brophy (ed.), *Advances in Research on Teacher Education* (2nd edn). Greenwich: JAI Press, pp. 305–347.

Witt, J.C., Elliott, S.N., Kramer, J.J. and Gresham, F.M. (1994) *Assessment of Children: Fundamental Methods and Practices*. Dubuque, IA: WCB Brown & Benchmark.

Wittgenstein, L. (2009) *Philosophical Investigations*, ed. P.M.S Hacker and Joachim Schulte (rev. 4th edn). Chichester: Wiley-Blackwell.

Woolley, G.E. (2006) Comprehension difficulties after Year 4: Actioning appropriately. *Australian Journal of Learning Difficulties*, 11(3), 125–130.

Woolley, G. (2007) A comprehension intervention for children with reading comprehension difficulties. *Australian Journal of Learning Difficulties*, 12(1), 43–50.

Woolley, G. (2008) Supported vocabulary development from context for children experiencing reading difficulties. *Proceedings of the Australian Teacher Education Association National Conference*, Sunshine Coast, 8–11 July.

Woolley, G. (2011) *Reading Comprehension: Assisting Children with Learning Difficulties*. Dordrecht, The Netherlands: Springer International.

Woolley, G.E. (2014a) *Developing Literacy in the Primary Classroom*. London: Sage.

Woolley, G.E. (2014b) Students with literacy difficulties. In M. Hyde, L. Carpenter and R. Conway (eds), *Diversity, Inclusion and Engagement* (2nd edn). South Melbourne: Oxford, pp. 107–128.

Woolley, G.E. (2016) Reading comprehension intervention for high-functioning children with autism spectrum disorders. *Australian Journal of Learning Difficulties*, 21(1), 41–58.

Woolley, G.E. and Hay, I. (2007) Reading intervention: The benefits of using trained tutors. *Australian Journal of Language and Literacy*, 30(1), 9–20.

Zhang, H. and Hoosain, R. (2001) The influence of narrative text characteristics on thematic inference during reading. *Journal of Research in Reading*, 24, 173–186.

Zheng, L. and Huang, R. (2015) The effects of sentiments and co-regulation on group performance in computer supported collaborative learning. *Internet and Higher Education*, 28, 59–67.

Zimmerman, B.J. (2002) Becoming a self-regulated learner: An overview. *Theory Into Practice*, 41, 64–70.

Zylka, J., Christoph, G., Kroehne, H. and Goldhammer, F. (2015) Moving beyond cognitive elements of ICT literacy: First evidence on the structure of ICT engagement. *Computers in Human Behaviour*, 53, 149–160.

INDEX